Revision

A Creative Approach to Writing and Rewriting Fiction

Revision

A Creative Approach to Writing and Rewriting Fiction

David Michael Kaplan

STORY PRESS

CINCINNATI, OHIO

Revision: A Creative Approach to Writing and Rewriting Fiction. Copyright © 1997 by David Michael Kaplan. Printed and bound in the United States of America. All rights reserved. No part of this book may be reproduced in any form or by any electronic or mechanical means including information storage and retrieval systems without permission in writing from the publisher, except by a reviewer, who may quote brief passages in a review. Published by Story Press, an imprint of F&W Publications, Inc., 1507 Dana Avenue, Cincinnati, Ohio 45207. (800) 289-0963. First edition.

Other fine Story Press Books are available from your local bookstore or direct from the publisher.

01 00 99 98 97   5 4 3 2 1

Library of Congress Cataloging-in-Publication Data

Kaplan, David Michael.
   Revision : a creative approach to writing and rewriting fiction / David Michael Kaplan.—1st ed.
     p.   cm.
   Includes index.
   ISBN 1-884910-19-X (alk. paper)
   1. Fiction—Technique.   I. Title.
PN3355.K35   1996
808.3—dc20   96-29202
                                                   CIP

Designed by Clare Finney

The permissions on the next page constitute an extension of this copyright page.

PERMISSIONS

The excerpt from "Story #2" by Josepha Conrad is reprinted by permission of the author.

The excerpt from "Pulled Triggers" by Tony D'Souza is reprinted by permission of the author.

The excerpt from "21 Days" by Erin Giannini is reprinted by permission of the author.

The excerpt from "Baby Killer" by Michele Kwiatkowski is reprinted by permission of the author.

"Bagpipes" was first published in *Mississippi Review*.

"Anne Rey" was first published in *The Ohio Review* and was later collected in *Comfort*, published by Viking.

"Piano Lessons" was first published in *American Short Fiction*, was broadcast on National Public Radio's "The Sound of Writing," was reprinted in the anthology *The Sound of Writing*, and was collected in *Skating in the Dark*, published by Pantheon.

For John Leggett, Doris Grumbach and
James Alan McPherson, who taught me

ACKNOWLEDGMENTS

First and foremost, I would like to thank the most important contributors to whatever I have to say about the art and craft of revising fiction. They are all the students with whom I've had the privilege of working in my writing workshops over the years. They've been a constant source of education and inspiration for me. Especially among these I'd like to thank Erin Giannini, Michele Kwiatkowski, Josepha Conrad and Tony D'Souza. My appreciation extends to David Wojahn, former director of the Indiana University Writers' Conference, and to Peggy Houston, director of the Iowa Summer Writing Festival, for the opportunity to present much of the material here as a series of lectures at their conferences.

My own fiction writing teachers at The Iowa Writers' Workshop provided inspiration and education, as well as giving me models of what a writer and a teacher of writing should be. They are John Leggett, Doris Grumbach, James Alan McPherson and the late Angela Carter and Angus Wilson. Bob Shacochis and Susan Dodd also gave me much advice and support. Later, my colleagues at Loyola University Chicago, Dean Young and Sharon Solwitz, and Sharon's husband, Barry Solwitz, have been a source of ideas and inspiration over many lunches and dinners. Suzanne Gossett, chair of the English department, has been supportive in more ways than I can enumerate, and I want to thank her. Loyola University Chicago, besides providing good colleagues, also provided a leave which allowed me to work on this book.

At Story Press, Lois Rosenthal first saw that there might actually be a book here, and then encouraged me to do it; Jack Heffron, the embodiment of editorial wisdom, taste and patience, guided it along. I also want to thank my agent, Gail Hochman, for all her help over the years. And lastly, my gratitude and love to my wife, Joyce Winer, a marvelous fiction writer and my first and best reader, who has provided love and inspiration and a continuing dialogue about what good fiction writing is and may be.

CONTENTS

INTRODUCTION

This is a book about revising fiction. Revising is what you do after you've written the first draft in all its fuzzy blush and warm promise of glory. It's what a writer does last; unfortunately, however, it's also often the last thing on a writer's mind. Much creative effort goes into writing the first draft of a story or novel. Having finished that, too often a writer—especially a beginning writer—considers the hard work over. Maybe a few brushups here and there, a check for punctuation, typos and spelling, and *voilà*—done! As I hope to show in this book, it is not done, nor is that really revision. Revision is an art, it is a craft, and moreover, it is a way of deepening your understanding of your fiction. Revision is the key process of writing. It's where stories are made. If you do not believe that, then you need this book. If you do believe it, but feel a bit (or a lot) at a loss for how best to proceed with revising, you need this book too. I believe I can help you.

Revision represents the less glamorous side of writing (although not, as I hope to show, the less creative or the less exciting). Revision is the imaginative rehearsals, with all their stops and starts, zigs and zags, stumblings and excisions and additions and polishings, before your story "opens" for an audience. Or to make an analogy from film-making, it's the editing process, all that's left on the cutting-room floor of your imagination and in the wastebasket by your typewriter. It's everything the audience—your readers—never sees, and the summation of what it does see.

In this book, I'm going to discuss how to think about revision in three ways: revising for *style* (which is often all beginning writers think revision to be), revising for *structure* (the nitty-gritty of revision), and revising for *meaning*. I'll look at common revision problems writers face, problems I've encountered any number of times in my own work and in the work of student writers in my workshops. Although I'm discussing fiction, the concepts and principles apply equally to creative nonfiction. Or journalistic nonfiction. Or playwrighting, or poetry. I'll talk about my belief that revision begins *before* you even write the first draft, when you're just thinking about your story. I'll discuss revising *while* you're writing the first draft. Then I'll take a look at common revision problems of first and subsequent drafts—how to spot them, what to do about them. These include such problems as lack of dramatization in the story, overwriting or underwriting scenes, unnecessary characters and action, out-of-sequence narrative events, weak openings and endings. And I'll talk about stylistics—how to revise language for more punch. I'll discuss strategies for what to do when you're stuck, and how to recognize when it might be good to quit a particular piece, for a little or a long while. Lastly, I'll take a look at revision *after* publication in the work of several noted writers, suggesting it as a model for how to look at our own ongoing growth as writers.

I'll give numerous examples of the revision process at work, mostly culled from my own fiction, which I use for two reasons. First, I don't have the successive drafts of James Joyce's short stories, or Ann Beattie's, or John Gardner's, but I do have mine. Secondly, even if I did have drafts of other writers' work, not being them, I couldn't fully explain their reasons for specific revision decisions. But I can explain the reasons for mine. You'll see my bumblings, infelicities, wrong turns, and false starts and stops on the way to the final story. If anything, I hope that seeing how one writer has toiled in the muck of revision might make it easier for you in your own work. And more fun. Because I don't want to give the wrong idea—revision is fun too. It's imaginative play, with no referees, no critics, just you and your story. No one's counting. No one's rushing you. You're free, you can try anything, and you get as many chances as you want to make it perfect. So doesn't it make sense to try?

An anecdote and a moral: My wife and I recently decided to remodel our kitchen. We were tired of the tired linoleum, the 1950s-style cabinets, the lack of a dishwasher, the knotty-pine paneling on one wall. We were tired of always bumping into each other while cooking because we didn't have enough counter space. So we talked to contractors and got estimates. And we discovered that there were two ways of going—the way we really wanted to do it, which would cost a hunk of change which we didn't have, and a scaled-down version, which would cost much less, not only in terms of money, but in terms of time and aggravation. It is no fun, as many of you probably know, to have workmen taking up all the available space and air in your house, as they can do even if they're only enlarging a closet. So, there was the decision: to go into debt, as well as endure the hassles of extensive remodeling, but to have the kitchen we really wanted . . . or to settle for the second plan, which was less bother and less expense, but which also—alas—was less kitchen.

It was a tough decision. We cogitated, and we debated. And we finally decided to go for the more expensive plan. It would be a pain, sure, but in the end we'd have the kitchen we wanted. The other way would have been easier—but we'd have always known that we settled for something less than what might have been, and less than what we wanted. And who knows? It might have been false economy anyway, because ten years from now, we might find ourselves tearing up the kitchen again, to do what we should have done in the first place.

You may see the moral toward which my little anecdote is leading. I think you're faced with the same decision in revising your fiction. You can really buckle down and work on a story until it is perfect, first class all the way. Or you can take the easier way, the way of less suffering and quicker "results." The story will be "done." Yet all you'll really have is a story that could've been better. Deep down, you'll probably know it, and if you don't, your readers will. We have to cook in our kitchens, and we have to live with our fictions. Spend the time and effort now and your story will fare better.

Consider this book to be a guide to "remodeling" your fiction. I hope to save you some time and trouble. Without straining the analogy too much, I hope to help you become your own best contractor. I also hope to be your coach and cheerleader. And to be your aesthetic Jiminy Cricket, your artistic conscience, nagging and nudging you never to settle for less than your best and not to give up until you've got it.

CHAPTER ONE

WHY REVISE?

I n an interview in *The Paris Review*, E.L. Doctorow tells of the time he had to write a school absence note for his daughter. He sat down, pen in hand, and began: "My daughter Caroline . . ." and stopped. *How silly,* he thought, *why say that, of course they know she's my daughter.* Again he began: "Please be advised . . . ," no, much too formal. He started again. The paper around him piled up, his daughter fidgeted, the school bus arrived, and finally his wife had to step in, snatch away his pen and scribble off a quick note, all to stop her husband from trying to create, in his words, "the perfect absence note." Was he crazy? No—just a writer doing what all good writers do, which is to devote themselves to revising their work, sentence by sentence, paragraph by paragraph, page by page, draft by draft, in order to make it—school absence note or *War and Peace*—the best possible work it may be. Mexican poet and essayist Octavio Paz has called revision "the senseless desire for perfection." Desire it is, but senseless it's not, as this book will try to show.

You need three things to be a good fiction writer. The first is talent, about which not much can be said, less done, and no books may teach you. I'm going to assume that all of you reading this book are supremely talented anyway. Secondly, you need a knowledge of craft. It does indeed help to know the basics of plot structure, characterization, conflict, etc., if only to deviate from them. For help here, you can find any number of excellent books, workshops and courses. The third thing needed—and just as necessary as talent and craft, especially if we take to heart the adage that art is ten percent inspiration and ninety percent perspiration—is a devotion to revision, to a merciless re-working of your writing until it is the best it can be, stylistically, conceptually and dramatically. The very sensible desire for perfection. Because believe me, talent and craft will only get you so far. A cellist or a bel canto singer might have talent and craft, but without endless hours of practice, as the hoary old joke rightly says, he'll never get to Carnegie Hall. (Tourist on street to man carrying a cello: "Excuse me, how do I get to Carnegie Hall?" Cellist: "Practice.") Just so a writer needs to devote himself to his "practicing," which is the revision of his story or essay or novel until it is, in Goldilocks' words, "just right." The pianist Vladimir Horowitz has said that if he didn't practice for a day, he knew it; if he didn't practice for a week, his fellow musicians knew it; and if he failed to practice for a month, the public knew it.

The same is true for writers, in a slightly inverse way. If we're content with the first draft, the world will know it; if content with one better than the first but still not the best it could be, our fellow writers will know it; if content with one *almost* perfect except for a few little glitches, perhaps, with luck, only we will know it. That's usually the state in which good stories are finished and eventually published anyway, with an unavoidable wart or two, much like the old Persian rugs with their occasional mistakes incorporated into the pattern as reminders that only God can make things perfectly. It's the *desire* for perfection, remember—not Perfection itself. Come to think of it, I'm not sure Perfection's true for God either. After all, He did send a flood to correct the mistake He'd made with humanity, thus being the universe's first and greatest Reviser.

It's in revision that good fiction is made. I'll say it again, even louder: *Only* through revision is good fiction made. If you imagine that stories fall plum-and-apple perfect from your imagination-to-pen-to-paper, like Athena fully formed from the forehead of Zeus, then you are either a genius (unlike most of the world's other acknowledged genius writers, who almost to a man and woman have stressed the importance of revision) and so have no need of this book nor indeed any book, course or workshop—or, like Bogart in *Casablanca*, you have been "misinformed."

The purpose of writing a story is to rewrite it. The purpose of a first draft is only to get us to the second; the purpose of the second, to get us to the third; the third to the fourth, and on and on and on, ad infinitum and often ad nauseam, although we hope to declare the story finished sometime before either nausea or eternity. If you talk with writers, if you read interviews with writers, over and over again you will hear this emphasis upon revision. Tolstoy wrote *War and Peace* eight times (without a word processor yet!) and was still making revisions in the galleys. James Joyce drove Sylvia Beach, his publisher, to distraction with his endless revisions of *Ulysses*. Raymond Carver says he's done as many as twenty or thirty drafts of a story, never fewer than ten or twelve. Truman Capote talks about believing more in "the scissors than in the pencil," and Isaac Bashevis Singer extols the wastepaper basket as "the writer's best friend." William Gass, the master stylist, swears he has to rewrite everything many times "just to achieve mediocrity." Doctorow maintains he doesn't finish anything in fewer than six to eight drafts. I myself have never finished a story in less than six drafts, in which case I count it as a "gift-from-God" story. Most take anywhere from ten to fifteen, and I have some that took more. A few have gone through twenty-odd drafts and still counting.

Yet the importance of revision is often hard for a beginning fiction writer—and many who aren't beginners—to understand. Wallace Stegner, the master writer and teacher of writing at Stanford, said that the hardest thing to teach someone is "Revise! Revise! Revise!" to which Irish short story writer Frank O'Connor might have added, as he did when asked if he revised his stories, "Endlessly, endlessly, endlessly." Dedication to revision is what makes the difference between a mediocre writer and a good one, and often between a good writer and a great one. The French novelist Colette has said that anybody can sit and put down everything that comes into her head. "But an author," she goes on to say, "is one who can judge his own stuff's worth, without pity, and destroy most of it." For the best interests of the story, of course. It's a paradox, this "destruction" that's really a creation. Sometimes I think writers would do well to imagine themselves like the tripartite Hindu godhead of Vishnu the Creator, Brahma the Preserver and Shiva the Destroyer. As writers, we have to be each at different times—creator, preserver and destroyer—for the sake of our work.

REVISION RELUCTANCE

As a longtime teacher of fiction writing, I can affirm Stegner's implication that writers are often reluctant to revise. Many think revising is simply retyping. To others, a word here, a word there, shift a few paragraphs around, put it through the spell checker—done! I've seen writers with talent, and not a little craft, balk at anything more extensive, when something more extensive is precisely what the story needs. I think this "revision reluctance" may happen for several reasons. Maybe the writer feels that a first draft, with a few minor touchups, *should* be the finished story—the Romantic idea of divine inspiration leading one to spew out line upon perfect line, as Samuel Taylor Coleridge professed to have done with his poem "Kubla Khan," dies hard. (In his preface to the poem, Coleridge says that the lines came to him in a dream "without any sensation or consciousness of effort"; when he awoke, he "instantly and eagerly wrote down the lines that are here preserved." Some of this, I feel, is a little Romantic mythmaking. And of course, Coleridge didn't talk about the revisions to the poem he *did* make, of which we have ample manuscript evidence!) "First thought, best thought," Allen Ginsberg has advised in a Beat echoing of this myth of divine inspiration, which has been misinterpreted to mean that whatever one first thinks *and writes* is best, and best left untouched. Of course, he meant only that the first thought may be best, not necessarily the first writing of that thought. For proof, just look at the studiously worked and reworked versions of his masterpiece poem, "Howl," now available for study in a holographic edition. And if you need further proof, read John Steinbeck's *Journal of a Novel*, which is an account of his struggles to write and revise *East of Eden*. Beguiled by Romantic and Beat myth, however, beginning writers may feel they're not "real" writers if they don't create an almost perfect first draft. But a real writer, to quote Colette again, is someone who "can judge his own stuff's worth, without pity, and destroy most of it."

Or maybe we're just too easily satisfied, too much in love with our own words, or too "frozen" by them. It's hard enough to see ourselves as others see us, let alone see our writing as they might. If we read our pages too often, they will take on what Annie Dillard calls a "necessary quality, the ring of the inevitable." And therefore the unchangeable. Or we may simply be in love with our own words. While commendable in some ways (after all, we *should* like what we're writing), this can become like the love of Narcissus for his reflected image—illusory, self-involved, and uninteresting to anyone else. (Also, it often masks an insecurity. We're afraid to be too critical with our work for fear we might see weaknesses we'd rather not acknowledge. Out of insight, out of mind.) Or maybe this "ring of the inevitable" is less like staring at Narcissus' image and more like staring into Medusa's: We become imaginatively frozen and can think of no alternate ways of saying and thinking about those words. Stare at a paragraph long enough, and its sentences start seeming inevitable; read a sentence enough times, and every word starts seeming preordained! If anything, I hope this book will suggest ways to "unfreeze" yourself imaginatively in revising your fiction.

Another possible reason for revision reluctance is the perfectly understandable desire to get something finished, done, perhaps even sent off for possible publication. Writing is a lonely business, yes indeed. We sit in small rooms and babble to ourselves. We long to find out if this babble means anything to anyone else, so we send it out. We're unwilling to hold back and wait, to take the second, third, fourth and God knows how many hard looks that will help make it less babble and more a meaningful imaginative experience. We're impatient, like little kids on a trip asking over and over again if we're there yet. The only problem is that we're the ones driving now. *We* have to decide if we're there yet. And it's tempting to tell ourselves we are when really we're only halfway there, or stuck with a flat tire, or on the wrong road entirely. If so, we must have the critical judgment to stop, take a breath, and find a map, a cop, a guidebook—something—to get us on course again. (And when *are* we there, you ask? When are we finished revising? When the story/chapter/novel is perfect, of course. No sooner. And how will we know when it's perfect? That's what this book will help you find out.)

Another possible reason we might not like to revise—which I hate to even suggest, but I must—is that we're lazy. Revision is hard work, after all, lots of muck and toil. Looking at our words and sentences until they no longer seem like English. Realizing that our characters belong in four different stories, and none of them this one. Fearing that this story, which was going to make us immortal, is only a rehash of a dippy, long-canceled TV sitcom. Thinking and rethinking, typing and retyping. Drinking too much coffee, and wanting desperately to be distracted by anything—the phone, the mailman, a book or a bagel. Unfortunately, there's no computer program for revision like there is for spelling. It's hands-on, imagination-intensive work. Revision is like putting up a house, then realizing that the walls aren't plumb and the windows don't hang right. What to do? Tear it all apart, start over? Who wants to? *But you must,* the good writing angel perched on your shoulder whispers. *Just leave it,* coaxes the bad writing angel on your other shoulder. *Maybe the owners won't notice.* Except you, my friend, are the owner. You have to live there. And maybe you can. But don't expect anyone else to.

There's a last possible explanation for our reluctance to revise, one that the rest of this book addresses: Maybe we don't really know *how* to think of revision, how to approach it, what to look for, what the common problems are. Writing workshops and courses teach you how to write a first draft, but not necessarily how to revise it. Indeed, at the very beginning of learning how to write, it may even be best *not* to revise too much, but simply to move on to the next story. This is because when we start writing, we have to write a certain number of Dumb Stories. I sure did. I call it "writing out your juvenilia," and it's something you have to do whether you're twenty-two or sixty-two. (The advantage of age is that you can possibly do it more quickly.) I used to mountain-climb. One day I was climbing with an old veteran, and we watched aghast as someone on another route climbed without belay ropes. He turned to me, shook his head, and murmured, "Dumb is forever." Some stories, unfortunately, are Dumb (I've written my share), and they're Dumb forever. No amount of revision will improve them, and it's just plain discouraging to keep trying. Discard them and move on. That's revision too.

But at some point you're going to write a story that doesn't seem Dumb, a story in which you really believe, which moves you and which you think has potential to move others. Now you *must* revise in earnest, and now it's helpful if you know some basic principles of revision. I believe these principles, both aesthetic and craft-wise, exist, and they're what I'm going to discuss in this book. I think they might help you with your own revision. After all, when you're looking at that metaphorical building that's a mess, you can either tear it down, start all over, and maybe make the same old mistakes, or you can look at some books on window-hanging and wall-plumbing and roof-raising, and try to figure out what went wrong and what can be done about it. It might save you some time and trouble and get you home a lot faster.

HOW TO THINK ABOUT REVISION

Now: I'm going to suggest a way of thinking about revision that may be different from how you've thought about it before. I think you revise for *style* (saying it in the most graceful way, which is often all people think revision is), and you revise for *structure* (saying it in the most coherent and dramatically effective way), and you revise—and here comes the way you might not have thought about it before—for *meaning,* for discovering what you really wanted to say in the first place, what the story's *really* about. After all, the roots of the word "revision" come from the Latin *revisere,* "to see again." To see what we're writing about in a new, richer, more meaningful way. In the most aesthetically expansive sense, revision is the opportunity we give ourselves in our writing to "see it all again," more fully, richly, deeply. Your first idea or draft is one vision, or version (from the Latin *vertere,* "to turn"). Then you revise—"re-see"—so that not only the story's words and structure, *but also its very meaning,* might change. And so you take a "turning," and produce another version, another draft.

You might think you should have nailed down what the story's about before writing it, but no, not necessarily, not necessarily at all. It may have needed more thinking out before writing that first draft— which is the subject of the next chapter, "Revising Before Writing." Or it may be that only through the act of writing the first draft, then seeing it again, mulling different possibilities for action and character, that we begin to understand what the story's really about. You thought it was about what a difficult man Grandpa was, how he was always so thoughtless and cruel to Grandma. But then, upon revision— "re-seeing"—you see it's better as a story about a man's frustrations and disappointments over his life's choices. And that story about a salesgirl debating whether to turn in the little girl she spots shop-lifting, which you thought was about a woman's struggle with her conscience, works better if she confronts the little girl and even helps her in her theft. And lo and behold! It's really a story about a woman realizing and giving in to the "criminal" anarchic impulses in herself.

Revision. Seeing again. In *On Becoming a Novelist,* John Gardner maintained it was only in the "on-going process of *seeing* what he'd said" that a writer figured out what he was trying to say. In psychotherapy, we don't expect to understand ourselves—the meaning of our experience—right away. We know, or should know, that it will take time and effort, and we will have to endure a period of some confusion and despair. Only gradually will we uncover, or "re-see," the meaning of our lives. Just so in revising fiction. Fiction, after all, is about finding the meaning of our *imaginative* experience. As T.S. Eliot said in *Four Quartets*, we can have the experience and miss the meaning. Revision, re-seeing our fictional ideas, is the means whereby we search for and find that meaning.

Let me give you another house remodeling parable. A few years ago I was getting estimates for painting the exterior trim of my house. One of the bids came from a burly, bluff, baleful Russian immigrant— let's call him Yuri—who looked at my trim with a cold eye, pronounced it in miserable shape, told me his crew would have to strip the windows down to the wood, and handed me an estimate that was three times as much as anyone else's. I was both astounded and amused by Yuri— his theatrical flair, his perfectionism, and his complete misreading of not only what I wanted and needed (a simpler, albeit less perfect, paint job), but also what the market would bear. As I retold the story to friends, I revised it for comic effect. I added and discarded and downright lied to make it a "better," if less truthful, story. Yuri became grander of gesture, more Dostoevskian in his passion for my trim. In my revision of the story, he shook his head and bemoaned it. I felt anxious. He took out his jackknife and cut off paint slivers. I asked questions, to which Yuri shook his head and darkly muttered. He microscopically examined the wood. I began to feel my case was terminal. Yuri told me his crew (hints here of illegal immigrants arriving by night on Canadian ships) would have to use—and here in my story he raised his hand like a pistol and cocked his finger—*heat guns!* They would burn off the trim. Then they would have to scrape, scrape, scrape. Sandpaper, sandpaper, sandpaper. It would not be easy, he sighed. It would take a lot of time. It will take a lot of money, I thought. I asked for an estimate. Yuri totaled up the cost. Three, maybe four, times as much as anyone else. I gulped and told him it was more than I anticipated. Yuri looked at me scornfully. Do I want the job done right? he asked. I felt guilty, like someone trying to get cut-rate surgery for a liver transplant for an only child.

In my retelling, my revision, the story became a comic encounter. But over time, I started to perceive—and then add—darker elements. I began to stress a fundamental misunderstanding between the Yuri character and the me-character. In the current version of my story he sees me as a rich American, which I'm not, who can surely afford and *who surely wants* the best-quality work, which, at his prices, I don't. I, not really understanding his Old World sense of craftsmanship, see him as a price-gouger. Over time and mulling and retelling—revision—my story has become less a comedy and more a bittersweet story of cultural misreading and miscomprehension.

And so over time I've revised the story more than once. It's been added to and exaggerated. Incidents have changed. The tone has changed. Dialogue that was never spoken has been added. Characters have changed: After all, I have no idea what the real Yuri had been thinking about me or the job. And most importantly, the story's meaning has changed several times. Indeed, the original incident *didn't even have a meaning*. Only retelling and revising gave it one. Katherine Anne Porter once said that it took her ten years to understand the meaning of something that happened to her. She could have given a narrative account of it right away, of course, but it couldn't become a true story until she understood what it all meant, and that took time and imaginative mulling. Revision. It's strange how we find this perfectly natural and acceptable in life, but not in our fiction writing. There, we expect the meaning to be apparent all at once, on the first draft. Or the second at most.

As I've tried to suggest, revising story elements changes a story's meaning. Revising story structure also changes its meaning. Conversely, seeing a new meaning in a story will necessitate revisions in its structure and elements. Let's say you've written a story about a woman being forced to give up her beloved child because of drug abuse. You thought it was a story about a woman's despair over the wreckage of her life. But you have a sudden insight: This could be a story about the redemptive power of a mother's love for her child. Because she is faced with giving up her child, this woman could summon the strength to begin to change her life. You like this story better. Imagining this new possibility, this new meaning, will naturally necessitate revisions in your story's plot. And sometimes it works the other way: You're mulling over your story and idly wonder what would happen if the woman told the social services worker to go to hell, instead of meekly demurring, when he suggests Child Welfare take her child. You like that, you get excited by it. And lo! it's now a story about a woman changing her life. Through revising a crucial story event, suddenly a whole new meaning for the story is suggested.

It's in revision—re-seeing our stories—that these changes can occur. And they begin, or should begin, before we even write the first draft. As I'll show you in the next chapter.

CHAPTER TWO

REVISING BEFORE WRITING

Here's Jack Kerouac in a *Paris Review* interview talking about how he prepared to write a story:

> You think out what actually happened, you tell friends long stories about it, you mull it over in your mind, you connect it together at leisure, then when the time comes to pay the rent again you force yourself to sit at the typewriter, or at the writing notebook, and get it over with as fast as you can . . . and there's no harm in that because you've got the whole story lined up.

Truman Capote once said condescendingly that Kerouac didn't write, he just typed. But that was unfair. Kerouac might not have done much revision *after* writing (and I really can't speak to that), but he seems to have done quite a bit *before*, in "mulling it over" and "connecting it together." It's probably here that the story was made for him. Maybe the rest *was* just typing, but it didn't matter. The important revision had already been done.

Mulling it over. Getting the whole story "lined up." I believe the most important steps in revising occur—or should occur—here, *before we even begin to write*. If, as I've suggested, revising is discovering what we really want to say, not just how to say it, then we can revise our stories by mulling and pondering them before we even sit down to do the first draft. Without tearing up and crossing out whole pages, we can change our characters, change their problems, change what happens to them. Before writing, it's easy to change the lonely teenager watching the Rollerbladers go by to a widowed old man. Or maybe a divorced middle-aged woman. As your *characters* change, so does the meaning of the story. Maybe your young divorcée traveling with her parakeet shouldn't get off the bus in Tucumcari, but should stay on it. How else will she meet that drifter who has dreams of being a bull rider? As the *events* of the story change, so does its meaning. Or maybe this story is better written from within the consciousness of the bull rider, not the young divorcée. As the *point of view* changes, so does the story's meaning. Often when we get the first idea for a story, we don't know what it's really going to be about. We may think we do, but often we don't. Remember the story idea I mentioned in chapter one about the saleswoman noticing a shoplifter? At first you think, ah, this is a story about a woman's struggle with her conscience. But when you mull and ponder it before writing, you try imagining other possibilities. What might happen if she finds herself sympathizing with the girl? Why would she? Because the girl looks poor? Or maybe because she herself has been overly proper and law-abiding all her life, and has unconsciously been chafing because of it? Or maybe because she hates her job? Or her supervisor? What if she *helps* the girl with her theft? This gets you excited, and soon you discover it's really a story about something you'd never even considered—a woman's discovery of her own capacity for crime.

Re-vising. Re-seeing.

I'll be honest and admit that writers differ on this business of revising before writing. Richard Ford, author of *The Sportswriter* and *Rock Springs*, has said his best stories are ones he's thought about a lot before writing. John Irving, author of *The World According to Garp*, says he doesn't begin a novel until he knows as much as he can stand to know without putting anything down on paper. Acclaimed short-story writer André Dubus, however, has said that he prefers just to begin writing and see where the story takes him. It's as if there are two kinds of travelers: those who prefer to land in a foreign country having done some planning and research beforehand, and those who don't. The latter just strike off somewhere, hippity-serendipity, trusting to fate and fortune. They may have some fine adventures. But they also may run into bandits, beriberi and fully booked hotels.

The other kind of traveler—most of us, I think—likes to have done at least a smidgen of planning. We'd like to know roughly where we're going and what we're likely to see. We'd like to know that there are ferry connections between Brindisi and Corfu, or that the best dolmens in Europe can be found in Brittany. So before embarking, we've probably thought and rethought about our trip and changed our plans—revised them—a dozen times. Shall we go here or there? Two days in Granada or one? Will we see a bullfight or not? Which is more important: the caves of Málaga or the Palace at Knossos? What's the best route to get there? We've settled these important details, then structured a "narrative"—an itinerary—for the trip. Most importantly, we've settled on what its "meaning" will be. Will our trip be "about" art and architecture? Cuisine? Surf and snorkeling? Natural wonders? Historical sites and monuments? In our imaginations we've revised our trip many times before we've even packed our duffles and left for the airport. And the journey goes that much smoother. We hope.

Just so in writing. Before writing, we can think about and revise our story's details, narrative structure (fiction's "itinerary") and meaning. Of course, we don't want to be overprepared. Part of the fun of any trip is the unknown. And that will happen anyway. Life at best is a planned mess, or as Beatle John Lennon once said, "It's what happens to you when you're planning for something else." But a little preparation still goes a long way.

STRATEGIES FOR REVISING BEFORE WRITING
In revising your story ideas before writing, first of all don't be in a hurry to write the first draft. Keep your options and your imagination open. Try getting to the "deeper" story by imaginatively doing the following:

1. *Change the characters.* Change their age, or their sex, or their physical characteristics or all of these. It makes quite a difference if the shoplifter in our earlier example is a nine-year-old girl or a thirty-year-old woman with two kids in tow.

2. *Change the point of view.* Maybe the story is better told by the daughter than by the mother. Or by the shoplifter than by the clerk. And maybe it's better in the first person than in the third.

3. *Change the setting.* It makes a different story if the shoplifter is in a fancy department store stealing perfume rather than in a convenience store stealing baby formula.

4. *Change the situation, or problem, at hand.* It's one story if the clerk in our example is a sixteen-year-old girl who has a difficult relationship with her parents. It's quite another one if she's in her early forties and has just lost a child to cancer.

5. *Change the conflict.* It's one story if the salesgirl is debating with herself whether or not to turn in the shoplifter. It's another one if she confronts the shoplifter, who protests her innocence and then turns violent.

6. *Mix and match any of the above.* For example, maybe the story that really excites you is one told from the point of view of a nine-year-old girl whose mother is shoplifting jewelry. The girl is apprehensive. They're confronted by the salesgirl. The mother protests her innocence. She and the salesgirl get into a screaming match, embarrassing the daughter mightily. Angered, frustrated and humiliated, she then betrays her mother.

Through playing with story possibilities, we begin to figure out and flesh out what the true story might be—before we even begin to write. From the very beginning, we're trying to avoid being frozen into the First Idea. A very important point: In all the examples above, we're changing *concrete* details, not abstract ideas. We imagine jewels or baby formula, a nine-year-old girl or a thirty-year-old woman, a salesgirl who hates a boss or a saleswoman who's lost a child to cancer. We don't think, *What if this were a story about Loss?* Or *Differing Concepts of Justice?* Or *Teen Angst?* It's through playing with the concrete details of the story that the abstract meaning changes, not the other way around. As the poet William Carlos Williams said, "No ideas but in things." Worry about the things first, and the ideas will take care of themselves.

Make notes. Or outlines. Or little sketches. Any way that allows you to develop most comfortably your ideas and alternate ideas. You can put them on index cards, as did Russian expatriate novelist Vladimir Nabokov, or on little slips of paper you keep in your pockets. You can dictate them on tape while you're driving. But for ease of access and prevention of loss, I recommend a notebook or a journal. If you don't have one for writing down dreams, images, ideas, things overheard and seen—anything that might become the "seed" idea for a story or might be used in revising the story you're working on—

I heartily recommend one. Mine are 5½″ by 8½″ artist's sketchbooks. They're portable (I take one everywhere), and the paper's thick and creamy and nice to write on. Whatever method you choose, get those ideas and alternate ideas down. You may think you can remember any *really* good one . . . but chances are you won't. They're like puffballs on a summer's day—here, pretty and gone. And that's not the point anyway. A good story idea often doesn't announce itself. It's only in mulling it over and mixing and matching it with other ideas, images, snippets of dialogue and so on, that it becomes a good one. Sometimes the yoking of two images from different times closes an imaginative synapse and creates an exciting story idea. My story "Anne Rey," which we'll examine in more detail later, began when I realized that the personalized license plate I'd seen on the Los Angeles freeway and copied down in my journal hooked up with an image I'd had of someone living on a sailboat at a marina. The two entries were years apart *and both forgotten* until I reread them while flipping through my journals, looking for story ideas. And hooked them up. Aha! The Anne Rey driving that car is also the one living on a sailboat. And the story developed from there.

So I heartily recommend regular browsing through your journals, whether casting for a new story idea or developing one in progress. Mix and match. The most unlikely notes, images, details, ideas will suddenly link up or fire your imagination. I've got a three-foot-long shelf of journals that I regularly dip into. I think of them as my ocean of story possibilities.

"BAGPIPES"

I'll try to make revision before writing clearer by using one of my stories, "Bagpipes," as an example. I'll trace with you the way it was much revised before I even started writing it. First, here's the story as published (beginning on the next page).

BAGPIPES

Someone is playing bagpipes again in the park across from my apartment. All this past week he's been coming here in late afternoon to play for awhile before it gets dark. Since he plays somewhere beyond the row of trees lining the park, I've never seen him. He always begins in fits and starts, sort of musical coughs or throat clearings. But then suddenly he'll really play, and the melody rises and falls like a strange dark bird. I turn off the lights in my apartment so I can listen better, and I listen.

I've been thinking about wolves. Their howling, I think, sounds just like bagpipes, sort of dark and lonely. It's funny— I've never understood how wolves can run in packs and be so sociable and all, yet sound so mournful, like each one was the last of his kind left on earth. Coyotes are like that too. I've got a theory about it—the most social animals always sound the loneliest. It's strange.

I've never seen a wolf in my life, but I know what they sound like because of Kate, a woman I saw for awhile after Sarah— my wife—and I finally split for good. Kate had an album of wolf calls put out by some wildlife preservation group. It was narrated by a movie star who used to make a lot of westerns. There was a picture of him on the cover hugging a big gray wolf.

"He looks pretty uneasy," I told Kate.

"Who?" she asked. "The guy or the wolf?"

Kate had lots of records of animal sounds: wolves howling, monkeys screeching, cockatoos jabbering like old men. You name it, she had it. It's funny—she wasn't *really* an animal lover. I don't think she even liked live animals—she didn't have a pet or anything, after all. But she did like turning off the lights and putting on one of those albums—the wolves were one of her favorites. We'd drink wine and lie on the sofa or the floor.

"Just pretend," she said, "that we're in the steppes of Asia, in a cottage, and there's a fire roaring and it's snowing outside and we hear the wolves."

Kate was always trying to pretend she was somewhere else, and I'd play along, even though it annoyed me sometimes. I mean, I was trying hard just to be exactly where I was, because life in those days right after the divorce was confusing enough, and I didn't need to make it any worse. I wanted to be right where I was, no place else. Anyway, we'd listen to the animals, and drink wine, and maybe even make love right there on the sofa or on the floor while the alligators thrashed or the wolves howled. One time Kate bit me on the lip, hard, and I yelped.

"What?" she asked, blinking, and I said, "You bit me." I couldn't believe it.

"You're bleeding," she said.

I licked my lip—sure enough, it tasted salty. She touched it. "Look," she said wonderingly, holding up her finger. "Blood."

I remember another album Kate had, one of humpback whale songs. Sometimes we'd sit in the dark and listen to them. You could hear ocean sounds on the record (I don't know whether they dubbed them in or what), so it was almost like we were underwater too. The whales' calls were really some-thing, not at all what you'd expect from such big creatures. They sounded as far away as the wolves, and just as sad, like big lonely babies. I told Kate that.

"They're not lonely at all," she said. "They're really very social animals."

There it was again, my theory.

"Do you know," she said, "that whales can call to each other across thousands of miles of ocean?"

I said, No, I didn't know that. For some reason, it didn't make me feel they were any less lonely. In fact, I was actually getting depressed about it.

"What're you thinking?" Kate asked. "You're so quiet."

"I feel like I'm underwater," I told her. I lay on my stomach and dog-paddled on the floor. I started making frothing, bubbly sounds. I flailed and thrashed. I think I really did just want to swim off, out of there, away. Kate thought it was funny and began giggling. I flailed harder.

"Help," I cried. "Killer whales! They're after me!"

"Don't be silly," Kate laughed. "Whales won't hurt you. They like people."

It's funny—Sarah and I tried to see whales once, years ago. We were staying on the Cape for a week the summer after we got married. Whale-watching trips left from Wellfleet, and one blustery afternoon we went on one. We didn't know it could get so chilly on summer days out on the open ocean, so we spent much of the time huddled together in a deck chair while the captain kept us cheerily posted on his lack of success in finding whales.

"Folks, I don't know what to say," he told us over the loud-speaker. "This is—I swear—the only time we've gone out all summer that we haven't seen any."

To be fair, he did find some eventually. But Sarah and I were below deck then, having a cup of coffee, and when we heard all the commotion and got back on top, they were gone.

"Where are they?" Sarah asked breathlessly.

"Just over there." An old man in a Red Sox cap lowered his binoculars and pointed. "Two of 'em."

We stared and stared but couldn't see them. I didn't care too much myself, but I felt bad for Sarah—I knew she was disappointed. I told her we'd come back another time, for sure we'd see some then, but we never got around to it. We were in love after all, and there were other things to do that week, and later, and later. We could always come back.

And then—so fast, it all seems so fast—it really was later and we were back on the Cape again, but everything was different. I'd just confessed to Sarah about Blake, the woman I'd gotten involved with five months earlier and whom I thought I loved too. Everything was confused, and we'd gone to the Cape hoping to get a little perspective, a little breathing room. It was my idea—I thought maybe it would help things. We were going crazy in our house crying and yelling and sulking and hiding out from each other. But of course being there, where we'd been happy before, just seemed to make everything worse. To top it off, the weather was just beautiful, clear and gentle and warm. We could've been having a wonderful time, if only we were two other people. After one really bad fight, I stormed out of the cottage, took a chair from the deck and went down to the beach. I planted it in the sand only a few feet from the water. The surf was soft, the sand squishy between my toes. Nobody was swimming, although two boys in bathing suits were standing on the last rock of the breakwater, daring each other to dive. I must have dozed, because suddenly I started, aware of something blocking the sun. I shaded my eyes. Sarah was

standing there in her swimsuit, snorkeling mask on her forehead, flippers tucked under her arm, holding a knife. "You're
not going to hurt me, are you?" I asked. A crazy thing to say.

"I'm going to get some mussels off the rocks for dinner,"
she said. "If we go out to one more restaurant, I'm going to
scream." She put on her flippers, and flip-flopped into the water,
stomach slightly thrust out for balance, like some ungainly bird.
Not hesitating a moment, she breasted the chill water, and
dove. I had to smile. *My brave wife,* I thought. She came up,
and waved. I waved back. It was better than anything we'd said
all week.

I closed my eyes and must have dozed again, or at least
was in that half-way state between dream and fantasy, because
suddenly I felt, I really felt, that I was out there swimming
with her. Or rather, I was on the surface, looking down at her
swimming below me. Large dark shapes were moving under
her, toward her, and I was frightened. I tried to cry out to warn
her, but my words were just bubbling sounds in the water. And
then, like a slide coming into focus, I could see everything
clearly: the dark shapes were whales, and they weren't at-
tacking Sarah at all. She was swimming toward them, and then
among them, without any fear, as if she belonged there. She
grabbed one by the flipper and stroked it, and I thought, *my
wife, my brave and gentle wife,* and even though we were
fathoms apart, at that moment I just couldn't understand how
anything beyond water could ever really separate us. I wanted
to call to Sarah, to tell her that. But already she couldn't hear
me, she was following the whales, sounding with them to where
no sound, no sound, no sound, neither of whales nor wolves
nor bagpipes, could ever raise her from the deep again.

•   •   •

"Bagpipes" is a story about a man's loneliness and regret over the
loss of his first and best wife. Its narrative structure consists of a series
of memories triggered by bagpipe music and then imagistically linked
through wolves and whale records and real whales to a final vision of
swimming with whales. Chronologically, the story goes back in time until
what's really bothering the narrator—the loss of his wife—is revealed.

But I sure didn't know any of this when I got the first idea for the story. I didn't even know any story was there.

It began with a dream. I used to live in Provincetown, near the migratory paths of gray whales, so whales were probably on my mind or in it way deep. And one April morning I woke up from a strange dream about whales, which I wrote down in my journal:

> April 7
>
> Dreams last night—in one the sea is huge and A. and I are standing on a dock or sheltered deck watching it. It's a huge tide and the sea is running in great swells, welling and falling. It is a bright turquoise color. Suddenly I see a fluke, and then the rising body of a whale breaching. I tell A., who immediately gets on her swim gear and mask and goes in. I'm very frightened and very anxious for her, especially when she doesn't come up. I see more whales rising and breaching, and I'm afraid they might have eaten her. But then I see her, next to a whale. She comes back on shore, or on the dock rather.

It's easy to see that this dream provided key imagery for "Bagpipes," especially the ending. But I didn't know that then. There was no ending, much less a beginning and middle. As a story scene, it's a little implausible. I mean, who swims with whales? As a dream it was halfway interesting, but probably only to me. As an editor once put it, "Tell a dream, lose a reader." So there it was, just a dream, just another journal entry.

A year and a half later, October. I was teaching at the University of Iowa, and my office overlooked a soccer field. In late afternoon I'd often hear a bagpiper practicing from somewhere on the field. I never saw him. He was probably somewhere within the copse of trees that bordered one end of the field, or behind an equipment shed at the other. Or maybe he wasn't on the field at all, but somewhere else, and only acoustical alchemy made it seem as if he were close. Now, I love bagpipe music. It makes me want to wail and weep and march to war all at the same time. So often on those purplish, hazy, chill fall afternoons I'd catch myself listening and dreaming as the field grew darker. And an image came to me for a character, a man listening to an invisible bagpiper and brooding. I made some notes in my journal (sections in italics are attempts to create a voice for this man).

Oct. 22

"Bagpipes in the Dark"—Every Thursday, I'd hear someone playing bagpipes in the dark, from somewhere on the playing fields, although I never saw who it was.

And I remember for some reason my first wife walking down the beach, a beach in—where is it?—Aruba, and she's carrying a spear gun. What are you going to do with that, I ask, she who would never kill anything.

"Where are you going?" I asked. "Where are you going now?" And the truth is she was going away, although I didn't know it then.

I loved her dearly. Although I didn't know that then either. I thought I loved her, sure, but it wasn't real knowledge. That only comes with loss.

I can never quite hold things as they happen. They drift away, like the bagpipe music.

And it seems like this room, this darkened room, is as wide as the ocean, and that I'm swimming in it too, near her, we are both swimming near some great shape that is beside us. We swim, the three of us.

I like doing things in the night. Sometimes when I'm restless, I'll get up and bicycle along the streets. I like the smells then, damp, almost decaying, tucked in for sleep, toasty, yeasty, fragrant like bread.

Who is this guy? What's his problem? Here, I'm trying to figure it out on paper. He hears bagpipe music and thinks of his former wife, okay. I've somehow connected that earlier dream of swimming with the whales to him, although I don't know why, or how it relates to bagpipes. I'm also considering possible character details and story events, such as his bicycling at night and his wife's carrying a spear gun, both of which later get revised—discarded in the case of the bike riding, changed to a knife in the case of the spear gun. Over the next few months, I made more notes and sketches as my image of the characters changed: For a while the wife was taking up scuba diving, the narrator was having insomnia and waking up in the middle of the night, he was having a nervous breakdown, etc., etc. All attempts to see and re-see the characters. Revisions.

Here's a journal entry only a few days after the one above:

Oct. 24

"Bagpipes"
He listens to the bagpipe music. *"I turn off the lights."*

"It reminds me of whales." He remembers his girlfriend who played animal records while they made love. Or it's his present lover . . .

"But I didn't marry her. I married another woman, gentler by far."

I think of her not in dark rooms, but in sunlight, and a specific sunlight, that of a summer at a beach cottage on the Massachusetts shore.

I'm trying to do two things here: figure out more about the characters and plot a possible story. At some point, you're going to want to do just this, to begin sketching out story events in some order—a plot. Here, I'm connecting bagpipes and whales and animal records and beach cottages, all of which find their way into the final story, although in what order, I don't yet know. And now the guy has a lover. But is she a girlfriend *before* his wife? Or a present lover? Or a lover after his wife and he have split? Or is he still married? Which one does he really love? Each possibility leads to a different story. At this point, I'm keeping things open, imaginatively unfrozen, trying to see the characters and the story in different ways. Because we rarely know what our stories are about right off. We have to discover what they're about.

For a while I seem to playing with the idea of it being a story about the *dread* of loss, as opposed to real loss:

The whales are migrating close to shore this year. We are happy, my wife and I . . . I'm so happy that suddenly I become sad, as if all this can quickly be taken from me, and had no more substance than the fog in the morning. I'm frightened, and all morning that fear is with me . . .

But a few days later, I'm seeing the story quite differently.

Oct. 26

I had already begun seeing someone else . . . we were at the sea . . . it was the summer the whales came close and my wife took up scuba diving.

I lay back in the sun and pondered what a wonderful woman my wife was. To be able to plunge into the ocean and come up with treasure!

He sees his wife in the ocean and thinks what a wonderful life, to be in love twice. And is filled with happiness. And then, suddenly, is terrified: *as if a cloud had crossed the sun and the air chilled. The world grew darker, and suddenly I was there with her, underwater, choking almost.*

Now the narrator is someone who's having an affair and is a bit smug and self-satisfied about it until he suddenly feels anxiety and terror. The story is no longer so much about nameless dread as it is about the guilty pleasures of adultery. Only a few days later, however, I'm seeing the story yet another way:

Oct. 28

"What are you crying about?" she asked, as if it was an affront to her somehow.
"I'm not young anymore," I said.
"Well, so what?" she said. "Everybody gets old." She said this, but I could tell she didn't believe it.

Now it's a story about despair over loss of youth! And a few pages later, I'm seeing it yet another way:

He dreams of her swimming with the dark shapes, and is afraid. Then sees her with the spear gun, and laughs. Is restored.

Now it's neither a story about dread nor despair nor guilt, but about their opposite—emotional renewal, the release from anxiety and dread! It's as if I'm consciously turning the story on its head—which, by the way, is not a bad idea when you're mulling and pondering your story before writing. Imagining it as its opposite can sometimes lead to very interesting ideas.

Well, in all these notes you can see I'm trying on different ideas for who this bagpipe-listener is, what his problem is, and thus what the story's ultimately about. Each is a different version, a "re-vision" of a possible story. Obviously, to explore all of these in full drafts would be pretty time-consuming. And frustrating. But here, before writing, whole "drafts" can be imagined, sketched out, changed. It's a bit like armchair traveling—you can get a rough idea about the Bushmen without having to go and live among them. Just so, you can revise your story now without having to commit prematurely to one version. You can have your characters be one way today and another to-morrow. No trip has yet been booked for them, no down payments made. So play with your characters and what happens to them. Make notes. Go over the notes and make new notes. When you feel ready, start outlining plot events. Then change them, shift them around. Sniff out the real, the best story.

How do you know when you're ready to stop revising and start writing the first draft? There are certain signs:

1. When the story as you've sketched it seems to hang together, to make sense.

2. When no other possibilities for character, setting, point of view, etc. seem plausible.

3. When the story starts to seem more like an actual memory than an imagined fiction.

4. Most importantly, when you feel excited and energized and can't wait to sit down and start writing it.

Back to "Bagpipes."

In a journal entry a few weeks later, I finally came back to the idea of loss:

Nov. 11

What is guilt but an inability to accept one's past, one's actions, one's experience?

"Did you ever stop missing someone you loved, even after you were divorced?"

After considering a lot of other possibilities, I was starting to get closer to what the story was really about—missing someone, and the irrevocable loss for which one feels responsible. Now here's the big, big irony. If we go back to the very first entry I made about the bagpipe-listener on October 22, we come across these lines, remember?

> *"Where are you going?" I asked. "Where are you going now?"*
> *And the truth is she was going away, although I didn't know it*
> *then.*

> *I loved her dearly. Although I didn't know that then either. I*
> *thought I loved her, sure, but it wasn't real knowledge. That only*
> *comes with loss.*

This sounds very close to what I'm now realizing the story is about on November 11. But I didn't know that back on October 22. I had to look at all those other imaginative possibilities for the story's meaning before coming back to this one.

Two interesting points here. First, I've often found that the key idea of the story, its emotional and imaginative core, often lies near the *beginning* of our notes and musings. It's just that we don't know it yet. Maybe we *can't* know it yet. Secondly, it's only through knowing what a story *isn't* that we begin to understand what it is. It's like meeting the girl or guy who's exactly right for you at your first freshman mixer, but not knowing it until you've dated many others. Without dating those others and having points of comparison, you wouldn't know. Just so we have to consider many re-visions and versions of our story ideas before we're able to return from "whence we started," as T.S. Eliot said, "and know it for the first time." So a word of advice: After you've thought and thought and thought about your story, seeing and re-seeing it in all different ways, and you're still stuck, go back and reread your first notes. Often what it's really about is right there staring you in the face. But only now are you ready to see it.

Back to "Bagpipes."

Concurrently with trying to understand the characters and the meaning of the story, I'd also been considering different ways of structuring its plot. What was going to happen, and in what order? I list key events in sequence, in a quick, sketchy way. You might want to make numbered lists or even a detailed outline. Whatever works. Among my key events for "Bagpipes," I had whale-watching, listening to bagpipes, listening to animal records, and dreaming of swimming with whales. How were they related to one another? Which were in the past and which in the present? These were giving me no end of problems. A huge one was this: How were the narrator, his lover and his wife related to one another, time-wise? Who came first, wife or lover? If the lover was concurrent with the wife, it led to one kind of story; if at least one of them were in the past, it led to another. In one journal entry, I try this sequence:

> Hears bagpipe—reminds of whales (present lover makes love to whale and coyote sounds)—"what are you thinking about"—"Mattapoisett"—his wife is scuba-diving—he's happy—she comes with her gear—she'll always be there—then he is suddenly afraid, afraid—back to present, his lover— "What's the matter?"—"Nothing."

This plot arrangement has him with a lover in the present, then remembering his wife, then returning to the lover. In another revision, I had the lover in the past and the wife in the present. Sometimes I had the whale-watching come before the listening-to-animal-records scene. Sometimes I had the dream of the whales come right after he listened to whale records. I don't know how many of these little plot summary sketches I made. Endless, endless. After one, I penned a despairing note to myself: "I'm not sure this is it." As indeed it wasn't. Big Frustration. I was excited by the story. I was getting to know more and more about the characters. I was pretty sure I now knew what it was about. I knew what the events were. But I couldn't get their chronology straight.

So I put it aside for a year. Not a bad idea if you're stuck. After all, there are other stories to work on too, right?

Flashback: A few years earlier I'd heard short-story writer Stuart Dybek read his marvelous story "Pet Milk" from his collection, *The Coast of Chicago*. It's about a young man drinking coffee and thinking back to his grandmother, and Chicago, and a love affair of his youth. I loved the way it was structured through associated images. Someday, I thought then, I'd like to write a story that was a series of linked images going ever further backward in time. And then one day, a year after my first ruminations about "Bagpipes," it struck me that this might be that story. What if *everything* in "Bagpipes" took place in the past, in his memory? So another chronology, another re-vision:

Nov. 22

He imagines the bagpiper–reminds him of whales—this reminds him of his lover, who listened to wolves singing, whales singing, etc.—reminds him of first wife, how they watched whales—they divorcing, having a bad time . . . she goes into the sea.

This felt good, this felt right! When the story begins, he has *no* wife, *no* lover. They're *all* in the past. He and his wife had split, then he had an affair with the lover who listens to animal records, and so on, the whole chain of memories triggered by the bagpipes. It would go *backward* to the core memory, the real problem, the loss of his wife. The whale dream would be the ending, of the story and of their marriage:

Nov. 25

There would be no sound, no sound, no sound that would ever make her come to me again . . . she was going to where my voice couldn't reach her.

This is very close to the published ending of "Bagpipes" and embodies what the story is really about—loss. And now, for the first time, the meaning of the original dream, the seed idea for the story, became clear. It was the final image of his loss.

Now I knew who the characters were, what the events were and their chronology, and what the story was about. At this point, and only at this point, did I feel that I knew enough to sit down and begin writing the first draft.

SUMMING UP

The most important revisions often occur before we even write the first draft, when we are giving ourselves the imaginative freedom to see and re-see our stories six ways to Sunday and back again. Film directors often say a film is made before the first frame is shot, in the writing and the casting. Write a good script, cast the right actors, and it's already ninety percent successful. The same is true of fiction: "Write" and "cast" your story as best you can *before* sitting down to write, and you're halfway there.

To summarize some key points and suggestions on Revising Before Writing:

1. Don't be in too great a hurry to write that first draft. Story ideas mature slowly, like wine.

2. Do as many imaginative permutations as possible of your characters, point of view, setting and conflict, until you feel you're really "onto something."

3. Make notes.

4. Sketch out possible sequences of events. Plotting, really. Add to them, subtract, shuffle them around.

5. Write some brief passages in the possible "voice" of the story, or of individual characters, to test them out.

6. Don't be reluctant to put aside story ideas that intrigue you but that don't yet seem "ripe," or ready. You can always come back to them. Move on to something else, and revisit them occasionally. Life—and your imagination—will eventually provide what's needed.

You may be a writer who just can't do all this, who has to write a draft, or maybe two or three, to know your characters, their problems, and what's going to happen. If so, good luck, Godspeed, and send me a postcard when you get there. It might take a while. Of course, some searching and changing *is* inevitable in writing the first draft, and subsequent ones, even if you've done your revision before writing. No matter how carefully we've planned a trip, we'll always make some changes en route. There's always the character who'll announce himself on page seven, or the sudden shift in plot that you never thought of until writing the first draft or the fifth one. That's the way it should be; that's part of the magic and the fun of writing. But if you have no itinerary, no map at all before beginning, you may have to resign yourself to spinning your wheels, or to going down roads only to find they're dead ends. All writing isn't done at the word processor or typewriter or legal pad, and all revising doesn't occur with a manuscript at hand. "Without premeditation," Octavio Paz has said, "inspiration just scatters."

CHAPTER THREE

REVISING WHILE WRITING THE FIRST DRAFT

You've done your Revision Before Writing. You've thought about your story every which way and feel you've got a good grasp on who it's about, what it's about, and where it'll go. Now you're ready to face the awful vacuity of the white paper or the blank computer screen and write the first draft. Again, this may seem like a strange time to talk about revision, since, after all, there is no first draft yet, and so nothing to "revise." But just as revision—in the sense of re-seeing—goes on before you write the first draft, so it goes on *while* you're writing the first draft. Even as you're writing it, you can have thoughts and afterthoughts about the story-in-progress. You start changing things—or rather, things start changing on you. Sometimes these changes seem inspired and exciting, but often they create anxiety, as your story starts to seem more and more like an ill-conceived, ill-written *mess*. Examples abound:

• You are on page six and suddenly you realize your Henry should be a Henrietta. Now you're going to have to go back and change not only the name—small matter—but also that opening scene of Henry with his pals in the bowling alley.

• You are on page eight and you feel your story hasn't yet gotten started. You are panicking, because at this pace you will not be writing a short story, but a work as long as Tolstoy's *Anna Karenina*—and you know it's not *Anna Karenina*. Or the opposite has happened: You're on page eight and the story's almost over. You fear you've maybe written a plot summary instead of a story.

- You are on page ten and you realize that a crucial scene has been left out. You need Gordy and Ruth to argue in the car *on the way* to the party. My God, how obvious! But of course that will also change the party scene, because now there will be that tension between them.
- You are on page fourteen and a character you've never thought of before, Georgette, suddenly walks into the story. Who's Georgette? Why, the heroine's cousin, her comic counterpart and essential foil. Georgette, of course, has not yet appeared in the other thirteen pages of the story, some of which will now have to include her.
- You are on page eighteen and suspect that your point of view is the wrong one. This story should not be in third person at all, but in the first. Now you have to go back and redo everything.
- You are on page twenty and realize the scene you're writing is better as the opening for the story, and the original opening is better in the middle. In fact, everything may now have to be rearranged to reflect your new insight about the Relativity of Time.

You get the idea. All of these, and many others I haven't mentioned, can occur to you as you're writing the first draft. (There are certain common ones that writers encounter over and over in the first draft, which I'll talk about later in this chapter.) These afterthoughts—these re-visions—often seem more like problems than insights, suggesting that you don't know where you're going, or what you're doing. Soon they start *weighing you down*. You fret, then worry, then despair. You think you're going to have to go back and change everything before you can ever go on. All your Revision Before Writing seems for naught. You've gotten off your map and are wandering in some strange jungle of narrative, hacking away as best you can.

Of course, these re-visions are both problems and opportunities. They are problems for the obvious reasons—we'll now have to change much of what we've thought about the story as well as much of what we've already written. But more than that, they are opportunities in that you may be re-seeing your story, reenvisioning it in a deeper, clearer, stronger way. As novelist and short story writer Bernard Malamud has said, "The fruits of afterthought are sweet." Often writing the first draft allows us to see what's really working and what isn't in a way that we couldn't do before writing it, no matter how much we've revised before writing. So even though they may cause despair, you must follow these re-visions of your story. There's a good reason, much of the time, that they're occurring to you now, after you've already thought a lot about your story. Henry probably *should* be Henrietta, or the story *should* be written from that other point of view. Better to discover it now than later, right? Anxiety-producing though they might be, these afterthoughts aren't something wreaked only upon you by a malevolent God of Writing. These are problems and opportunities shared by all writers. To resist them is to resist your deeper creative impulses trying to get your attention.

SHOULD I REVISE AS I RE-VISE?

Before going any further, let's address the Big Question hovering like a foul furry moth behind all this: In the first draft, should you *revise*—in the sense of cleaning things up, getting things straight, making things congruent and correct—as you're *re-vising*, in the sense of re-seeing and reimagining your story in some fundamental way? (By the way, whenever I use the word *re-vise* in this book, I mean it in this sense of re-seeing and reimagining—as opposed to *revise*, no hyphen, which refers to making specific kinds of revisions.) It may be all well and good that you now know more about what your story needs, but should you stop right here, go back, and change what you've already written? If, for example, the point of view is all wrong, should you now go back and rewrite everything from the new point of view?

I don't think so. In the first or any subsequent draft, you should do all the re-vising (in the sense of re-seeing) you want, but not much, if any, revising (in the sense of making congruent) *until that draft is finished and you begin the next one.* Then make the changes. I believe in getting through the first draft as quickly as possible. After all, its only purpose is to get the story told, out and down on paper, imperfect and strange and disorganized as it might be. Dotting the *i*'s, crossing the *t*'s, making everything perfect before first getting the story out will . . . slow . . . you . . . down, and it is important not to slow down here. You should think of first drafts the way the King of Hearts in *Alice in Wonderland* advises Alice to tell her story: "Begin at the beginning, go through to the end, *then* stop." (Italics mine.) Don't stop at Go. Don't mess with Mr. In-Between. Playwright Horton Foote has said that in the first draft he goes "right ahead," doesn't stop, and resigns himself "to making the biggest fool of myself as possible." No matter what confusions and infelicities those afterthoughts may cause you in your first draft, don't worry about them. You'll fix everything later, in subsequent drafts.

Why is it important not to get slowed down in revision here? First, to give yourself a sense of accomplishment. You can point to your draft, confused as it may be, and say to yourself, "I wrote a story." As Dorothy Parker said, there's no feeling like Having Written. A story half written may be abandoned prematurely; a story completely written will encourage further work. John Steinbeck thought "re-writing in process" was often an excuse for not going on. I think this is especially true of novels. If you stop to revise a novel as you go, you may *never* finish, and it's important in such a long project to have that sense of completion. You can point to your foot-high stack of manuscript pages and say, "It may be a mess, but there it is." People climb mountains because they're there. But as a writer, you first have to make the mountain. Then you can go climb it.

A second reason: When you're writing the first draft all the way through, you're allowing the story's energy and excitement to carry you along to the end. It's like a good following wind for your creative sails. If you stop to change sails, you will go into a luff, slow down, maybe stall. It may be hard to pick up the wind and fill your sails again. Instead of excitement and energy (and a certain bravado and whistling in the dark) carrying you through, you can succumb to all the doubts and despairs that a first draft occasions: *I don't write well . . . this is a stupid idea . . . I'll never get the characters straight . . . the time line is completely screwed up . . . I'm overwriting . . . I'm underwriting . . .* and on and on, all voices of those demons of creative despair who sit on our shoulders and whisper, *What makes you think you can even write a shopping list?* Stopping to revise as you go is like the old joke about Orville and Wilbur Wright's first airplane flight of 120 feet. One less-than-enthused spectator turns to another, shakes his head, and says, "Well, I don't know . . . it's sure gonna to take a long time to get to Chicago this way." Just so. It's hard to get to the finish of your story and feel that special sense of satisfaction of Having Written unless you plow through to the end as directly and quickly as you can.

There's a third reason for not stopping to revise as you re-vise: Until you finish the first draft, you still don't have a full sense of what it may need anyway. Who's to say if you went back and rewrote everything from Randolph's point of view that a little later on you wouldn't decide that it should really be written from his wife's? Who's to say that the scene you're sure is the opening of the story later turns out to be expendable? You'll waste a lot of time fixing, and then fixing the fixing, and on and on. It's like Zeno's Paradox: If you always have to cover half the distance to get somewhere, and then half of that, and half of that, etc. ad infinitum, logically you can never get there. Or at least it can seem that way.

Some writers can't do this. They have to stop and *revise* before they can go on. William Styron talks about his "neurotic need to perfect each paragraph," and Anthony Burgess talks about doing one page many times before moving ahead. But they seem to be in the minority. When discussing their working methods, most writers more or less say they close their eyes, plunge in, and finish the damn thing before worrying about making it good. In her excellent book on fiction writing, *Bird by Bird*, Anne Lamott says everyone should be allowed the luxury of writing "shitty first drafts." After all, you've got to have *something* to do in all those later drafts, right?

So—if Henry wants to become Henrietta, have her *be* Henrietta from that point on—a quick sex change on page six—and don't worry about fixing up "her" earlier scenes. If you think of a character on page twelve who will now have to appear earlier in the story, worry about putting her in earlier later. If you decide on page thirteen that the story is best told in first person, make the change from that point on and don't worry about the previous twelve pages. The goal is to get that first draft out, done, *fini*. As Malamud says, writing a first draft requires "the ability to accept the imperfect until it is better." Don't expect yourself to be perfect at this point. You're just writing a first draft. Nothing is fixed in concrete, and no one will ever see it, unless you become famous and scholars pore over your papers, and then it won't matter anyway.

COMMON FIRST-DRAFT ANXIETIES

Let's look now at some of the more common first draft re-visions that can cause all that revision anxiety.

Slow Starts. You've written three or four pages and realize you haven't yet gotten to the story. This may be bad, may be good. Maybe you really need those pages to set the scene. Maybe you're writing a more leisurely paced story than you imagined. Maybe you're writing a novella. Maybe a novel. Several novels began as short stories that, like Topsy in *Uncle Tom's Cabin*, "just grew." On the other hand, you may be indulging in literary "throat clearing," i.e., warming up on paper, just as a public speaker or singer warms up. If you seriously feel you're not moving forward, if it feels like too slow a pace, then stop right there and *get going.* Start writing the first scene that you know has confrontation and conflict. Don't worry about transitions. You'll radically condense or eliminate the initial throat clearings in the next draft.

Digressions. There you are, rafting down the Mississippi of the story, and all of a sudden you find yourself on a tributary (better at any rate than running aground). On one hand, this digression may be a mistake—you're drifting away from the real story. On the other hand, strange and unexpected and wondrous things may be found on this tributary. The real story may even lie here. So you have a duty to follow it until it runs back into the main story or runs out. In which case, stop right there, go back narratively to where the digression began, and *go on.* You'll trim or eliminate it later.

Character Changes. You're pages into the story and find that your main character or characters are the wrong age, or sex, or occupation or whatever. This is almost always good: You're that much closer to understanding who they really should be. Now just wave your wand of imagination, and voilà! From this point on, they are transformed. He is a she. The jewelry salesman now sells computers. The teenage girl is now eight years old. Don't worry about going back and changing everything to match up with their new sex, age, occupation, diction, whatever. You'll do that on the next draft.

New Characters. You discover halfway through the story that the heroine really needs a saucy friend, or the absent mother very much needs to be a present mother. Deal with it the same way as above—bring the new folks on stage at this point and *go on.* Now they're here—hooray, and welcome! In the next draft you'll stick them in the front of the story too.

Underwriting. You suspect that scenes you've already written need to be expanded and fleshed out. You are tempted to go back and do it now. Maybe good, maybe not. If you know *exactly* what should be done, and are eager to do it, and think it may really help the forward momentum of the story, then go ahead. Just don't get hung up back there—remember, the important thing is to get the whole story out. You can always go back and expand that scene (or condense or delete it, if you have an unnecessary or overly developed scene). I like putting a few handwritten notes in the margins of the questionable scenes, something like, "Expand this scene," or "Put in business with the dog and the sunglasses," or "Have them argue more about the artichokes." On the next draft, I'll go back and do it. One writer friend purposely omits extended dialogue scenes, which he hates to write, in the first draft. He'll just make a note in the manuscript—"Dialogue Here"— and plow ahead. A scriptwriter I knew who wrote for one of the hospital shows on television would insert "Doc Talk Here" into her scripts to indicate medical dialogue about which she had no idea and which bored her silly anyway. She didn't stop writing to call the doctors who were the show's technical advisors, read them the script, and get their advice on what the Doc Talk should be. It wasn't really important. The most important thing was first to finish the script, then go hunt up the docs and get some Doc Talk. Your particular bête noire scenes which you might like to leave for later development could be dialogue, or description, almost anything. Me, I hate to write description, so often I'll go light on describing a setting in the first draft, knowing I'll flesh it out later.

Overwriting. Your story seems to be . . . slowing . . . down. You're spinning words like cotton candy, page after page, but nothing much new is happening. You realize you've spent two pages describing the convenience store Joe and Helen have stopped at for gas, when you should be getting them to Albuquerque and the argument with Joe's mother. Or Helen and Joe's mother have been talking for four pages and still haven't gotten around to arguing. You aren't digressing really; it's more like you're spinning your wheels. Or wading through molasses. Do you go back and trim everything that needs trimming? No. You *get on with it.* Have them put the pedal to the metal and get out of the store pronto. Make Helen and her mother-in-law start arguing *right now.* Later, in revision, you'll both condense what's overwritten in the scene (or take the scene out altogether) and smooth the transition to what's important in it.

Missing Scenes. You realize an important scene is missing from an earlier part of the story. A valuable insight, and easy to deal with.

Either make a note about it and *go on*, or write it now, right where you are. Who cares about narrative continuity? You'll put it in the right place later. I usually flag these scenes to myself in the first draft by the header "Put before," which tells me that the scene that follows is supposed to come earlier in the story. When I've finished writing that scene, I type a tag, "Back to," and return to the story from the point I began the inserted scene.

Out-of-Order Scenes. You realize that you've got scenes out of sequence. Putting them in the right sequence will of course subtly change what happens in them. Again, this is simple. Either ignore it and go on writing, or make quick little notes by the scenes that this one comes before that one, and so on. Don't worry about all the little changes within the scenes. Just *go on*. You'll reshuffle and fix everything on the next draft.

Alternate Scenes. You don't know which way a particular scene should go. Should Antonia's lover argue with her in person or on the telephone? Should he stomp out or slap her with the teddy bear he'd won for her at the fair? If you can't decide, you might try writing it both ways in the first draft. I usually write the scene one way, then put a big header, "Or," then write it the other way. If you do it both ways right away, it usually becomes apparent which is the right one, and you can go on with the story, humming happily.

Point of View or Voice or Verb Tense Changes. You realize you're writing in the wrong point of view. Or with the wrong voice—the narrator should be less smart-alecky, or less pompous, or more naive or whatever. Or you're writing in the wrong verb tense. In any of these cases, make the change right there, whether you're on page two or page thirty-two, and *go on*. Don't worry about the earlier pages with the wrong point of view, voice or tense. You'll fix them later. Besides, you may even realize that that first point of view was the right one after all, and you'd just have to change everything back again.

Style Anxieties. A special word about style. This is often the A1 anxiety producer in the first draft. You realize as you're writing that your syntax is tortured, sentences don't parse, your vocabulary is fractured, your language is clunky and insipid. Your words are lead, your thoughts ungraced. You are writing gibberish, not metaphorical gibberish, but real, honest-to-God gibberish. You are a *bad writer*, no two ways around it. How can you continue like this, consciously

39

creating a sow's ear out of what was to have been a silk purse? Shouldn't you stop and go back and revise and make everything apple-pie and spit-and-polish perfect before going on?

No, you do not. You *go on*, and style be damned. My first drafts are utter gibberish. Here, see for yourself (from the first draft of "Tidewatcher" in my collection *Comfort*):

> I've been spending a lot of time at the beach lately. It's only twenty-five minutes away to get to the South Shore, two streets down, a quick trip on the Expressway, a few miles over, and I'm there. I should say that it's winter now, and so I never really get out of my car on these cold, blustery days, instead I stay in the car and watch the tide coming in, going out. It changes every day, according to some schedule that is unknown to me (although I suppose I could find out if I bought a newspaper, but what would be the point of it, since I don't really want to know, it just interests me, that's all), so that I never know quite how it will be when I arrive, some days it's quite high, and laps the sand about thirty yards from the concrete parking area, empty now except for the few others who come here, and on other days it has gone out, leaving the ocean denuded for as much as fifty yards into the sea, and I can watch gulls and ducks pecking in small flocks out at the farthest rim, where the last lick of ocean meets the receded sand . . .

See what I mean? Run-on sentences, vague language (and wordy at that!), graceless phrasings—it's all there. But I'm not worried about this on the first draft. I just want to get the story told. No writer writes well in the first draft, with the possible exception of a few geniuses, of whom it's best not to speak, even in hushed tones. If you want further proof, look at just a few writers' draft pages that are used as frontispieces for their interviews in the *Paris Review Writers at Work* series: pages covered with deletions, insertions and chicken scratches. Remember: The important thing on the first draft is not to say it well, but *just to say it.* To make a silk purse out of a sow's ear, you first need the sow's ear.

A CAUTION, AND A COMFORTING THOUGHT

I hope I've allayed some of your anxieties about the first draft. Many of the problems you encounter there—digressions, wrong point of view, scenes out of sequence—are actually re-visions, and very important to the enrichment and development of the story. You can't ignore them. Just don't let them unduly worry you at this point. And don't let them lead you into premature revision fussing. First drafts are expected to be a mess. The true measure of the artist is not the muddle of the first draft, but the elegance of the last one. And consider this: Concern about the messiness of your first draft is a good sign. It shows that you have the right critical attitude toward your work, since right off the bat you're thinking about ways in which the story can be made better. You haven't fallen into the trap of feeling smug and secure about your first draft, as some inexperienced writers—and some who should know better—can do. Like the newest born baby in a family, their story seems beautiful and perfect. Their words have already taken on that "ring of the inevitable" that Annie Dillard has cautioned against. If you find yourself thinking this way about your first draft, my best advice is to pat yourself on the back . . . then cool it. Put the story away for at least a month. Then look at it again. If it's still perfect, or nearly so, maybe you've written one of those gift-from-God stories. Give it to a few trusted—and tough—readers, and see what they think. Chances are, however, that time and a cooler critical eye will make apparent problems you hadn't seen in the flush of first draft infatuation.

However, if like most writers you're only too aware while writing it that your first draft is a mess, take comfort: The lousy first draft, the sow's ear, is usually not as bad upon rereading as you imagine it while writing. As so often happens in life, disaster imagined is greater than disaster realized. I don't know how many times I've finished a first draft and said to myself, Well, nothing there, and nothing to be done. Only to discover upon rereading that it's not quite as bad as I thought. The writing can be cleaned up, yes; this character is mildly interesting, especially after I give her a gecko for a pet, yes; the scene in the Gap store can be enlivened by having Cory flirt with the cashier, yes; the description of nighttime driving on Cahuenga Boulevard has some good images, yes; the scene on page six is mannered and cliché-ridden, but the dialogue in the next one is good . . . and so on. Yes, yes, yes. Don't give in to the early no's. And that will get you to the second draft, and new problems of revision.

CHAPTER FOUR

FIRST REVISIONS, AND OPENINGS IN PARTICULAR

You've finished the first draft. It's a mess you know, but that's okay, and there it sits. Maybe you've put it aside for a few days, or weeks or months, so you can approach it with fresher, more objective eyes. I heartily recommend this: Fresh from the fire of creation, your words can easily have Dillard's "ring of the inevitable." There are two critical times in which your words can seem forever cast, either in gold or in dulled bronze. The first is right after you've finished the first draft; the second is after you've revised draft upon draft upon draft and are fresh out of ideas for seeing your words differently. Both occasions require perspective—and a deep breath. One editor of a respected literary magazine has said that he sees way too many obvious early drafts in stories submitted. So put the story aside for a while, then come back to it. You may be able to more easily discern its strengths and weaknesses.

Done that? It's at least a couple weeks later? Okay—now it awaits your revision. So where do you begin? What do you do?

At first, very little. I suggest reading the story through once just to reacquaint yourself with its overall shape and pace and feel, and to get a sense of its main strengths and weaknesses. Don't get bogged down making notes and changes, and don't be too critical. Chances are it will (a) read better than you feared, but (b) have loads of problems, big and small, you can spot right off the bat. Now read it through again, this time making some quick marginal notes. Don't worry too much about the small stuff. Confine your note-making to big problems or new ideas suggested by these read-throughs. You may see new possibilities in scenes and for characters. You may get ideas for *new* scenes and characters.

Take a look at the early read-through notes I made on one page of a short story of mine:

> The train slowed and lurched around the Sheridan curve.
> George looked out the window into the greenish, almost lunar
> light of the apartment, and saw a man sitting at a table,
> alone, his hands pressed flat on the table, eyes closed,
> almost in prayer. He might have been a monk in a cellar
> devotion. In another apartment, in an almost identical
> kitchen, a woman was spraying her daughter's hair, fluffing
> it, then spraying. None of them, man, woman, daughter,
> looked out their window as the El went by.
>
> ~~Again,~~ Helen bumped against him as the train lurched
> by, and he ~~almost~~ recoiled, the contact almost distasteful. ~~He
> almost resented her sitting beside him~~ Even though they'd
> said almost nothing since boarding the train, even though
> her eyes were still closed—did she find their marriage as
> wearying as he did?—he resented her presence, she seemed to
> take up the space that should have been occupied by his
> thoughts and fantasies. This was his time after all.
>
> Tired, tired. He was tired all the time. He wanted to
> lie down on sofas and sleep. He found himself nodding off
> at the office, found himself staring at telephones, date
> pads, windows, seeing nothing, not knowing how long he'd
> been sitting there, or whether or not he'd been sleeping.
> He slept at night and had dreams of walls and long
> corridors; he awoke and felt as if he hadn't slept at all.

[marginal notes, left:] make his remind him of the man in the deli?

Out on p. 7

Out on p. 7

And now she'd followed him on the El

Put earlier

[marginal notes, right:] All momentarily, perfectly illuminated in greenish fire, like the mechanical ghosts & goblins who lurched at you in a fun house ride

He went into rooms and forgot why he'd gone there.

You can see that almost two whole paragraphs have been scratched—it was obvious right off that they were superfluous. I also made a marginal note ("Put on p. 7") to move the top paragraph and the first sentence of the next one to another page   wrote a marginal query to myself: "Make this [the incident described in the top paragraph] remind him of the man in the deli [a scene later in the story]?" And I made a few other marginal notes concerning scene and character: "He went into rooms and forgot why he'd gone there," and "All [the scenes seen from the El] momentarily, perfectly illuminated in greenish fire, like the mechanical ghosts and goblins who lurched at you in a fun house ride. . . ." But other than these quick jottings, I've made no detailed revisions.

After you've done these first read-throughs, you're ready to revise in earnest. Now some people wonder what's the best physical method for revision. Should I do it by hand, on paper drafts? Or directly on the computer screen? Of course, if you write longhand or use a typewriter you don't have much choice. You're stuck with producing successive drafts, probably working on each one in the same scribbly, interlinear, marginal way you've just seen me do. If you work on a computer, however, you have the choice of revising directly on the screen, consigning all deletions and changes to cyberspace, or printing out drafts, working on them by hand, then entering revisions back on the master draft in the computer. With the former method, you end up with one draft only, the final one; with the latter, you also have all your intervening ones. I prefer the printout method, for three reasons. First, I find it very satisfying to be scribbling, slashing and marking up on paper. I like seeing those sentences with lines through them, those arrows showing one paragraph switching places with another, those little carets pointing to inserted words and phrases. It's fun, it's play, it's making a mess in the name of art. I always envied my artist friends two things: that they could listen to music while working without becoming distracted, and that they got to make a mess. Revising by hand is the only way writers get to make a mess— unless, of course, you're a practitioner of outré compositional methods, such as William Burroughs, who sometimes cuts up sentences, tosses them in a hat, pulls them out randomly, and writes them down in that order. Or so he says.

Second and more important, when you revise by hand, the original sentences, words, paragraphs, phrases *are still there* under the chicken scratches—they haven't been jettisoned into cyberspace. You can see not only how you've changed a sentence, but also what it was like to begin with. You can compare. You may decide the first version was better after all. And last, if you don't print out and mark up your successive drafts by hand, how will future critics of your work have anything to study?! Sometimes I imagine these poor scholars of the next millenium staring at the immutable, final and only version of a masterpiece on the writer's hard drive. Sad, sad, sad. The imaginative process that led to that final version, once traceable in an author's successive drafts, can now never be studied. So give these future critics and scholars a hand, and revise by hand. It's fun, it's practical, and it'll give them something to do when you become famous.

So here you go, revising your story.

REVISING OPENINGS

First, some considerations. What should an opening do, after all? And just how long should it be?

Think what you do when you introduce two friends to one another, a social "opening," as it were. Ideally, you tell each who the other is, possibly where they live and work, and then you mention something interesting about each one that you hope will spark interest. Thus: "Patsy, this is my neighbor, Joe Headline. Joe's a correspondent for the *Tribune*, and he's just back from covering the wars in Rootabaga Country . . ." etc. You introduce them, you interest them in each other, you keep it short, and you stand back.

Just so in a fictional opening. An effective one usually does three things: (1) It *introduces* us to the main character(s) and at least intimates something about the situation she/he/they are in, i.e., the conflict that will provide dramatic gristle for the story; (2) it gets us *interested and involved* in these; and (3) it does it all in a timely fashion, i.e., it stops being an opening as soon as possible and *gets on with the story*. The opening should be exactly as long as necessary to introduce and interest, and no longer. Thus, a short story's opening may be as brief as a paragraph or as long as a page or two, but rarely much longer. If it is, it may be too long and more appropriate to a novella or novel. For a novel, however, the opening may be an entire chapter or two—think of the very leisurely openings, replete with rich, extended descriptions of landscape and cityscape and family history, that often begin Victorian novels, as in the famous opening to Charles Dickens' *A Tale of Two Cities*.

It was the best of times, it was the worst of times, it was the age of wisdom, it was the age of foolishness, it was the epoch of belief, it was the epoch of incredulity, it was the season of Light, it was the season of Darkness, it was the spring of hope, it was the winter of despair, we had everything before us, we had nothing before us, we were all going direct to Heaven, we were all going direct the other way—in short, the period was so far like the present period, that some of its noisiest authorities insisted on its being received, for good or for evil, in the superlative degree of comparison only.

And so on, for some pages. If you've written a couple of chapters like this, however, and the story *still* hasn't moved along, you may be in trouble. It can't be emphasized enough that readers want to Get On With The Story, to have a sense that things are happening, changing, for the characters. In general, they'll have more patience with a novel Getting On With It, much less with a short story.

Look at the opening to Raymond Carver's short-short story, "Little Things":

Early that day the weather turned and the snow was melting into dirty water. Streaks of it ran down from the little shoulder-high window that faced the backyard. Cars slushed by on the street outside, where it was getting dark. But it was getting dark on the inside too.

He was in the bedroom pushing clothes into a suitcase when she came to the door.

I'm glad you're leaving! I'm glad you're leaving! she said. Do you hear?

It's quick, but it does all an opening should do: It *introduces* us to the characters and where they are, shows us that they've got problems, and *interests* us in these problems. And it does all this in three short paragraphs. After this, the story is off and running, as the conflict between the husband and wife escalates with disastrous results.

Another example of a quick opening, from "The Use of Force" by William Carlos Williams (although he is known primarily as a poet, Williams also wrote some wonderful short stories).

> They were new patients to me, all I had was the name, Olson. Please come down as soon as you can, my daughter is very sick.
>
> When I arrived I was met by the mother, a big startled looking woman, very clean and apologetic who merely said, Is this the doctor? and let me in. In the back, she added. You must excuse us, doctor, we have her in the kitchen where it is warm. It is very damp here sometimes.

The main characters are introduced—the doctor, the mother, a sick child—as is the setting, the house of a poor family (we know they're poor because the kitchen seems to be the only warm room). And the problem is presented: The child is sick, the doctor must attend her. It's his efforts to do so, and her resistance, that will provide the conflict in the rest of the story.

Here's the more leisurely opening to my short story "Doe Season":

> They were always the same woods, she thought sleepily as they drove through the early morning darkness—deep and immense, covered with yesterday's snowfall which had frozen overnight. They were the same woods that lay behind her house, *and they stretch all the way to here,* she thought, *for miles and miles, longer than I could walk in a day, or a week even, but they are still the same woods.* The thought made her feel good: it was like thinking of God; it was like thinking of the space between here and the moon; it was like thinking of all the foreign countries from her geography book where even now, Andy knew, people were going to bed, while they—she and her father and Charlie Spoon and Mac, Charlie's eleven-year-old son— were driving deeper into the Pennsylvania countryside, to go hunting.

Again, the main characters are introduced: the little girl Andy, her father, Charlie Spoon and Mac, his son. The ages of the children are established, both subtly (we infer Andy is eight or nine because of the way she imagines the immensity of the woods), and directly (we are simply told Mac is eleven—later we'll also be told that Andy is nine). The setting is established—they're in a car driving in winter through the great woods of Pennsylvania—as is the situation. They're going hunting.

Soon we read this exchange.

> Charlie Spoon was driving. "I don't understand why she's
> coming," he said to her father. "How old is she anyway—eight?"
>   "Nine," her father replied. "She's small for her age."
>   "So—nine. What's the difference? She'll just add to the noise
> and get tired besides."
>   "No, she won't," her father said. "She can walk me to death.
> And she'll bring good luck, you'll see. . . ."

Here, we are introduced to the conflict between Andy and Charlie
Spoon, with her father as her champion, which will play itself out in
the story. This conflict, we already feel, is about Andy's place, literally
and psychologically, in this world of men. Through *dramatizing* the
argument between her father and Charlie and not just telling about
it, I'm also obviously trying to interest and involve the reader in the
story.

Let's look at a *very* leisurely opening, that in Edgar Allan Poe's
classic short story "The Fall of the House of Usher":

> During the whole of a dull, dark, and soundless day in the
> autumn of the year, when the clouds hung oppressively low in
> the heavens, I had been passing alone, on horseback, through
> a singularly dreary tract of country; and at length found myself,
> as the shades of the evening drew on, within view of the melan-
> choly House of Usher. I know not how it was—but, with the
> first glimpse of the building, a sense of insufferable gloom per-
> vaded my spirit. I say insufferable; for the feeling was un-
> relieved by any of that half-pleasurable, because poetic,
> sentiment, with which the mind usually receives even the
> sternest natural images of the desolate or terrible. I looked
> upon the scene before me—upon the mere house, and the
> simple landscape features of the domain, upon the bleak walls,
> upon the vacant eye-like windows, upon a few rank sedges,
> and upon a few white trunks of decayed trees—with an utter
> depression of soul which I can compare to no earthly sensation
> more properly than to the after-dream of the reveller upon
> opium: the bitter lapse into everyday life, the hideous dropping
> off of the veil.

Poe continues in this vein, describing the ominous scene and analyzing his reactions to it, for again as long as the section quoted. He
then describes a letter he received from Usher urging him to come,

and *then* expatiates at some length about his past relationship with Usher ("Although, as boys, we had been even intimate associates, yet I really knew little of my friend. . . .") and upon the Usher family history ("I had learned, too, the very remarkable fact, that the stem of the Usher race, all time-honored as it was, had put forth, at no period, any enduring branch. . . ."). After all that, he again returns to the gloominess of the House and its surroundings, and his reactions to it:

> Shaking off from my spirit what *must* have been a dream, I scanned more narrowly the real aspect of the building. Its principal feature seemed to be that of an excessive antiquity. The discoloration of ages had been great. Minute fungi overspread the whole exterior, hanging in a fine tangled webwork from the eaves. Yet all this was apart from any extraordinary dilapidation.

It is only after this, after we're a good three pages into the story, that the narrator finally rides into the castle and gets off his horse! And it's yet another page, after equally atmospheric descriptions of the interior of the castle and the room into which he's shown, that we finally encounter Usher, who, we learn, has "terribly altered." Poe describes him in the same minute detail that he's already lavished upon the setting:

> And now in the mere exaggeration of the prevailing character of these features, and of the expression they were wont to convey, lay so much of change that I doubted to whom I spoke. The now ghastly pallor of the skin, and the now miraculous lustre of the eye, above all things startled and even awed me. The silken hair, too, had been suffered to grow all unheeded, and as, in its wild gossamer texture, it floated rather than fell about the face, I could not, even with effort, connect its Arabesque expression with any idea of simple humanity.

It is only after this extended description—five pages into the story—that Usher begins to talk about why he wanted the narrator to visit him and about "the nature of his malady." Only now are we out of the opening. For all of this *has* been the opening, the leisurely kind more often encountered in novels than in short stories. Poe has taken his time setting the scene, introducing and describing the characters and intimating the problem. And of course, interesting us. Because even with so "slow" an opening, we are interested, primarily because Poe has so masterfully painted a foreboding atmosphere of decay, ominousness and gloom—as well as hinted, through this mysterious letter, of trouble at the House of Usher—that we are on tenterhooks. We want to know what's going on. We feel terrible things are bound to happen, and we want to stick around to see them.

Whether you're writing a snappy, let's-cut-to-the-chase opening or a more leisurely one, thinking about what effective openings should do provides clues for what can go wrong with them. I believe almost all problems with openings boil down to *a failure to introduce the characters and their conflicts in a timely fashion, and/or a failure to interest us in them.* So it follows that there are three questions you must ask yourself when revising your opening:

1. Am I introducing the characters and the conflict?
2. Am I doing it in a timely way?
3. Am I doing it in a way that will interest the reader?

All three are inextricably knotted together. If you fail to introduce, you will probably also fail to interest, just as if you fail to Get On With It, you will also fail to interest.

Let's look at some ways in which early draft openings can go wrong. We need search no further than my own work.

DELAYED OPENINGS

Here's the first-draft opening, in all its purple prose and prolix glory, of my short story "Piano Lessons":

> There are certain inevitabilities to growing up, and certain events which mark them, and mark a change, a transition to something, somewhere, or someone we've not been before. For a young boy, the first pair of long pants, the first time he can go hatless in winter, taking off the hated cap his mother has always made him wear—these are signal events that like the flight of birds south in the fall, or the first frost in October, signal that something is turning, changing, where change was never imagined before, and life existed, except for the change of seasons in a sort of fluid fixedness, an ever-changing now. There are certain common passages that all children of the middle-class, at least when I was growing up, perhaps still so

today, underwent, passages that were so common, so universal, that they were taken for granted, and aroused no particular interest on the part of other children. For girls, there were the inevitable ballet lessons and baton-twirling; for boys, freer it seems from the dreams of their parents to achieve some sort of grace, there were Little League baseball and other organized sports. For all of us, there were braces on the teeth. And for many of us, there were music lessons.

During the winter of my seventh year, the year that I was in second grade, my mother decided I should take piano lessons. I can't remember why.

There are some good things here. The writing has an avuncular omniscience, a voice I don't often use, but one which I admire tremendously when done well, as Dickens and George Eliot and Gabriel García Marquez can do. There's some egregious purple prose ("a sort of fluid fixedness, an ever-changing now" ... *yecchh!*) that would have to come out, but there are also some happy turns of phrase ("the first pair of long pants, the first time he can go hatless in winter ... signal that something is turning, changing, where change was never imagined before. . . .").

Well. All this, good stuff and bad, the *whole* first paragraph, was junked between the first and second draft. "Piano Lessons" as published begins like this:

> When I was seven years old, my mother decided I should have piano lessons—why, I don't know. We had an upright piano inherited from an uncle of hers on the side porch, and I think she felt it should be used. My father didn't like the idea at all. I'd never shown any interest in music, he said; it was a waste of time and money. Most of all, he didn't like the idea of the nuns.

I didn't even get to these lines until paragraph two of the first draft. Why did I decide to throw away all of those grand musings about Time and Change? Because it was *talking* about the story rather than Getting On With It. It wasn't introducing the specific characters, a young boy and his parents, and their conflicts: his problem learning to play the piano, which leads to a confrontation between the boy's teacher and his father, and ultimately within himself. The original opening only delayed the true beginning of the story. In a novella or a novel, this ruminative first draft opening might be okay. Remember Dickens. Even in some short stories it might be okay. Remember Poe. But in what is ultimately a ten-page story, that opening looks like gargling and throat clearing at best and cracker-barrel philosophizing at worst.

I think many writers in their first drafts edge into stories like this. They clear their throats and do verbal warm-ups and stretching exercises before plunging into the story in earnest. Maybe it's because they don't yet know what the story is and are casting around trying to find out (which won't be the case with you, since you'll have pretty much zeroed in on that in your Revision Before Writing). Or it could be because it's just hard to plunge in. Like someone standing at the edge of the ocean, you first have to look at the water, then wade in to your ankles, then up to the thigh, the waist, the chest, and finally, finally, take the plunge into the breakers. But we all know this is torture. Better to plunge in and Get On With It.

Incidentally, there's also another big problem with the first draft opening of "Piano Lessons," which you may have spotted. Its tone of omniscience, its divagatory Jamesian syntax, are unlike the true voice of the narrator in the published story. This voice is much more plain and terse. The difference between the two is jarring, and so one has to go, or be drastically modified, and it's obvious which one. (Funny— whenever I try to strike an omniscient voice or High Style in my fiction, it never seems to work. I would love to be able to Muse and Ponder the way some other writers do. But I always wind up crossing it all out. It never seems to fit with the real voice of my stories, which is a lot more simpleminded, I fear. As Henry Miller once said in a *Paris Review* interview, "Out with the vast and pompous learning which I haven't got!")

So ask yourself, Am I introducing the characters and the conflict, and with due dispatch? Or could this story really start later? Could I eliminate or radically condense the first paragraph? The first page? The first chapter? Anton Chekhov said that a writer had to cross off the beginnings and endings of stories, because often they just weren't relevant. Do this imaginative experiment: Take away that first paragraph or two, maybe even the first page, of your story. Or even the first chapter of your novel. See if it really hurts if they're gone, or at least drastically condensed. What you're really looking for is that first sentence or paragraph, that first description, event or line of dialogue, that is *impossible* to do without. In "Piano Lessons" that first line was "When I was seven years old, my mother decided I should have piano lessons." For Franz Kafka in "The Metamorphosis," it was "As Gregor Samsa awoke one morning from uneasy dreams he found himself transformed in his bed into a gigantic insect." This is the true beginning of the story. Ask yourself, Where does the story really take off? It's as close as possible to that takeoff point that you want to be. Think of your story as a 737 rolling down the runway. The rolling, the gathering speed to the first moment of liftoff—that's your opening. You don't need to see the plane getting fueled, the food and baggage loaded, the passengers boarding, and the plane taxiing to the runway. And you certainly don't need to see it holding for clearance to takeoff.

OVERLY DETAILED AND/OR REPETITIOUS OPENINGS

Here's another first draft opening by a student writer. The story concerns a young woman who leaves for a theatrical audition and bumps into an old lady who's locked out of her apartment. The young woman tries to help her, with comic results.

> Christi, wrapped in her soft white towel, stepped out of the shower. She combed her long brown hair with a wide toothed comb and then shook her head vigorously, her fingers brushing and shaking the hair. Christi dabbed cream on her cheeks, forehead and chin, and then carefully and calmly, with her manicured fingers, spread each dot in all directions. Around her eyes she put a special, more rich cream. Then she smeared body lotion on her broad and bony shoulders, her small firm breasts, her tight skinned hips and freshly shaven legs. Her feet she powdered. She rolled a cold stick on her armpits and then rubbed her arms tightly back and forth against her body.
>
> Christi walked into the closet, pushing the hangers back and forth looking for something suitable to wear for her Steppenwolf audition that afternoon. Something plain and simple, not showy, nothing to draw attention, but still, to draw attention. She settled for a tight black T-shirt that accentuated her shoulders and slim arms, and black dress pants that fit

tight around her small waist, but then hung down loosely and straight to her ankles.

In the bathroom, Christi pulled her makeup basket out of the cabinet, and skillfully began to apply light foundation to her fair, flawless skin. Only underneath her eyes did she need to cover up slight shadows, which were visible only when she tilted her chin to her chest. Christi noticed a hair that was not part of the perfect high arch of her left eyebrow and plucked it with her shining silver tweezers. Then she brushed mascara on her long lashes and dabbed Bordeaux lipstick on her small but well-defined lips. Her teeth she rubbed with her fingers and then tried to compare the white with the white of her eyes, which almost matched. Turning around in front of the mirror a few times, she smiled at her accomplishment. Everything was so subtle, yet pronounced.

In the kitchen Christi sat carefully drinking Evian, her head tilted back and her mouth wide open, not to smudge her lipstick. She arranged her mail on the table, checking the latest dates for payment on her bills and arranging them in piles of importance. The postcards from her friends and the letter from her mother, who wrote in small print on both sides of each thin yellow tinted paper, she put in the third pile. Then Christi arranged her black leather purse, checking for her wallet, her planner, and the right color lipstick. Christi put on her thin black coat, grabbed her keys and opened the two locks on her apartment door, noticing the *Chicago Tribune* in its blue plastic bag. She pulled it off the doorknob and put it in the corner of her entrance where she had a stack of papers in their plastic bags. Simply no time, no time at all. Christi closed the door, turned the top lock twice with the key to the right, and then the bottom one. Quickly she walked down the two flights and went through the front door.

Even though it's only a page or so long and serves to vividly describe Christi, there's something about this opening that seems, well, *slow*. What is it, and why?

For starters, it seems slow because it has a problem similar to the first-draft opening of "Piano Lessons." While it introduces us to the character, it doesn't get us to the conflict, to the *problem,* fast enough. Things won't happen to Christi until she gets out of the apartment and onto the street. So why all this attention to the details of her dressing and makeup? Is it really needed? Will it have bearing on what happens to Christi later? Does it show us an essential side to her character? Is it creating an interesting mood, as in "The Fall of the House of Usher"? As we discover, what's important in the story is what happens to Christi *after* she gets out of the apartment. So why not get her, and the reader, out there sooner? To do that, the writer doesn't need to take us through all of Christi's morning routines. They could be radically condensed. This opening makes us uneasy. Will the writer be this detailed about *everything?*

Watch out for your openings getting bogged down in excessive and extraneous detail. It's easy to do, because we feel we have so much to do at the beginning. After all, we have to create a whole universe from scratch, with believable people, places and problems. So we are tempted to overwrite. I can't tell you how common it is as a teacher of writing to read short stories that begin with the finely detailed writing that you might expect from a Victorian novel—and then suddenly changing, becoming sketchier and sketchier as the writer realizes he's really writing a short story, pages have gone by, and it's time to Get On With It. It leads to stories that seem grossly out of balance—ten pages of opening and the rest of the story wrapped up in four pages.

But there's something else that makes our example opening slow—the *repetitiousness* of the description. In the first paragraph Christi is applying makeup. Then she goes into her closet to choose some clothes. Then back to makeup again. We feel we've read this before, and start to get a little antsy. A useful exercise in revising your openings—and any other part of your story, for that matter—is to seriously question anything, from individual details and actions to whole scenes, that have been shown before. Of course, some repetitions serve excellent dramatic purposes, such as showing obsessive or ritual behavior. I said "question." Always remember you're going forward, not looking back.

As with Delayed Openings, another useful imaginative exercise in avoiding repetitious, overly detailed openings is to decide which scene of your story first introduces the problem, the conflict. Then see how quickly you can get to it, or at least intimate it. Question the necessity of every sentence and paragraph before that critical scene.

UNNECESSARY HISTORY AND BACKGROUND

Another variant of the opening that fails to introduce characters and conflict and then Get On With It happens when the writer feels he has to give the entire familial or personal history of the character(s) before getting to the story at hand. I remember a workshop story about a young couple who wanted to marry despite their immigrant families' protests. But before getting to that problem, the writer took six or seven pages—of a fifteen-page story—to describe the parents' lives in their respective Old Countries, their respective trips to America, their struggles when they arrived, their meeting and marriage, assorted family births and deaths, the hero and heroine's childhoods and so on. This approach might be fine in a novel, or in a story that chronicled the passage of an immigrant family through America (although then it would have had the opposite problem, I fear, and would have read more like a sketch for a novel). But since the story was really about the young couple's marriage problems, and that's where it focused after the opening historical narrative, those pages seemed all the more tedious and unnecessary. The writer just wasn't Getting On With It. Once she realized this and cut much of that historical background, the story started more dynamically, with the young lovers and their problem. Beware, especially in short stories, the temptation to tell everything that happened before the story started. For that matter, be suspicious of it in novel openings too. Often it just isn't relevant to the real conflict of the story. And if it is, try to work it in later, in bits and pieces, well after the narrative is off and running.

UNNECESSARY FLASHBACKS

Flashbacks are tempting to use in openings because they seem like a good way to provide necessary exposition. We can start in the narrative "present," then show readers what happened before the present of the story began. But they can create problems too. The unnecessary flashback is one of them, and still another way openings can fail to Get On With It. Here's an example from a workshop story:

> The light flickered like some strange Morse code over her face in the dark as she lay back on the beery mattress. She scratched another mark to the growing line of slashes on the wall with the jagged, bitten end of her fingernail. There were

twenty-one of them now, the duration of her time with him.

She turned from the wall, curling up, like a fetus, struggling for air on this stinking mattress.

He took her to a dimly lit restaurant (the first of many shadowy places she found herself); walls a beautiful soft beige, and everyone spoke in well-bred whispers. The waiters were charmingly arrogant and the food was fashionably late. He mumbled sweet things over romantic Muzak that she could never decipher and the candlelight obscured his eyes. In her mind, the words didn't matter, anyway; it was the soft voice and the soft glow that surrounded his head, the little flames of the candles making rainbows of the raindrops that clung to his wooly, black hair. He looked like an angel.

He slammed into the room; his fraternity letters, done in red with gold thread stitching, glared dully in the double darkness of his black sweater and the room itself. He came toward her with his arms outstretched.

"Honey, I'm sorry."

She didn't turn from the wall.

He sank down into his favorite chair with a sigh, the old cracked leather groaning as he shifted his weight to get comfortable. "I don't know what came over me. I saw you standing there, telling me you wanted to maybe see other people."

She heard his feet swishing through the cigarette-singed shag and the creak of the springs as he sat next to her. She stiffened, as his hands gently worked the tangles from her hair, moving down to caress her shoulder. "Honey, relax," he said. "I'll never hurt you again. I love you, and you're mine."

He took her to a fraternity party. The stale smell of spilled beer and old cigarettes hit her as she walked through the door. She wanted to run away.

She remembered, with some embarrassment, how she had mocked her best friend, as they got ready to go to school during the long, stifling days of August, when she had mentioned joining a sorority. "You really want to spend your time going to stupid frat parties?" she'd said. "All they do is drink and belch and make sexist remarks."

One of his brothers materialized through the cigarette haze, let his eyes slither over her, then whispered something in his ear. They bellowed goatishly. . . .

And so on, as the flashback goes on for another three-plus pages before we return to the present of the story, the woman and her boyfriend in the bedroom. Here, the story has opened, and character and conflict are introduced. A woman is crying in a bedroom. Our interest is whetted. And then almost immediately the writer slips into a flashback about a restaurant date with the heroine's later-to-prove-abusive boyfriend. Then back to the woman crying, and the boyfriend coming in. And then into an even longer flashback about their date at a fraternity party. It's not until page six that we return to the story proper, the woman and her boyfriend in the bedroom, and the conflict advances.

Beginning a story and then almost immediately going into a flashback, particularly one that lasts longer than the paragraph or two that opened the story, is almost always suspect. First, it usually stalls the main story. And if it's a long flashback, by the time we get back to the main story, we've often forgotten it. A woman crying in the bedroom? Really? Secondly, the reader can't help wondering: If the flashback is so important that we have to leave the story's "present" and get to it lickety-split, then why didn't the story simply start *there?* For that matter, why isn't *it* the main story? So . . . be *very suspicious* of any immediate flashbacks in your opening, especially ones that do go on. Ask yourself if they wouldn't be better (a) dispensed with; (b) condensed radically; (c) broken up into smaller flashbacks interspersed throughout the story; (d) transformed into the beginning of the story, not a flashback at all; or (e) incorporated into the "present" of the story. (For example, the woman here could tell a friend later how angelic her boyfriend had seemed on their first date.) In general, I look on *all* flashbacks—beginning, middle and end—with suspicion. They stall the story's forward motion. They could almost always be more effective dramatized in the story's "present."

Now, there are exceptions to everything I've been talking about. Sometimes flashbacks are necessary. Sometimes introducing characters and conflict can be postponed, and there are several great short stories that do it. For example, in J.D. Salinger's "A Perfect Day for Bananafish," we don't see a main character, Seymour Glass, until halfway through the story. But he and his incipient madness are still very much present from the beginning in the phone conversation his wife has with her mother, in which they discuss Seymour's behavior.

"What'd he say, though? The doctor."

"Oh. Well, nothing much, really. I mean we were in the bar and all. It was terribly noisy."

"Yes, but did—did you tell him what he tried to do with Granny's chair?"

"*No,* Mother. I didn't go into details very much," said the girl. "I'll probably get a chance to talk to him again. He's in the bar *all* day long."

"Did he say he thought there was a chance he might get— you know—funny or anything? Do something to you!"

"Not exactly," said the girl.

Even though Seymour's not there, he is. As are his problems. And in Joy Williams' story "Cloud," we're not aware of a key conflict—that the narrator's little sister Steffie is dying—until the very end, in these paragraphs:

> It would get harder for Steffie, everyone knew, even Steffie. There wasn't anything to do about this. Outside, a breeze made the palm fronds rustle. It was one of the prettiest sounds there was.
>
> Every time Rusty came back, Steffie was stopping one more thing.

But even if the full extent of the conflict hasn't been revealed until now, it doesn't matter, because the vapid, superficial world of Rusty and her friends, against which Steffie's impending death will be ironically juxtaposed, has been so brilliantly dramatized earlier in the story that we've been totally involved with it.

EFFECTIVE OPENINGS: THE TEASER AND THE GRABBER

Effective openings, besides introducing character and conflict, must also interest and involve the reader. Call it what you will—building narrative drive, creating suspense—you have to interest readers enough to propel them out of the opening and into the story proper. You've got to make them turn the page. How to do this is hard to say. There are a thousand and one ways to interest a reader in your opening paragraphs. The best way of getting a feel for it, as with almost everything else in fiction, is to read a lot of good stories and see how their openings work. Are they leisurely openings? Quick? How do they introduce characters, setting and conflict? Above all, ask yourself how the writer is interesting us in the story, so that we want to continue reading it. Is it through tension created by atmosphere and mood, as Poe does so well? Is it through action? Through a quirky, fascinating character about whom we want to learn more, as short story writer Flannery O'Connor almost always does in her openings? Through dialogue that hints of coming conflict, as Salinger did in "A Perfect Day for Bananafish"?

I think the thousand and one ways in which openings can interest, however, fall into two basic categories: openings that tease and those that grab. The Teaser goes something like this (from Sarah Orne Jewett's "A White Heron"):

> The woods were already filled with shadows one June evening, just before eight o'clock, though a bright sunset still glimmered faintly among the trunks of the trees. A little girl was driving home her cow, a plodding, dilatory, provoking creature in her behavior, but a valued companion for all that. They were going away from the western light, and striking deep into the dark woods, but their feet were familiar with the path, and it was no matter whether their eyes could see it or not.
>
> There was hardly a night the summer through when the old cow could be found waiting at the pasture bars; on the contrary, it was her greatest pleasure to hide herself away among the high huckleberry bushes, and though she wore a loud bell she had made the discovery that if one stood perfectly still it would not ring. So Sylvia had to hunt for her until she found her, and call Co'! Co'! with never an answering Moo, until her childish patience was quite spent.

The scene is calm and bucolic, a little girl bringing her cow home. The narrative pace is leisurely—time to talk about the cow's stubbornness and other characteristics, which goes on for some length after the passage quoted. And yet, despite the languid pace, we sense the potential for conflict. The hour is late, after all, and the road dark. The cow doesn't obey well. They are striking into the dark woods. We are uneasy. Something might happen. It's not evident what, if anything, but this pastoral scene may contain a surprise. We're being teased into reading more, to see if that's so.

Another teaser is the opening of Kate Chopin's short story "Désirée's Baby," set in antebellum Louisiana:

As the day was pleasant, Madame Valmondé drove over to L'Abri to see Désirée and the baby.

It made her laugh to think of Désirée with a baby. Why, it seemed but yesterday that Désirée was little more than a baby herself; when Monsieur in riding through the gateway of Valmondé had found her lying asleep in the shadow of the big stone pillar.

The little one awoke in his arms and began to cry for "Dada." That was as much as she could do or say. Some people thought she might have strayed there of her own accord, for she was of the toddling age. The prevailing belief was that she had been purposely left by a party of Texans, whose canvas-covered wagon, late in the day, had crossed the ferry that Coton Maïs kept, just below the plantation. In time Madame Valmondé abandoned every speculation but the one that Désirée had been sent to her by a beneficent Providence to be the child of her affection, seeing that she was without child of the flesh. For the girl grew to be beautiful and gentle, affectionate and sincere,— the idol of Valmondé.

It was no wonder, when she stood one day against the stone pillar in whose shadow she had lain asleep, eighteen years before, that Armand Aubigny riding by and seeing her there, had fallen in love with her. That was the way all the Aubignys fell in love, as if struck by a pistol shot. The wonder was that he had not loved her before; for he had known her since his father brought him home from Paris, a boy of eight, after his mother died there. The passion that awoke in him that day, when he saw her at the gate, swept along like an avalanche, or like a prairie fire, or like anything that drives headlong over all obstacles.

Monsieur Valmondé grew practical and wanted things well considered: that is, the girl's obscure origin. Armand looked into her eyes and did not care. . . .

I know, I know. This story goes immediately into a flashback, of which I said to be wary. Well, it only proves that there are no hard and fast rules in fiction writing. As Flannery O'Connor said in *Mystery and Manners*, her excellent book of essays on fiction writing, "You can do anything you can get away with, but nobody has ever gotten away with much." At any rate, this flashback effectively teases us: Désirée came to the plantation under strange circumstances. There is a mystery in her origin that might have implications for her marriage, and her baby. Will this be so? We want to read on and see.

The second kind of opening, the Grabber, goes more like this (from Ray Bradbury's short story "The Veldt"):

> "George, I wish you'd look at the nursery."
> "What's wrong with it?"
> "I don't know."
> "Well, then."
> "I just want you to look at it, is all, or call a psychologist in to look at it."
> "What would a psychologist want with a nursery?"
> "You know very well what he'd want." His wife paused in the middle of the kitchen and watched the stove busy humming to itself, making supper for four.
> "It's just that the nursery is different now than it was."

Here we're plunged right into a dramatic situation. Conflict is there from the first two sentences. Something's wrong with the nursery. What could it be? For that matter, what kind of a nursery is this, after all, that needs a psychologist? Here, a problem is presented right away, and we're hooked.

Short stories, because of their length, use grabber openings more than novels, which usually feature more leisurely, teasing openings. But here's a grabber from Alice McDermott's *That Night*, a novel about young love and loss:

> That night when he came to claim her, he stood on the short lawn before her house, his knees bent, his fists driven into his thighs, and bellowed her name with such passion that even the friends who surrounded him, who had come to support him, to drag her from the house, to murder her family if they had to, let the chains they carried go limp in their hands.

If there's ever been an opening sentence that more forcefully grabs a reader's attention, I sure don't know what it is. We've *got* to find out who this guy is, who the girl is whom he's come to claim with such passion and force, and just what has happened that has led to this scene of violence.

There are dangers, of course, in both kinds of opening. The teaser's potential problem is that it goes on teasing too long and never follows up on its promised conflict. The grabber's problem is that it can seem overly dramatic, hokey and contrived, like the shrill, aggressive spiel of a carnival barker. Something like:

> "No, no, no, you'll never make me marry him," she cried, as she ran from the living room where her parents sat, aghast and astounded. She slammed the door behind her, and the crockery shook on the wall.

This smacks of artifice and melodrama, of a self-conscious attempt to grab us. If you're starting off like this, I suggest taking a deep breath, relaxing, and toning it down a notch or two. Keep in mind that the grabber opening has to do it almost without letting us know.

Another kind of opening that tries to grab us but fails is the one that gives away the story. Execrably exaggerated for effect, it can go like this:

> As he waited for the sleeping pills to take effect, Sam thought of the wreckage of his life, especially the last horrible days in which Emma had revealed to him her affair with Charly, her plans to leave him, and her determination to take with her Buster and Brownie, their pet kinkajous.

The writer is attempting to grab our interest: Look at all the horrible things that have happened to this poor man! And we are interested. Where will it go from here? we wonder. Imagine our dismay when the story *doesn't* go on from here, but instead goes back to show us precisely these last five horrible days in which Emma reveals her affair to Sam and tells him of her plans to leave and take their pet kinkajous. Since we already know this, and that Sam will wind up committing, or trying to commit, suicide, what's to be interested in? Where's the suspense? It's like coming in at the end of a mystery movie, then having to watch it all the way through from the beginning. You already know who did it, so what's the point? Just imagine Hemingway's short story, "The Short, Happy Life of Francis Macomber" beginning with a line like, "Just when he had achieved a new sense of his manhood, Francis Macomber was shot by his wife"? Intriguing, yes. But ultimately unsatisfying, since it betrays the surprise and deflates the irony to come. And can you imagine Shirley Jackson's classic story "The Lottery" beginning with a line like, "The annual lottery in which a townsperson was sacrificed was one of the stranger customs in the small New England village." All the power in the revelation of the seemingly innocent lottery's sinister purpose would be lost. Instead, "The Lottery" begins bucolically, masking the horror to come:

> The morning of June 27th was clear and sunny, with the fresh warmth of a full-summer day; the flowers were blossoming profusely and the grass was richly green. The people of the village began to gather in the square, between the post office and the bank, around ten o'clock. . . .

Summary openings make readers *very* anxious, since we desperately hope there will be something more to the story, that *everything* hasn't been given away. If everything has, we will feel really cheated.

To sum up, getting a good opening, one that introduces, interests and Gets On With It, is critical for the revision of your story because the opening sets the tone and pace for all that follows. If it has the wrong voice, the rest of the story might have the wrong voice too. If it's too long, the rest of the story might also suffer from prolixity. Or might seem "too short" by comparison—you've spent eight pages setting up your characters and conflict in a too-leisurely opening, then wrapped up their story in only three pages. With the right opening, however, you and the reader are effortlessly compelled and propelled into the story's ensuing dramatic complications.

CHAPTER FIVE

CUTTING WHAT'S NOT ESSENTIAL

Michelangelo was asked once how he created such beautiful sculptures out of unformed blocks of marble. "All I do," he replied, "is carve away everything that isn't the sculpture." This answer can seem either wiseass or profound. I think it's profound and applies to revising fiction as much as to sculpting. To revise, all you have to do is take away everything that isn't the story. (Well, that's not *all*, of course—you may have to add stuff too, but that's the subject of the next chapter.) Playwright David Mamet put it another way when he said that good writers take out what mediocre writers leave in. (He added that good writers also leave in what mediocre writers take out—but again, that's another subject.) At any rate, cutting what's not essential to the story should be an early revision focus.

The first few times through your draft, I suggest you make a special point of identifying and cutting out *big* blocks of stuff that aren't necessary. I'm not talking here about individual words and phrases—that's for fine-tuning later on. No, look for *big* sections that aren't really relevant to the story and get rid of them. I'm talking about whole scenes or sections of scenes, entire characters (often minor ones), rambling dialogue, philosophic pronouncements, anything overly extended or overtly unnecessary or extraneous.

How do you spot these, you might ask?

Well, you've got to develop a sensitivity. And such sensitivity requires first of all that you're not so overly enamored of your own words that you can't bear to make these *big* cuts (Dillard's "inevitablity" again). It's easy to change a word or two. It's tougher to take out a whole scene. It's especially tough to take out a scene that may be very good, but bad for the story as a whole. I gave an example of that in the last chapter with the opening of "Piano Lessons." Even though it had some potentially good writing, out it went. You must develop ruthlessness. "Kill your darlings," some writer (it's been attributed to several, including Anton Chekhov and Dorothy Parker) once said, meaning that you've got to have the objectivity to strike out scenes/characters/dialogue that you gave birth to, that may be quite good, that you even may love, if they aren't helping the story. Hemingway was referring to this objectivity when he said you must find the most beautiful sentence in your story and take it out. That may be a bit draconian, but the attitude toward revision it indicates is well taken: You can't be afraid to cut that which may be beautiful if it isn't right for the story as a whole. It isn't just the bad stuff that comes out in revision. Good stuff can get cut too. More about this, with examples, later in this chapter.

The big reason you're cutting what's not essential, of course, is that your story has to move, has to Get On With It. Some stories move fast, some move at a more leisurely pace, but all have to move. A reader may be on the rapids or on a languid river, but she must sense that she's getting somewhere. John Gardner, in his book of advice and instruction *The Art of Fiction*, called this "profluence," and every writer has to develop a keen nose for it. If there's no profluence, no sense of movement, a reader gets bored, like a sailor becalmed in the Doldrums or Horse Latitudes.

What are some common examples of nonessential writing that interfere with the profluence of the story?

THE PHILOSOPHIC RAMBLE

One kind of nonessential writing we've already seen in the first-draft opening to "Piano Lessons": the *Philosophic Ramble* or Rumination, in which the writer suddenly seems to take time out for some cracker-barrel philosophizing or narrative commentary. Passages that *talk* about the story rather than *dramatically express* it through what characters do or say or think may be ready for the ax. Now it's a different story (to make a pun) if the philosophic asides are an ongoing, integral aspect of the narrative, the author in effect becoming a character himself, like Dickens or Henry Fielding or Leo Tolstoy, the avuncular authors of eighteenth- or nineteenth-century English or Russian novels. If they're not, these passages may be gratuitous and self-indulgent.

Sometimes these little rambles where you're ruminating about the story rather than dramatizing it can be very sneaky and hard to spot. Look at this one from the first draft of my short story "Turk." It's told from the point of view of an eleven-year-old boy who's both attracted to and repelled by his mother's lover, a mysterious truck driver named Turk. In this scene the boy and his young friend Jonquil are musing about Turk:

> We walk across the Dixie Roadway, past the houses where the Haitians live. They seem like ghost people sitting on the stoops or leaning against the wall, talking softly to one another, no one's voice very high, not like in Whatleyville, the section of town where most of the black people live, where there always seems to be noise and cars backfiring and music coming from windows and in the alleys.
>
> "Maybe she'll marry him," Jonquil says. The idea seems to please her. "Maybe he'll be your daddy."
>
> I think about that. "She'd never marry him," I say.
>
> "Why not? Doesn't she love him?"
>
> *I don't know. I don't know anything about love. I've never thought of my mother as loving Turk. Being with him, sleeping with him, but not loving him. Turk is someone who comes into our home and stays awhile and then leaves, and each time he leaves it seems for good, he's gone like a stone in deep water that plunges just right, so that it doesn't leave a ripple. Or like a stone that's skipped just right off the water, so that rather than drop, it seems to pick up velocity with each skip, going further and further out and way, barely touching, barely disturbing the water as it flies. When he's gone Mom never mentions him, it's as if he's never been there, so that sometimes Turk seems more like a dream than anything, and I wonder whether or not I've dreamed him.*

The whole last paragraph (in italics) was cut in revision. Why? Because it's *talking* about Turk, rather than *showing* him. It's *talking* about, rather than *showing*—the way his dialogue does—the conflicted way the boy feels about him. There's another reason too. The language and insights here are inappropriate, off-key, too mature and philosophic for a boy of eleven—or at least this boy. He wouldn't say this, and he wouldn't think this. It's as if another character—the author—momentarily took over the boy's consciousness. Which is exactly what happened. So out it goes.

"PIANO LESSONS"

Before going on, I'd like you to read another short story of mine, the aforementioned "Piano Lessons." We've already looked at problems with its original opening in the preceding chapter. Because I'm soon going to be using other sections from an early draft as illustrations of what to cut (and will be referring to the story again in later chapters), the ensuing discussions might make more sense if you have the final version in mind.

PIANO LESSONS

When I was seven years old, my mother decided I should have piano lessons—why, I don't know. We had an upright piano inherited from an uncle of hers on the side porch, and I think she felt it should be used. My father didn't like the idea at all. I'd never shown any interest in music, he said; it was a waste of time and money. Most of all, he didn't like the idea of the nuns. Except for Mrs. Kresky, who lived thirty miles away in Schuylerville, the nuns at St. Stanislaus were the only piano teachers in the county, let alone Tyler, the little town in western Pennsylvania where we lived. "I don't like him being over there with them," my father said, but my mother was insistent.

"For God's sake," she told him, "what do you think they're going to do? Convert him?"

So on Wednesday afternoons that December, my father waited after school to take me to my piano lesson. As our Packard coughed and spluttered like an old, tired beast, we'd drive across the bridge to the Third Ward, the side of town where St. Stanislaus was. I'd crane my neck and look down at the frozen French River, its ice mottled and dirty. Once I asked my father where it went. "Nowhere," he said, and I thought, *The river is going nowhere.* We'd pass tired houses, their yards littered with broken toys, empty doghouses, rusted iceboxes and washers, cars slowly being stripped to skeletons. In one yard, a gutted deer carcass hung by chains from a child's swing set. Often their lights weren't yet on, and I wondered if anybody really lived there, and did they have children like me who also took piano lessons.

"Mind now," my father warned as he handed me a dollar for the lesson, "if those nuns try and teach you anything besides piano, you let me know."

I didn't know what he meant. I knew nothing about nuns, had never even been close to one until I started taking piano lessons, and his words frightened me.

"You just tell me," he said, "and we'll put an end to that. I don't care what your mother says." Then he'd leave me to go wait somewhere—I never knew where—while I had my lesson.

I'd knock on the priory door and be ushered into the music room to wait for Sister Benedict. The room had a stale, waxy smell and was always too warm, the radiator sporadically hissing like a cornered cat. The drapes were kept closed, and shadows seemed everywhere. Above the piano a wooden Christ gazed down on me in agony. Sometimes I'd hear doors softly opening and closing in the hallway, but I never saw any people pass by, nor did I hear voices, or the sound of pianos being played by any other children taking lessons. What I did hear was the rustle of Sister Benedict's habit in the hall, and then she'd be there, hands folded, lips thin and unsmiling, smelling like old sweaters and my mother's laundry starch. She'd nod and sit beside me on the piano bench, and uncover the keys. "Let's begin," she'd say.

I always played badly. Meter was a mystery to me. I was either going too fast or too slow or losing the count altogether. "Do it again," Sister Benedict would murmur, and I would try, but still I couldn't get it right. Sometimes when I played particularly badly, she would pinch the bridge of her nose between her fingers and rub. "Again," she'd tell me, tapping her pencil on my music book in an attempt to mark the beat. I would blink with frustration as I struggled to find the proper rhythm. I rarely finished an exercise. "No, no—like this"—Sister Benedict would interrupt—and then demonstrate. "Do you understand now?" I'd nod, even though it was still a mystery and a secret, and I didn't understand at all.

Afterward, my father would be waiting for me in the car, its motor running so he could keep warm: after the first lesson, he'd never gone back inside the priory. "Did those nuns try and tell you anything?" he'd ask. I would shake my head.

And then one afternoon everything changed. Snow was falling thickly when my father dropped me off for my lesson. "I have something for you," Sister Benedict said when she entered the music room, and she was smiling, something she'd never done before. She went to the closet and came back with something I'd never seen, a wooden box with a metal shaft and scale. "I got this for you," she said, putting the metronome on top of the piano. "Maybe it will help." She wound it and pressed a button on the side. The shaft clicked back and forth like an admonishing finger. "Play," she told me. "Try keeping up." I tried, but the metronome only made things worse. Like a shaming, clucking tongue, it seemed to mock me. I stopped playing.

Sister Benedict stopped the metronome. "What's the matter?" she asked.

"I—I can't keep up."

"Let's try it slower," she said, and adjusted the metronome. But still I couldn't find the proper beat. I felt myself sweating underneath my shirt.

Once more she reset it. "Try again," she urged.

But it was always gaining on me, pushing furiously onward with a pace and a will of its own. My fingers missed more and more notes, the page became a blur, and still the metronome marched on, and with every tick it seemed to say, *You will do this again and again and again; you will never get it right; you will be in this music room forever.*

My fingers froze. I began to cry.

"What's the matter?" Sister Benedict asked anxiously. "Why are you crying?" I couldn't reply. I sat with my hands rigidly by my side, chest heaving, my face hot with tears.

"Jonathon—" she said, using my name for the first time, "please." Her hand fluttered, as if she would touch me, then fell into her lap. "I don't understand," she said. "Please stop crying." But I couldn't—I couldn't stop at all.

"Stay here," she murmured and, as much to herself as me,

"I'll get Mother Superior." She left and soon was back with an older nun, who wore a white shawl over her black habit.

"He just started bawling," Sister Benedict told her. "He won't stop."

"What's wrong, child?" the other nun gently asked. I shook my head. I couldn't say what was wrong.

"He has trouble," Sister Benedict said. "He gets frustrated."

The older nun put her hand on my forehead. "He feels hot," she said. She stroked my hair. "He should go home today."

"His father should be coming for him shortly," Sister Benedict said.

"Would you like to rest until your father comes?" the older nun asked me. I nodded. She took my hand and led me down the hallway to a narrow room with mullioned windows that looked out onto a courtyard lit by a single lamp on a post. The snow was still falling fast and had already covered the bushes, the ground, the benches. I'd stopped crying now but was still sniffling hard. "You can lie down over there until your father comes," the nun told me, pointing to a settee by the window. I went over and lay down. She softly closed the door.

I heard a high-pitched yell in the courtyard. I rose to my knees and looked out. Four nuns were standing in the falling snow. I couldn't see their faces clearly because of the thick flakes, the poor illumination, and my breath, which kept misting the pane. One nun had thrown a snowball at another, who was laughing and pointing her finger accusatorially. She bent over and made her own snowball and threw it back at her assailant, who shrieked and dodged. And then they were all making snowballs and tossing them awkwardly at one another, laughing and running about like excited children. One tall nun scooped up a lapful of snow in her skirt. Making a chugging sound, she chased the one who'd started it all, who squealed and tried to escape, only to slip and fall in the snow. Her attacker flipped up her habit, dumping snow on her. Then they were all upon her, furiously shoveling snow with their hands. "No, no," she screamed, and laughed, and they were all laughing, until one by one they collapsed, panting, their black habits powdered white with snow. For one moment, no one and nothing moved in the courtyard except the snow falling from far above and far away, and all of it—courtyard and snow and nuns—looked like a miniature scene in the snow globes I'd seen at the five-and-dime. *If I breathe,* I thought, *they will vanish.*

And then they rose, and brushed themselves off, and quietly walked across the courtyard and into the dark.

I heard voices in the hall, the loudest my father's. The door opened, and there he was. "Let's go," he said, his lips tight. We saw no one as we left.

We got into the car and drove away from St. Stanislaus. My father gripped the wheel tightly with both hands. The streets were silent except for the scrunch of our tires.

"Goddam snow," he muttered. A muscle in his jaw twitched.

Everything looked different, I thought. The houses in the Third Ward seemed transformed, the cluttered yards now soft undulating hillocks of snow, the stripped cars fantastic caverns, the gutted deer on the swing magically rimed and glistening and frosted. Lights were on in the houses; people lived there after all.

"What happened?" my father asked. "What did those damn nuns say to you?"

"Nothing," I murmured, as I stared at the houses. Through one window I could see a man brushing his wife's hair with slow, gentle strokes; in another, a young couple danced languidly while a little boy drove a toy car around their legs. I thought: *I have never seen any of this before.* We crossed the bridge. It was too dark to see the river, but I knew it was there and that below its ice it was flowing, away from Tyler, and even though I didn't yet know its destination, still—it was flowing somewhere.

"They must have said *something,*" my father said, looking at me hard. "They told me you were crying."

I thought of the nuns playing in the snow. The car seemed hot and close, and I rolled down my window a crack. The sliver of cold air felt bracing. And I wondered, Could Sister Benedict have been one of those nuns in the courtyard? And I just hadn't seen, hadn't known? I thought and thought but couldn't decide.

"Well, that's it," my father said, making a cutting motion with his hand. "No more piano lessons! You're through with that." He slapped the steering wheel. "I'll just have to have it out with your mother."

But I wasn't listening anymore at all. I laid my head against the window and closed my eyes and felt the rest of my life come rushing toward me, like the French River flowing back on itself, and I knew with a shiver approaching wonder that all of it would be both more terrible and more wondrous than anything I'd ever been told before.

•　•　•

Okay. Now let's get back to our discussion about Cutting What's Not Essential.

REPETITIONS

This is something we've seen before, in the chapter on Openings. But of course repetitions can occur anywhere. Here's another passage from the first draft of "Piano Lessons" (sections later cut in italics):

> During the winter of my seventh year, the year that I was in second grade, my mother decided I should take piano lessons, why, I don't know. We had a piano—a small upright one—at home, and for as long as I can remember, no one touched it. It was simply a piece of furniture that one never uses, like an ornamental breakfront, or the chairs—carefully covered in plastic by my mother—that we never sat in. We moved through our house in a kind of ritualistic ease, careful not to put something on one table, nor sit in that chair, and to walk carefully around the edge of that rug. *The piano was the same way, rarely opened. At any rate, no one used the piano, and maybe that gave her the idea that I should have music lessons. Maybe the piano had been waiting, like a locust buried in the ground, for my coming of a certain age, wherein its purpose could be revealed. I was to have music lessons, and learn to play it. I'd never expressed any interest in it—I can't remember a time, before I took lessons, when I'd plunk on it, although I do remember it smelled of disuse.*

Why did I cut all this, more than a half-paragraph's worth? For one reason: It was *repeating* what I'd already written. In the first part of the paragraph, you notice, I'd already written that the narrator was to have piano lessons, and that the family piano had been unused until then. The bottom half of the paragraph then repeats that ("The piano was the same way, rarely opened," and "At any rate, no one used the piano . . .", etc.). It's slightly different, sure, but basically I'm saying the same thing. I'm spinning my wheels. These passages of *repetition*, of circularity, are ripe for cutting.

And would you look at this. In the beginning of the very next paragraph, here I go again:

> Nevertheless, despite any lack of interest, it was decided one day that I should take piano lessons. I don't remember being asked if I wanted to take lessons. All I remember is that one day I found myself going to my first lesson.

Good Lord, how many times do I have to say this! I'm on page three and for all purposes still saying the same thing. So all of this can go too. And in the rest of the paragraph, I'm really just repeating the same philosophizing of the opening paragraph we discussed in the preceding chapter:

> In our family, I was adored, but not consulted, and things often happened as if they were fated, and I was in the hands of some more inscrutable destiny understood by my parents, but a mystery to me. Dental appointments, braces, polio shots—all arrived on some mysterious schedule, unknown to me until they happened, and I was being trundled off in our old Buick to yet another appointment, yet another interruption from whatever I was doing. They were the interruptions of childhood, unannounced, tolerated, and music lessons seemed to be another of them.

Just more repetition, and more need for cutting.

Have I made my point? Don't repeat yourself. If you've described the kitchen of the old farmhouse once, you probably don't need to do it again. If you've shown that Melvin is cruel to animals by his shooting nightingales with his pellet gun, you probably don't have to have him shoot squirrels too. If Fluella has told her good friend Joanie of her dislike for her mother-in-law, you probably don't have to have her say it again to another friend. Fiction isn't a philosophic argument, where it's often necessary to explain the same thing again in another way. Fiction is a series of ongoing dramatic events. It thrives on change, not repetition. In an early draft of my story "Glory," a divorced mother who's trying to enlist the help of men in protecting her son from a school bully is successively rebuffed by her former husband, her boyfriend, the school principal and a YMCA instructor. I eventually eliminated the scene with the principal. Three scenes effectively dramatized her growing frustration. Four started to seem repetitious and boring. Enough already.

TANGENTS

Back again to "Piano Lessons," draft one, to see another kind of passage ready for cutting:

> I remember my parents arguing. They seemed to be arguing over many things that fall and winter, and they would continue to argue into the spring, and then with the melting of the snow in late April a kind of reverse internal weather set in, a silence and a frostiness, in which they argued no longer, but rather endured each other in silence, so that silence hung heavy in our house, like a thickened air. It was the year before my parents separated, and later divorced, and it was the year in which I began my music lessons.

Here, I'm describing an unease in the parents' relationship, the harbinger of a future divorce. Indeed, as I was writing the first draft I thought this might be important dramatically, so I did more with it, showing them arguing and the boy listening:

> I'd go upstairs to my room and try to organize my stamp book or build the model I was working on, and still listen through the heating duct to their voices, muffled now, but every now and then I could make out some word or phrase. Their arguments were never loud, their voices never rose, they were too well-bred, too tolerant for that; but they argued nonetheless, my father's neck muscles tightening and my mother's lips pursed together, her eyes staring in a strange way past my father to the wall behind, so that often I'd look there too, to wonder what she was seeing while he talked. . . .

But as I thought more about the story, I realized that the tension between the parents was a dead end and distracted from what the story was really about, which as we've seen is the conflict between the father's bitter view of life and the young boy's emerging realization of its possible wonders. The parents' conflict was a sideshow, a distraction. A similar thing happens a little later in the first draft:

> We were the only Jewish family in town, something which I wasn't really aware of, since we never made much of our Jewishness, never going to synagogue (the nearest one was in another city, some twenty miles away). I don't think I was really conscious of being Jewish for some time, and after I was, found that it didn't much affect my life. None of my friends was Jewish, and I'm not sure they even knew I was Jewish. I'm not even sure they knew what a Jew was. If they were prejudiced at all, it was an assumed prejudice, something which one adopts without thinking and without having any personal stake in, nor any real targets to vent it against. If they agreed that they disliked Jews, they still would have liked my father, who was a popular man in town, judging by the way people greeted him when I walked with him down the street or the way the barbers greeted him when we went for our weekly trim. We were Jewish, but it seemed to mean nothing, and so it surprised me when my father seemed disturbed at my going to have piano lessons with the nuns, and I wondered both what being Jewish meant, and who were the nuns.

Again, all this business about being Jewish and the conflicts and complications it creates were interesting, but ultimately not in this story, I decided. Here, they muddled things, created conflicts and raised issues that didn't really pay off dramatically. The real story, again, was elsewhere. So out they went.

Still later in the first draft came this somewhat rambling paragraph:

> Oh, my gentle, my suffering father! He wanted nothing more in life than to please my mother and to make us happy, and yet it was something that he never could do, and it gnawed on him, and soured his stomach, and lined his face. I can see him now with his tape measure over his neck—measuring how much a hem had to be taken in, bending down close to the ladies' knees, his white, white fingers gently holding the hem while taking a pin from his mouth and carefully, as if he were afraid he might prick her, pinning off the material. Later, when he and mother divorced, I'd visit him in Pittsburgh, where he settled, and would almost cry as I, taller than he now, saw him with arms

akimbo, looking at me, smiling sadly, as if taking my measure, as if somehow he could, if he only tried, find me the perfect suit, tailored to my needs, cut to my bones.

Again, this was cut in the next draft. Not only does this Philosophic Rumination-cum-Flashback interrupt the narrative drive of the story, it also, as you know from having read the final version, presents a completely different father. Here, the father is all-suffering, slightly beleagured, basically good-hearted. Upon re-vision, I saw that he was *not* the father who was best for the story. That father had to be more narrow-minded, pessimistic, soured on life and its possibilities. So out went the wrong father—and this paragraph.

One more example. In this paragraph from the first draft of "Piano Lessons," the narrator talks about his irrational childhood fears:

When I walked along the sidewalk I'd often find terrible thoughts welling up from some dark place inside me, and they terrified me. One time I was walking on a summer evening, happy, the smell of hollyhock and fern in the air, and from down in the park below Indian Head the sounds of the older boys playing baseball. I would be going down to Isaly's to buy a popsicle. And as I was walking along, looking down at the sidewalk and the cracks through which grass was pushing, I was suddenly afraid that unless I got to the end of the block before another car came around the curve, my mother would die. It was a thought from nowhere, and it almost took my breath away with its terror, and I ran to the end of the block, hoping that no car would come around the curve, and none did, and so—I was convinced—I had saved my mother from sure death. Where had the thought come from? I was as frightened of that now as of anything, and wished that I would never have that thought again, or any other like it, but every now and then they came burgeoning to consciousness, and try as I might not to think of them, I couldn't stop them.

Again, this paragraph was cut because it presented a psychological aspect of the narrator that in the long run seemed wrong. Upon re-vision, I realized this boy is not really obsessed with thoughts of death, which is what I was toying with in this draft. Instead, he's a boy who without knowing it feels constricted by his world. That's his conflict, which has little to do with these obsessions about death. So this paragraph—and others showing the "wrong" boy—went out too.

I've given so many examples because this aspect of Cutting What's Not Essential is important. These cut paragraphs illustrate the *Tangent*, the narrative tack that leads nowhere, extraneous and unnecessary to the real story. Sometimes these go on for a paragraph or a page, sometimes they're developed throughout the story. When I revised "Piano Lessons," *re-saw* it, I realized divorce and family breakdown, or the problems of being Jewish, or an all-suffering father, or the child's obsessive fears, had very little to do with what the story was about. They were possibilities I had to try out in the first draft, but they led nowhere. They weren't the true conflict, the true characters, and so not the true story. And anything that is not the true story must be cut.

Sometimes you find out tangents are tangents while you're writing the first draft. Then you just stop writing them, they slough away like a snake's dead skin, and it's easy to cut them in revision. Sometimes, however, you discover they're tangents only after you've more fully developed them in the first draft, as I did with the parents' conflict in "Piano Lessons." The first draft of "Piano Lessons," while I was exploring all these story possibilities, these tangents, was three times as long as the final version! One of the reasons my first drafts are so long is because even after doing all my Revising Before Writing, I still have to try different narrative possibilities as I'm writing. I have to explore possibilities for what the story might be in order to see better what it isn't. So I'll always have tangents. And they must always be cut.

USELESS AMPLIFICATIONS

Other passages ripe for cutting are ones of *Useless Amplification*. They're sections where basically you're just overextending a scene, going on too long. Overkill. As a writer, you have to cultivate a fine sense of the right length for scenes, and thus when to shorten one.

Take a look at another scene from "Turk." Here, the boy and his friend Jonquil are engaging in some awkward prepubescent sexual explorations. The paragraphs I cut are in italics.

> . . . She takes my hand then and guides it under my shirt—
> I resist, but she tugs harder, and so I let her put it on her chest.

"Feel?" she says. I feel swelling on her nipples, small and hard, like two hard plums.

"Sure," I say. I try to withdraw my hand, but she holds it there. I can feel her heart beating.

She takes my hand away. "That's enough," she says, suddenly shy. She sits up. She tucks her shirt back in her shorts, not looking at me. It's like she's mad, and I don't know why.

"Hey," I say. "Let's call up people in the phone book, and say something stupid."

"Like what?" she asks, without much interest.

"We can ask them if John's there, and when they say No, we'll say, Well, where do you go to the bathroom then?"

She stares at me. "That's funny?"

"Sure," I say.

"You just hang up?"

"Yeah."

"What's the point?" she asks. "If you never get to hear what they say?"

We don't do anymore hugging or kissing or anything. What happens is that we fall asleep. Both of us, right at the same time. We only wake up later when suddenly the light's on in the trailer, and there's Jonquil's mother standing there, her waitress uniform still on.

The whole last paragraph is Useless Amplification. It makes the scene go on too long. It carries it past the dramatic core, the sexual fumblings of the boy and his friend Jonquil, and so vitiates its power. Every scene has a dramatic climax. Here it seems to come with Jonquil's irritated questions (" 'What's the point?' she asks. 'If you never get to hear what they say?' "), which resonate like the aftertone of a bell, rather than with what she and the boy did later—falling asleep—which seems more like an afterthought. When you're debating about where to cut a scene, consider that they're best ended *without addenda,* and by addenda I mean explanations of what just happened, or summaries of what just happened, or summaries of what happened right after the key moments of the scene. These all fall under the category of Useless and Unnecessary Amplification.

Another example, a first-draft scene from "Glory." The woman narrator is talking on the phone with her former husband, who left her and his son to run off to Arizona to join some New Age movement. The subject is their son's problems with school bullies (again, later cuts are in italics):

> He's silent for a moment, then says, "Maybe he should get into meditation."
> "What the hell does that have to do with it?"
> "It may be his aura," he says. "Maybe he's putting out some kind of negative energy that brings out their hostility."
> I'm stunned. "Are you siding with them?"
> "Carrie, I just think maybe if he'd, you know, meditate a bit, he'd feel more comfortable with himself, and then—"
> "You mean he'd learn to *like* getting beaten up?"
> "No, of course not—"
> "Jesus, this is your son we're talking about."
> "Is it? Maybe you're mad about the child support payments," he says. "That's it right?"
> "Yes, I'm mad about them, but that's no—"
> "You're really hostile," he says. "You always have been. Did you ever think maybe that's why he's got problems?"
> I feel like crying. Everything is getting twisted around again, and suddenly it seems that we're married again, and he's right in the room with me, not two thousand miles away, and we're having one of those endless, endless arguments, in which somehow I'm always the heavy, the bad guy, and he's the victim whose strength of ideal and purity of purpose are being stomped on. *Sometimes I feel like I just have to go away and become a monk, he'd say. I feel I'm losing the divine glory within me.*
> *What divine glory? What are you talking about? It scared me when he talked that way, as if he were about to take vows or something.*
> *It's just a metaphor, he said. I just feel like there's too many demands on me—I can't think somehow. I can't be alone. There's something inside me that I can't tend to. A voice I can't hear.*
> *Well, now he's alone—or is he? The last time I called a woman answered the phone. And as far as voices, he gets to ignore the one that says send his child support payments. . . .*

Why was all this cut? It's not that it was tangential—after all, her memory of their former arguments does shed light on their relationship and on Paul's selfishness and narcissism. It's not really repetitious either. The problem is that this second argument, in the past, isn't really needed, and deflects energy away from the main scene, their present argument on the telephone. It's Useless Amplification. Do we really need to hear them argue in the past to understand their problems now? For that matter, there's just too damn much argument. They start to seem a bit like the old cartoon characters Maggie and Jiggs, always arguing.

Look at another phone conversation from my story "Homecoming" (cut sections in italics). Here, the narrator has broken into the house that he and his ex-wife used to live in, now empty and for sale again. Missing her, he calls her from inside the house.

> You ought to come over, I said. You're only fifty miles away.
> You're crazy, Eddie.
> Wouldn't that be something? You and me back here.
> I'd have a hard time explaining it to Peter.
> Is he there?
> Of course he is.
> How're things with you two?
> I told you. Fine.
> You don't sound too enthusiastic.
> You're still reading things into everything I say, she said.
> *I was silent.*
> *We have problems like everybody's got problems. So what else is new.*
> *I'm sorry to hear that.*
> *It's nothing special.*
> Good old Peter.
> *He's OK, Eddie.*
> *Different from you and me, huh?*
> *Sure, different. Of course, different.*
> *You've got a nice place where you're at?*
> *It's nice.*
> *A house, I bet.*
> *Sure.*
> *Fixed up nice? You get to do everything with it you wanted?*
> *We're working on it. We don't have as much money as you and I had.*
> Tell me what it looks like, I said. Your house.

Again, the dialogue isn't tangential and isn't repetitious. It just goes on too long. The ping-pong quality of the repartee starts to grate. The reader starts to feel it's the writer who's keeping the dialogue going, not the characters themselves. They need a little bit of silence, and the story needs to Get On With It and not get bogged down in talk-talk. If readers feel you're overly extending a scene—not repeating yourself necessarily, more like just going on and on—they'll not only get a bit restless, they'll also wonder at its veracity. Aren't these people a bit *too* verbal? After all, real talk is often punctuated by hesitations, silences, and stabs at what to say. We don't just go merrily on and on. Dialogue that seems too arch, quick and ping-pongy, in which no one ever seems at a loss for what to say, often needs some tightening and some silences. Similarly, dialogue that goes over the same territory (unless you're showing characters' obsession with what's being discussed) probably needs some cutting. Less is more. This is true whether your characters are debating the proper way to cut a pastrami sandwich, reacting in amazed horror to a car accident, or admiring the view from the top of the Witchee-Watchee Bridge.

A TIME OUT FOR A TALK ABOUT TALK

This may be a good time to have a little talk about talk. I don't have a separate chapter on revising dialogue because throughout this book, as above, I'll be talking about it, usually in the context of a larger point about revision. As we've just seen, problems of dialogue often embody other problems: useless amplification, repetitiousness, etc. But it might be helpful here to take a look at what good dialogue does. Here's a section from J.D. Salinger's short story "Uncle Wiggily in Connecticut." Eloise and her friend Mary Jane have been reminiscing about their youth while getting drunk:

> "This is my last. And I mean it," Mary Jane said, picking up her drink. "Oh, listen! You know who I saw last week? On the main floor of Lord & Taylor's?"
> "Mm-hm," said Eloise, adjusting a pillow under her head. "Akim Tamiroff."
> "*Who?*" said Mary Jane. "Who's he?"
> "Akim Tamiroff. He's in the movies. He always says, 'You make beeg joke—hah!' I love him . . . There isn't one damn pillow in this house that I can stand. Who'd you see?"

"Jackson. She was—"

"Which one?"

"I don't know. The one that was in our Psych class, that always—"

"Both of them were in our Psych class."

This snippet of dialogue provides a master class in how to write dialogue that sounds "real." When people talk, they often don't stick to the subject: Here, Eloise brings up Akim Tamiroff, just to make a joke. Indeed, sometimes people seem as if they're not listening to each other at all. Their attention wanders, as does Eloise's when she wonders aloud where a pillow might be. Talk is often elliptical. Thoughts remain unfinished and drift away ("I love him . . ."). Often people are at a loss for what to say. They stumble and fumble. As I showed in the dialogue quoted from "Homecoming," they often have pauses and silences in their talk. Quick and witty is *not* how people talk. Also, they interrupt one another, as Eloise interrupts Mary Jane; they don't always wait politely for the other person to finish a sentence.

Good dialogue, besides not succumbing to any of the other problems discussed heretofore and hereafter, most likely takes into account these features of the way people talk. If it doesn't, it can sound unreal. Which leads to a special case of "unreal" dialogue, and another area that can use cutting, namely, Unnecessary Stagey Dialogue.

UNNECESSARY STAGEY DIALOGUE

This is dialogue that exists solely to provide information, usually background, to the reader, not to the characters themselves, because presumably they would already know whatever is being discussed. You can always recognize this dialogue by its "staginess"—and by what I just said, that the characters would already know it. In highly exaggerated form, it looks like this:

"I'm sure glad to see you," Jeff said to his wife, Anne. "It's almost time to go to the party the Donovans are having tonight for their niece, Trudy, who just came back from California where she's been studying beekeeping. Let's take the green Lexus this evening, since the Toyota's in the shop getting the fender fixed after that accident you had last week in the Safeway parking lot, when you skidded on the ice and rammed into the mail truck."

> "I'm surprised you're in such a good mood," Anne said. "Especially since you dislike Tom Donovan so much since that time he borrowed your pruning shears and didn't bring them back. They left for a vacation at Moon Lake, and you had to break into the garage to get them."

Now really, folks—wouldn't Anne already know about the reason for the party? And that their Lexus is green? And that she had an accident with the Toyota last week? By ramming into a mail truck? And wouldn't Jeff know why he dislikes Tom Donovan? And what happened when the Donovans left for Moon Lake? All this dialogue exists not for the characters, as dialogue should, but for us, the readers. It's unreal and must be radically revised. How? First delete *everything* the characters would already know. Yes, everything. That might leave our dialogue pretty spare, but also believable:

> "I'm sure glad to see you," Jeff said to his wife, Anne. "It's almost time to go to the Donovans' party. We'll have to take the Lexus."
> "I'm surprised you're in such a good mood," Anne said. "Especially since you dislike Tom Donovan so much."

And what do we do with all that other information about nieces and pruning shears, which we'll assume is necessary to our understanding of the story? We either put it into narrative ("Anne had just found out from Elsa Donovan that Trudy was studying, of all things, beekeeping . . ."), or into characters' thoughts ("Beekeeping! Anne thought. And her father had wanted her to be a lawyer!"), or into dialogue that *is* believable, that shows us character and conflict instead of just imparting information. Using these techniques, our revised scene might read like this:

> "I'm sure glad to see you," Jeff said to his wife, Anne. "It's almost time to go to the Donovans' party."
> "What's that niece of theirs studying out in California anyway?"
> "Beekeeping."
> "*Beekeeping?*" Anne laughed. "God."
> Jeff tightened his tie. He was thinking they'd have to take the Lexus this evening, since the Toyota was still in the shop after Anne's accident last week.

> "Why so grim-faced?" Anne asked. "Is it because you'll have to see Tom Donovan?"
>
> "Yes . . . I mean, no." Jeff sighed. "OK. I'll be honest. I was just thinking that I hope the Postal Service doesn't sue us."
>
> Anne pouted. "You're still mad about the accident. I *skidded,* I told you."
>
> "Good thing the mail carrier was out of the truck."
>
> Now it was Anne's turn to sigh. She flung up her hands in resignation, and went to the hall tree for her coat. She didn't wait for Jeff to help her on with it.

And so on. Here, information is being given, but through thoughts and dialogue that also show Tom's brooding about the accident and his simmering conflict with Anne over it. Later his dislike for Tom Donovan can be shown either in his thoughts or through his dialogue with and actions toward Tom at the party:

> "Jeff!" Tom shouted heartily from across the room almost as soon as they stepped through the doorway. Jeff winced, and took a deep breath. Tom seemed to bound over, and before Jeff could avoid it, his hand was being shaken mightily. He forced himself to smile. As soon as Tom released his hand, Jeff pulled off his coat. Taking it into the bedroom would give him a chance to escape.

You get the idea. There's no rush to tell everything at once. Especially through stagey dialogue.

Ruminations, Repetitions, Tangents, Useless Amplifications, Stagey Dialogue—what other passages lend themselves to block-cutting?

DREAMS

Ah . . . dreams. I think you should *always* question your dream scenes. Remember that editor I mentioned in chapter two who said, "Tell a dream, lose a reader"? I think that's good advice. Some dreams, of course, do advance the story and give us new insight into a character—but not many. Dream scenes suffer from either being too obscure or muddled—the reader is as baffled by the dream's imagery as the character might be—or too obvious, wearing their symbolism right on their little dream sleeves. What's more, whatever they show of a character's state of mind could usually be done better—and much more powerfully—through that character doing or saying or thinking something while awake. I think beginning writers get fixated on dreams because they seem like a chance to Really Write, with Deep Symbolism and Surreal Panache. But the symbolism is usually either obscure or hokey, and the surreal writing pretty mannered. Anybody can have a character dream about running naked through Niagara Falls pursued by a herd of winged lawnmowers. What's tougher is to show that character's anxiety through what she says or thinks or does while awake. Dreams are cheap ways of trying to reveal character, and so they usually don't.

You don't believe me? Look at this dream the narrator has in the first draft of "Glory":

> I think of things I've never thought of before, violent images that creep around the edge of my mind, just as I'm falling asleep, so that I start awake again, the TV still on. One image was a wolf suddenly looking up and snapping, lunging at me, its breath reeking from something terrible and bloody it had just eaten when I'd surprised it. Oh, what was it that it was eating? I was terrified, and I had to know, but the wolf's body blocked it from my view, and his snapping and growls kept me at bay. In another sort of half-dream, I'm running along a carnival midway, and at various intervals a clown's face bobs out, like the old witch's in haunted houses, and scares me, so that soon I'm apprehensive of where and when the next one will pop out, and I'm always glancing to the right and the left, but no matter how closely I watch, how cautious I am, the clown face manages to surprise and startle me. And then suddenly I have something in my hand, something huge, and I look: it's a bomb. Now it's my turn to grin. The next time he pops out, I'll throw the bomb. And he does, and I do, and then I realize, just before the bomb goes off, that the clown really meant no harm after all, he was just teasing me, and I've done something terrible in killing him.

Well. A lot of dream pyrotechnics—all x-ed out in the next draft. I decided that the narrator's sense of being pressured and pursued was better shown through scenes depicting her frustrations while awake, e.g., that phone conversation with her husband. Which leads to an interesting point. If you dramatically show conflicts while your characters are awake, which you should do, then dreams have a redundant feeling, a certain sense of overkill. Still another reason to regard them with suspicion.

UNNECESSARY CHARACTERS AND EVENTS

Now we come to an important juncture. The kinds of passages we've been talking about are basically ones that prevent us from Getting On With The Story. Now we've got to look at some that may work very well, but should still be cut because they're not best for the story. I mean *whole* scenes, not just sections, and entire characters. These are the hardest to spot and the hardest to cut because they seem so vital, so much a part of the very warp and woof of the story, when maybe they aren't. As I said, you can't get overly attached to *anything*. To illustrate, because this is very important, I'm going to have to go into a bit of detail from the first draft of a story of mine, "Anne Rey." And again I'm going to beg your indulgence by first asking you to read the story as published. This is necessary to explain the decisions I made in revision.

ANNE REY

When Anne Rey was a little girl and her mother read her fairy tales from a large purple book, her favorites had been those in which the hero embarked on a journey by boat; in later years, after consulting the I Ching, Anne always felt a special thrill when she received a hexagram advising "crossing a great sea." So perhaps it was not surprising that shortly after her mother began complaining about the "funny little hat" on the side of her head, Anne Rey—twenty-eight years old, single, an art restorer specializing in prints and drawings—decided to give up her small apartment and move onto a sailboat.

Her mother had just undergone a battery of skull X-rays, angiograms, and CT scans. "Sometimes the sensation of scalp tingling or phantom pressure comes from a brain tumor," the neurologist, a Dr. Gans, told Anne. "Maybe malignant, maybe not. I'd hoped that's what it was." He saw her expression. "I don't mean I *hoped* we'd find something, you understand. But now I can't tell you anything." He gestured to the ghostly films of Anne's mother's skull on the light box behind him. "There's nothing there."

"What's going to happen?" Anne asked.

"What can I tell you? There's no pathology. No pathology, no prognosis." He leaned back in his chair. "Maybe it's psychosomatic. Maybe it'll go away."

Anne looked at the films of her mother's skull and felt she was staring into realms of light and shadow that she had never known existed.

Dr. Gans leaned forward, his chair creaking. "Look—if it's real, it'll show up eventually. If it's not"—he shrugged—"well, let's just wait and see."

Two days later Anne Rey began looking for a sailboat on which to live. She spent an afternoon at the marinas putting up neatly typed notices in ships' chandleries, sailing schools, convenience stores, and laundromats:

BOAT SITTER. RESPONSIBLE PROFESSIONAL WOMAN WILL GUARD

YOUR BOAT AND PERFORM LIGHT SERVICE IN EXCHANGE FOR

LIVING ON IT. IMPECCABLE REFERENCES.

And she left her phone number.

She received three calls: one from a man who soon made it clear he wanted Anne to live with *him* on his boat; another from a woman who wanted rent, despite the clarity of Anne's notice. The third caller identified himself as Lou from the Ship-Shape Shop in Long Beach.

"You asked me if you could put up a notice, remember? I was putting beer in the cooler."

"Oh, sure," Anne said.

"You want to boat-sit, right? Well, I was over at San Pedro yesterday, out by the number two marina. Me and a friend got a hull-cleaning business, part-time. The guy whose hull we were doing said he had a friend who was going on a long trip and wanted his hull cleaned while he was gone. And he was worried about his boat being broken into. I told him I knew somebody who wanted to boat-sit, if his friend was interested. Well, he called him, and the friend's interested. I can give you his number, if you like."

"That's great," Anne said.

"It's a real nice boat, from what I hear. Thirty-eight foot Coronado. That's counting the bowsprit. It'd be real nice for one person. There's just you, right? That's what I told him."

"Just me," Anne said.

Adam Samuelson, the boat's owner, was an entertainment contract lawyer who wore glasses frames too big for his eyes and sandals too big for his feet, so that they flip-flopped against the pavement as he walked. He was fascinated with Anne's being an art restorer.

"Like old masters, right?"

"Well, not really," Anne said. "I just handle prints and drawings. An occasional watercolor. Oils and tempera I don't do at all."

"I didn't know you guys got so specialized," Samuelson said.

He wondered why she wanted to live on a boat.

"I've wanted to since I was a child," Anne said. "And now's a good time. I feel like I need to simplify things, get more control. You know, make things smaller."

"It's small, all right," he laughed.

They went to see the boat, the *Estelle*. "It used to be *Esther*, after my first wife," Samuelson said. "But I had to change it when I remarried. Lucky I could still use the first three letters." The boat moved languidly in its slip, held fast by anchor and spring lines. The mast creaked slightly as it bobbed; its stays hummed in the breeze. Below, it was much lighter than Anne had expected, due to several oversized portholes. The main compartment consisted of a galley ("Good stove, always lights"), a chart table, and long side couchettes which transformed into a dining table. There was a head in the forward compartment ("No shower, but you can take them free up at the marina") and a large captain's quarters aft, with bunk beds, built-in lockers, and a small fold-down desk. Everything seemed close at hand, manageable. Anne ran her fingers along the wood paneling; as if responding to her touch, the *Estelle* rocked gently, cradling her. Anne felt safe.

"Like I told you, it's small," Samuelson said, misinterpreting her silence.

"I want it that way," Anne replied. "It's wonderful."

Within a week, Anne had moved aboard the *Estelle*. She held a yard sale which rid her of much of her furniture, appliances, and wardrobe. Goodwill collected still more. She donated most of her books to the local branch of the Los Angeles City Library and gave her records to a friend. What could neither be kept, given away, nor sold was boxed and taken to her studio basement. Anne came to the *Estelle* with two suitcases, a garment bag, half a box of books, a print of Ulrich's *Etcher in His Studio*, and a cassette player with some of her favorite records dubbed onto tape. She put the print over the chart table, her clothes in the built-in drawers and lockers. The books fit neatly into the shelf along the bunk bed. She examined the charts rolled up in pigeonholes under the table. She liked the one of Avalon Harbor West, so she unfurled it along the table and clamped it flat with the parallel rulers on one end and a spring clamp on the other. Everything was in its place. Anne was satisfied.

She called her mother from the pay phone at the marina.

"They won't tell me anything at the hospital," her mother said. "I think they know I've got something bad—but they won't tell me."

"Mom, I've spoken with Dr. Gans. They really can't find anything wrong. Be glad."

"Well, I know there's something wrong, even if they don't. But I think they do. They look at me funny. They whisper."

Anne sighed. "Mom, that's not so. You've got to quit talking that way."

Her mother was silent.

"You still feel it?" Anne asked. "The little hat?"

"Oh, you know—I put it on, I take it off."

Anne didn't like the way the conversation was going. "I've moved onto my boat," she said.

"Oh, really?"

"Yep. Just finished. It's nice. You'll have to come down and see."

"Where are you calling from? I thought you weren't going to get a phone."

"I'm not. I'm calling from a pay phone at the marina."

"I don't like you not having a phone. What if I have to get in touch with you in the evening?"

"You can call the marina. Somebody's there till eleven. And

you can always leave a message on the answering machine at the studio."

"By the time you get all these messages," her mother said, "it could be too late."

"What do you mean, Mom?"

"If there was an emergency."

"What emergency?" Anne laughed nervously. "Are you planning on having an emergency?"

"You never know."

Anne rubbed her hand across her forehead. "Mom—it frightens me when you talk like this."

And now her mother laughed. "Well," she said, "I wouldn't know you cared."

Anne made herself a cup of hot chocolate after the phone call, and while the gas stove hissed, she pondered all her mother had said. Its meaning disturbed, yet eluded her. Like the X-rays on Dr. Gans' light box, either something was there— unseen—or was not there at all. "I can't think about this now," Anne said aloud: talking to herself was something she'd recently begun doing. She took her hot chocolate to the captain's quarters, read a few pages from *Swann's Way*—her summer reading project—and felt cozy and snug. She was soon lulled to sleep by the *Estelle*'s gentle rolling.

The Callot engraving sent over from the Oldershaw Galleries puzzled Anne. From the French school of the late sixteenth century, it depicted a landscape with two farmers pulling a heavy plow. Clouds roiled above the fields in thick fibrous masses. On the left side of the engraving, near the rooftops of a distant village, a reddish stain had appeared; several smaller ones dotted the fields. Anne had never seen stains like these. No mold, climactic condition, or pollution of which she was aware had caused them. She thumbed through Plenderleith's *Conservation of Antiquities and Works of Art*, but had no luck identifying them. Anne put on a Bach violin partita and looked at the Callot through a magnifying glass over the light box. She shook her head, and brushed back strands of blond hair that fell over the magnifier.

"Well, there's got to be a cause," she said aloud. "It's got to be something." She put a beaker of water for coffee on the hot plate where she heated chemical solutions. Gingerly, Anne touched the largest of the red stains; it was just the size of her fingertip. She drew back her finger and looked at it, half expecting to see the stain transferred there, then went over to the sink and washed her hands until the skin burned. "Crazy," she murmured. She sat down with her coffee. She decided to send photographs of the Callot to her old mentor, Preston Hamblin, at the Columbia Academy for Conservation in New York. Restless then, Anne paced the studio. "I don't want to work anymore today," she said. She turned on her answering machine and returned to the *Estelle*. She tried to take a nap, but kept thinking about the Callot. Still restless, Anne got up and ran the engine to recharge the boat's batteries, and after that waited for night to come.

Summer evenings on the *Estelle* became a solace for Anne Rey. More and more she left the studio early to return to the boat, picking up something along the way to cook for dinner. After a shower, she changed into jeans or cotton shorts and a workshirt and sat with a beer in Samuelson's deck chair that said HOTSHOT LAWYER on the back. As shadows spread like oil across the water, Anne watched the harbor come to life. Arc lights illuminated the great ships' holds, exposed like the gutted ribbing of monstrous sea creatures. Giant cranes lifted pallets of boxes, crates, barrels, sometimes entire railway cars. The ships were often overhauled at night, and workers in canvas slings and gleaming helmets swung like acrobats against the hulls, acetylene torches sparking wildly. The water wove a silent cocoon around everything, while the evening light flattened the scene into a mezzotint. Anne watched until the breeze became too chill. Then she went below, put on her hooded sweatshirt, and climbed into her bunk in the captain's quarters to read until she fell asleep. The *Estelle* rocked in the slip, gently groaning and creaking. Anne's childhood seemed very near in the small cabin: footsteps on a porch, a hand on the bedroom door, adult voices heard through walls and floors—all seemed redeemable just beyond the wooden hull. Here she could sleep, guarded and protected.

No one ever came to the boat, and it suited her.

Her mother refused to come. "I'm afraid of water," she told Anne over the phone.

"Mom, what are you talking about? You've never been afraid before."

"You should be too. Boats sink, you know."

"Not in a harbor, Mom. I'm tied to the dock. It's safe."

Her mother grunted skeptically.

Anne sighed. "How are you feeling, Mom?"

"My head hurts."

"It hurts?"

"Yes."

"Where the little hat was?"

"There—and other places, too."

"What does the doctor say?" Anne asked anxiously.

"Nothing."

"He doesn't say anything?"

"No—he says it's nothing. It's always nothing."

"Well, thank God," Anne said, relieved.

"But I know he's lying."

"Oh, Mom—not this again." Anne was exasperated.

"I can tell. I can see them passing signals to each other."

"Mom, that's crazy!"

"I know what I know," her mother said smugly.

"You've got to stop thinking that. Please."

Her mother was silent.

"Please, Mom. Promise me you'll stop thinking this."

"Do you remember Cleo Springs?" her mother asked.

Cleo Springs. It was where they had lived in Oklahoma before Anne's father died when she was three. After that, they'd moved to California, staying with a great-aunt until her mother found work as a bank secretary.

"I got stung under the eye by a wasp," Anne said. "That's all I remember."

"We lived in a white frame house with a big porch that ran all the way around it. I loved that porch. I'd sit with you, and we'd watch the rain come down. You'd try to grab the rain. I'd lean over the porch railing with you, and you'd reach for it. Do you remember?"

"No."

"Well—you did." Her mother sighed. "I don't know why you changed."

"What do you mean, Mom?"

"You don't care about things anymore. You don't care about me."

"Mom—that's just not true. You know that's not true."

"I know what I know!"

"Don't say that!" Anne snapped.

"That's the only place I've ever really been happy," her mother said softly. "On that porch. What a shame it came at the beginning of my life."

Anne was staring again at the Callot: the stains always seemed to be getting larger. At least once a day, she would take out her triangular scale and measure them, but they never changed. The phone rang, and she jumped. It was Preston Hamblin from the Columbia Academy for Conservation. His voice was as she remembered it—austere, patrician, as dry as a leaf in autumn. Anne imagined him sitting in his Shaker chair, cigarette burning in the ashtray beside him.

"I've examined your Callot photographs," he said, "and I've made some inquiries. I think I have at least a partial answer. But it's not good, I'm afraid."

"Okay," Anne said.

"Yes, well." Hamblin cleared his throat. "You know that during the sixteenth century papers were made that often had a high acidic content. The fibers tend to disintegrate over time if not properly preserved—magnesium carbonate and all that. But there are certain kinds of paper from this period that are more troublesome. Especially a batch made around 1645 in the mills at Fontainebleau."

"Fontainebleau," Anne repeated. She wrote it down.

"We don't really know what the basis of the acid is in that paper, but it shows itself as those reddish stains. You don't usually run into it in prints of the period, although my friends at the Huntington say it's quite common in books printed then. Well, you see where I'm leading. Callot must have gotten ahold of some. Usually he used a better quality paper. The Courtauld ran into some Le Creuzes like this a few years back. Had everybody scratching their heads."

"What can I do?" Anne asked.

"I'm not sure. It's given everybody a problem, I know. But— I'll be talking to my friends at the Courtauld soon, and I'll ask how they've come along with it. And I'll get back with you."

"Thanks so much," Anne said.

"So—how is sunny California?"

"Fine. I'm living on a boat now."

"Ah—" Hamblin said. "How sybaritic."

Some days later Anne's mother called at the studio. "I just don't feel right," she said, "and I can't pretend I don't. There's something bad wrong with my head."

"What is it, Mom? Is it the headaches?"

"No. This is worse. There's something growing inside me. It's pushing my brains out." She sounded in tears. "I've tried not to think about it. I didn't want to bother you."

"I'll come over," Anne said.

When she arrived her mother was sitting calmly in her wing chair and sipping black cherry tea. She seemed smaller, more frail, and she blinked when Anne came in, as if she couldn't quite see her.

"How are you, Mom?" Anne asked.

Her mother shrugged, waved her hand. "It's all right now. I'll get used to it, I suppose. If you want some tea, you'll have to put the water on."

Anne hadn't been to her mother's apartment for three weeks. Everywhere—on the counters, the table, the floor—were Dixie cups turned upside down. She filled the kettle with water, put it on the stove, and lifted one of the cups: a cockroach slithered away, its antennae feverishly poking the air. She turned over another cup on the counter, then one on the floor. Under each, a cockroach.

She walked back into the living room. "Mom, what's this all about?" She held out one of the cups.

Her mother folded her hands primly in her lap. "I'll be honest with you. I just don't want to kill them anymore."

"You don't want to kill them?" Anne sat down.

"Oh, I guess I'd like to. But I just don't want to bother with it anymore. I've been killing cockroaches all my life."

Anne tensed, unsure what was happening. "Mom, you've got

to do something with them. You can't keep putting cups over them."

She looked at Anne, a hint of challenge in her eyes. "Well, what would you suggest?"

"Jesus!" Anne cried, and stood up, accidentally knocking over a cup near the sofa: the cockroach underneath didn't run, but rather stood on its hind legs, antennae twitching, as if performing a trick. Both women stared at it. It scurried away.

Anne drew a deep breath. "Mom, I think you should go back to the hospital for another checkup. If it hurts—"

"They'll say there's nothing wrong," her mother interrupted. "It's in there"—she tapped her head—"but they'll never admit it. I know that now."

"That's crazy, Mom. They haven't found anything *wrong*. Why in the name of God don't you believe them?"

"And I know why they won't admit it."

"All right—why?"

"They won't tell me because they *put* it in there." She tapped her head again. "They put it in the very first time I was in the hospital. When they gave me that test. When they gave me that injection—"

"The CT scan," Anne said numbly.

"—that's when they put it in. That's how they did it. With that needle."

"What, Mom? Put what in?"

Her mother shrugged. "What's inside me. What's making me crazy."

Staring at her mother, Anne saw the future as a large light-filled room whose great door was slowly being closed. She and her mother sat in opposite chairs outside that room, revealed to one another only by its reflected and fast-diminishing light.

"Oh, Mom—" Anne went over and knelt beside her, placing her hands on her mother's arm. The older woman's skin was dry, papery.

"Let's go back to Cleo Springs," her mother said, staring hard into Anne's eyes.

"Mom—"

She grasped Anne's arm with both hands. "I can show you where we lived. When you were a baby. I can show you everything you've forgotten." Anne shook her head. Her mother gripped her arm tightly, almost painfully. "I'll get better there."

"Mom, Mom," Anne murmured.

"Don't you want me to get better?"

Anne stood, and her mother rose with her, still holding her arm with both hands. *I will have to pry her fingers away*, Anne thought desperately. But then her mother let go, all at once, and sat back in the chair. She smiled, a smirk almost, and Anne had to look away. Pressure marks from her mother's fingers mottled her arm. Anne rubbed them, rubbed them, but they wouldn't go away.

"You only think of yourself," her mother said. "Oh, I know you now."

Anne returned to the studio and called Dr. Gans. He was in a residents' conference. "Is it an emergency?" the switchboard asked, and she said "Yes," and then quickly, "No," and left her number. *Be calm*, Anne told herself. *There are things that can be done.* She put a Handel organ concerto on the record player, made some coffee, and tried to go back to work. But she couldn't concentrate. She unscrewed jars of chemicals and forgot what formula she was preparing. Once she feared she'd put an eighteenth-century English hunting print that she was retouching into a bath for removing fox-rot, a fungus. She gave up and tried to pay bills—only to find herself staring blankly at her checkbook, unable to remember whom she was paying. Then she remembered she hadn't yet checked her answering machine. She got up and flipped it on.

There were two hang-ups, an inquiry from a client, and then the voice of Preston Hamblin. "Yes, well . . . ordinarily I'd call again, but I'm off to Belgium in a bit, and I wanted to get back to you." He cleared his throat. "I've talked to my Courtauld friends, and the news, I'm afraid, is not good, not good at all. The bottom line is this: there's not much you can do with this paper. The stains can't be eradicated, and they can't be stopped. Only stabilized for a while."

"Stabilized," Anne repeated. Mechanically, she wrote it down.

Hamblin went on to outline recommendations for further treatment, which Anne tried to copy. He seemed to be speaking a language she no longer understood. While he droned on,

Anne stared at the Callot on the easel. The late afternoon sunlight raked it at such an angle that the reddish stains were almost obscured; if she squinted a bit, they seemed to disappear altogether.

". . . so I'd give it another two hundred years or so," Hamblin was saying. "Then it'll just be a horror. But—look on the bright side. By then maybe our techniques will be better. Science marches on, you know. I don't think the damage will ever be restorable, however. The paper has just eaten itself up, after all."

Anne turned the machine off. She looked again at the Callot.

"Just rotting away," she said. "Everything rotting, rotting, rotting."

Her mat knife lay on the workbench. Anne picked it up and approached the Callot. *I could slash it*, she thought, and just the thinking of it gave her a kind of joy. She needn't stop there, she realized. She could slash all the prints and drawings. It would be easy. She would become an ally of time and destruction; she would become her own instrument of inevitability.

Her hands began to tremble, as if they had a quick will of their own, and Anne clenched them. She felt she might choke, and then—incredibly—she was choking and gasping for breath. Panicked, she stumbled to the sofa and lay down. Her breath came in short, harsh rasps. She tried to breathe deeply, willing calmness to return, and after some minutes, it did. She looked at her hand: the mat knife had slipped out and was lying on the floor. The Callot rested undisturbed on its easel.

"There's just nothing I can do for you," Anne said. "I'm sorry." She picked up the knife and put it on the workbench.

"I'm going to be alone soon," she murmured.

Anne returned to the *Estelle* and got under the comforter in the captain's quarters. Outside the porthole a dirty gray gull preened on a piling. Anne couldn't bear to look at it and pulled the curtain.

There is nothing to do, she thought. She could only wait for everything to happen that would happen. Anne remembered Dr. Gans' advice: *If it's real, it'll show up—let's just wait and see.* She would wait. She would see.

Anne rocked gently, the comforter wrapped around her shoulders, for what seemed like a long time. Then, cautiously, she opened the porthole curtain. The gray gull was still there, head under its wing, asleep.

She would wait. She would see. She could extend herself no further.

• • •

Okay. Now read the following scenes from the first draft of "Anne Rey." In the first scene, Anne has a phone conversation with "The Brazilian," an enigmatic, godlike client she's never met:

> "I was just working on your hunting prints," Anne said.
>
> "Good, good." He sounded genuinely happy. "I was sitting here, I was thinking, How is she coming? Is it too big a job? Too hard? My wife tells me that I'm always asking her questions too. But she's—forebearant?" It sounded like a question.
>
> "I think I can get most of the varnish off."
>
> "They're hand-colored," he said. "Did I tell you?"
>
> "No, actually they're not," Anne said.
>
> "No? Not hand-colored?"
>
> "No. You couldn't tell beneath the varnish. But it's a repro-duction. Not hand-colored at all."
>
> "Life is strange," he said. "Just this minute when you said they weren't hand-colored, I looked out my window and two horsemen went by. Dressed almost exactly like those in the hunting scenes. In English habit. Do you ride, Miss Rey?"
>
> "No," Anne said.
>
> "Neither does my wife. I used to ride a lot. But you get older, things don't seem to interest as much. I seem to lose interests with each year. One year it's horses, the next year it's some-thing else. I will be a true Catholic before I die. Do you sin, Miss Rey?" Before she could answer, he was speaking Portuguese to someone who must have entered the room. . . .

Anne then meets Shmuel, an Israeli who paints custom designs on vans and RVs, and they become lovers:

> She and Shmuel spent a lot of time on the beach, going to movies. He loved to drive Anne's small Toyota—he never had had a car, he explained. "In Israel," he said, "no one can afford it. Not the gas either."

"How do you get around Los Angeles?" she asked.

"I have friends. They are always traveling. Coming and going, everyone's visiting. Someone always has a car I can borrow. And there's my cousin's van." He smiled, his lips slightly cracked from their day in the sun. "Now I can borrow yours."

"I don't know about that."

He reached over and patted her thigh. "Only when you let me. You are a strong woman."

Their relationship, however, is rocky. Shmuel thinks that Anne keeps the world—and him—at bay. In one critical scene, they argue:

"All these pictures," he said, the same thing that he had said when he first came to the studio. "All old. It's all the past. You think too much about the past."

"No, I don't," Anne said.

"You spend your time poring over old pictures. Touching them up a little bit. For rich men." Shmuel lit a match from the box at the bunsen burner. Anne thought he was going to light it, but instead he walked over to the Callot hanging on the drying rack. "I should burn them all," he said, extending the match to one corner of the Callot engraving. Anne felt her heart turn cold. She watched, transfixed. Shmuel looked at her and grunted, then held the match closer. "Why not?" he said. "Let's burn the past. You'll marry me and we'll go to your place."

"Shmuel, if you burn that print in the smallest degree, I will kill you. I will find a knife, and when you're sleeping, I'll kill you."

Shmuel laughed and shook the match. It went out, leaving a sulfurous smell. "It's like I say, you're a strong woman. It's lucky I love you. This place makes me crazy. If you think I'm crazy enough, you won't let me near these. We'll have to go to your place. Wherever you live."

Later Anne gets a phone call from the hospital. Her mother has tried to commit suicide:

The nurse that had conferred with the duty nurse came through the door, stethoscope wrapped around her neck. The two nurses came over to Anne. The new nurse extended her hand, and Anne reached forward with hers, thinking that she wanted to shake it. But the nurse handed her a pill.

"These are what she took," she said matter-of-factly. "A whole lot of them."

Anne looked at the capsule, pink as a slug in her hand.

"What is it?"

"Diet pills."

"Where did she get them? She wasn't fat."

The nurse shrugged.

"Is she okay?" Anne asked.

"She should be. As best we can tell."

Please don't ask me why she did it, Anne willed. . . .

While she waits for further news of her mother's condition, Anne has a brief encounter with a teenage couple:

When she went back out to the waiting area, it had emptied considerably. The teenage couple were still there, the wife no longer leaning against her husband, but asleep in the chair, her head lolling on the other side, snoring. What vigil were they keeping? Anne wondered. The boy was staring grimly ahead. She walked over to him; he looked up when she stood before him, the first movement she'd seen him make.

"Excuse me," she said. "Did it hurt? Getting that tattoo?" Anne pointed, and the boy stared at it slowly as if noticing it for the first time, wondering himself how it had gotten there, as if it were a spider crawling on his arm. He grinned. One of his front teeth was chipped halfway off.

"Nope," he said. "Hardly at all."

"I wondered," Anne said. "I wondered because I'm thinking of getting one, you see."

"Lots of women do," he said.

"I just . . . I just think that it's very beautiful," she said. Her voice trailed off. "There's nothing to be ashamed of."

The boy nodded, and closed his eyes sleepily.

Wha? I hear you saying. Who *are* these people? Who's this Shmuel, The Brazilian, this kid with the tattoo? What visit to the hospital, what attempted suicide? I don't remember *any* of this in the published story! You're right. During revision, I took them all out. Not because they were so bad as scenes and characters. The Brazilian is enigmatic, Shmuel an abrasive delight. Given her psychological state, her mother might have attempted suicide. The scene of Anne wanting a tattoo is resonant with her pain. I would have loved to have used these characters, these scenes. I'd *still* love to use them somewhere, in some story, sometime. Maybe "Anne Rey 2." But in this story, it was no go. How come?

First, because the story is really about Anne and her mother. At heart, it's a two-person drama, and all these other characters— Shmuel, The Brazilian, the teenage couple—tended to diffuse that. In re-vising, in *re-seeing* the story, I realized this. The Brazilian was easily dispensed with; he wasn't a major character anyway. Good as he was, when he came on, the story seemed to slow down. It was like da-dah! Intermission! while The Brazilian did his little number, then back to the main story. Shmuel was more problematic, since he *did* figure as a major character. I cut him because his conflict with Anne tended to obscure and weaken Anne's true conflict, which was with her mother and with her own fears and anxieties. This is not to say that a character can't have conflicts going with several different people. But in this particular story, as I kept re-seeing and reimagining it, it seemed more dramatically effective to have Anne become increasingly solitary and isolated. As much as anything, this is a story about running away from people and problems that will find Anne anyway. The more she actually *is* alone, without contact with lovers, friends, clients, anyone except her mother, the better.

The mother's attempted suicide and the scene with the young man and the tattoo, while good, were also abandoned for dramatic and thematic reasons. It seemed more dramatically resonant that the story end with Anne's mother still alive, a quasi-demonic presence, and Anne in a state of suspension, tension, *waiting* for the other shoe to drop. Having her mother attempt suicide—almost a cliché itself— vitiated this tension. Also, the hospital scene brought Anne out into the "real" world a bit too much. Her world is the boat, her retreat. Upon re-vision, it seemed dramatically better to end with her there, anxious, alone, wondering and fearing what was going to happen next.

It's interesting—not everything is lost from these cut scenes. Like palimpsests or pentimenti, we can see echoes of those cut characters and scenes in the final version of "Anne Rey." For example, some of The Brazilian remained in Anne's mentor, Hamblin, who also speaks to her like the voice-of-God on the telephone. Shmuel's anger at the prints, his desire to burn them, to escape the past, became Anne's own impulse to destroy them and escape. Aspects of his character are introjected into her, where they really belonged. It is she who's struggling with her isolation after all, not he.

What's the moral? That you not only must eliminate whatever is repetitious, tangential and overly amplified, but also must always keep in mind *what your story's really about,* and ask yourself whether characters and events are dramatically enhancing that meaning or not. Ask yourself of each scene whether it's helping to develop and deepen the conflict that dramatizes that meaning. Sometimes, of course, you don't fully understand what a story is really about until you start re-vising and re-seeing it. But once you do, it becomes easier to identify and cut everything that, recalling Michelangelo, "isn't" that story.

CHAPTER SIX

ADDING WHAT
IS ESSENTIAL

L ess, as we've just seen, can be more. But more can be more too. There seem to be two kinds of first-draft writers: those who overwrite, whose chief revision problems are mostly ones of cutting, and those who underwrite, whose problems are more ones of adding to, expanding and fleshing out. I like the image of thickening, as in making a soup. "Thin soup," we say, to denote something tasteless, textureless and bland. Good thick rich robust soup—that's what satisfies. Just so in storytelling. "But what about minimalism?" I hear someone saying. Minimalists, contrary to popular misconception, never advocated writing too little (an oxymoron, if you think about it). Raymond Carver's *tone* is spare and laconic, but his prose is often richly descriptive. His characters talk; they have physical presence; they exist in evoked settings. They come to life maximally. Ernest Hemingway, the granddaddy of the terse school of writing, may have eschewed a florid style—although you can find passages in which he's as baroquely lyrical as, say, William Faulkner—but he never failed to describe, to fully appeal to his readers' senses, and by so doing to create for them a rich imaginative world.

Which is the point. As John Gardner said so well in *The Art of Fiction*, the task of the writer is always to create a vivid, continuous imaginative dream for the reader. You may write as expansively as Henry James or as sparely as Hemingway, but your task as a writer is always to make a reader *believe* in this imaginative dream world's reality (or in its surreality, if you're a fantasist or postmodern writer), so that the reader becomes sufficiently interested in it to continue reading. This can't happen unless, in Conrad's phrase, you make the reader "see, really see" your characters and the world they inhabit. How do we really see them? Through how they look. Through how their world looks. Most importantly, through what they say, do and think. For a particular writer, some of these will be more richly rendered than others: Carver's style emphasizes dialogue more than description; Henry James' characters think more than they talk. But every writer has the same task, which he can't fudge: He must create that vivid imaginative world. Every writer is a maximalist in that sense, and can never do less. This is what's essential, what must be there, what can't be skimped on. If it's not there, you must add it.

Beginning writers, I've found, almost always under—rather than over—write. It takes time to realize that merely because *you* can see it in your imagination doesn't mean that the reader can. She can't— not without your making her "see, really see." You may see a tired horse listlessly stomping its feet in a wooden corral under a hot August sun, but unless you write each of those words, one reader will see a young stallion friskily prancing around, while another will see an old mare in a cold barn. This seems so obvious that it doesn't need to be said, but it does, because this is the undoing of so many stories: *Unless you put it there, in vivid, concrete, sensory detail, the reader will not "see" it.*

With beginning writers, I often hear the protest, "I don't like to describe my characters or setting too much. I'd rather let the reader use his own imagination to fill in the blanks." Well, I tell them, isn't that your job as a writer? Why do you expect a reader to do it for you? They're *your* characters, it's *your* story, after all. And readers won't do it for you anyway. Believe me, a reader will always read something that lets him *really* use his imagination, which is what a writer allows when she richly creates an imaginative world in which that reader may participate. A reader wants to wander imaginatively through the streets of Dublin as Leopold Bloom in James Joyce's *Ulysses*, or become Ahab and Ishmael and Queegqueeg on the doomed *Pequod* in Herman Melville's *Moby Dick*. But he's never been to Dublin or been a mad sea captain. How can he be unless you create that world and those characters for him? Ahab didn't exist until Melville richly evoked him—through more words, not fewer—so that he can again and again come alive in our own imaginations. In first describing

Ahab, Melville didn't just say, "He was a thin, gray-haired man with a scar on his face, who didn't say much." Instead, he writes:

> He looked like a man cut away from the stake, when the fire has overrunningly wasted all the limbs without consuming them, or taking away one particle from their compacted aged robustness. His whole high, broad form, seemed made of solid bronze, and shaped in an unalterable mould, like Cellini's cast Perseus. Threading its way out from among his grey hairs, and continuing right down one side of his tawny scorched face and neck, till it disappeared in his clothing, you saw a slender rod-like mark, lividly whitish. . . .
>
> . . . Captain Ahab stood erect, looking straight out beyond the ship's ever-pitching prow. There was an infinity of firmest fortitude, a determinate, unsurrenderable wilfulness, in the fixed and fearless, forward dedication of that glance. Not a word he spoke; nor did his officers say aught to him; though by all their minutest gestures and expressions, they plainly showed the uneasy, if not painful, consciousness of being under a troubled master-eye. And not only that, but moody stricken Ahab stood before them with a crucifixion in his face; in all the nameless regal overbearing dignity of some mighty woe.

Simply put, Melville *takes the time* to show us Ahab, to make us "really see" him. This is what good writers do, whether they are maximalists or minimalists. Here's the so-called minimalist Raymond Carver describing a drive into the country in the short story "Feathers":

> It felt good driving those winding little roads. It was early evening, nice and warm, and we saw pastures, rail fences, milk cows moving slowly toward old barns. We saw red-winged blackbirds on the fences, and pigeons circling around haylofts. There were gardens and such, wildflowers in bloom, and little houses set back from the road. . . . On the left side of the road, I saw a field of corn, a mailbox, and a long, graveled driveway. At the end of the driveway, back in some trees, stood a house with a front porch. There was a chimney on the house.

Nothing minimal here. Again, Carver takes the time to really show us this countryside, which is important, since it represents the kind of bucolic life these characters will never have. Lesser writers don't take the time. They skimp.

A novice writer who believes in letting the "reader do it all" might write: *He saw an animal moving on the rise.* So? What kind of an animal? A camel? A squirrel? A Gray's gazelle? An ostrich? Doesn't it make a difference? And what kind of a rise? A grassy hill? A bump in the prairie? A sand dune? A far ridge on the next mountain range? And moving how? Trotting? Crawling? Hobbling? Gamboling? Galumphing? Don't *all* of these make a difference? If they don't, why is it worth writing about, or reading, for that matter? If the writer doesn't show me, so that I may imagine *exactly* the animal and movement and setting she wants, I could imagine an anteater trudging through the tall grass, and my friend might see a grizzly bear chugging through the Rockies, while what the writer meant all the time was an emu running across the savannah.

Too extreme an example, you say? Here's one even more extreme, to make my point: If we *really* believe in letting the reader construct it all, then an ideal short story might look something like this:

> A man was sitting thinking. He had a problem. It involved other people as well as himself. Eventually a lot of things happened, and then it was over.

Let the reader imagine not only the man, but also his conflict, the other characters, everything that happens in the story, and how it all gets resolved! For one reader the man is a sailor on a ship trying to figure out how to outrun a hurricane. For another, he's a man in Seattle sitting in his car trying to decide whether or not to leave his wife. Who knows? Who cares? Presumably the writer does. Then why won't he just do his job and take the time to write it, really write it?

I think my examples, while extreme, are instructive. Without specific concrete details, without rich evocations of what characters look like, think like, speak like, and do like, writing fails to evoke and to interest. More is more.

Okay—we've got that behind us.

Now, in their early drafts, some writers consciously underwrite. They're interested in getting through the hurdle of the first draft as quickly as possible, or they've come to a section that puzzles them, or just plain bores them, and they'd rather skip ahead. They may hate to write dialogue, even though they know they have to, and so would prefer to skip those sections where their characters, they know, just gotta talk. Me, I hate to write description, whether of characters or of setting. But this is fine. Dialogue haters *know* they're going to have to come back and have those characters talk, so they'll grit their teeth and do it when they begin revising. I know I'll have to put in description where needed. Most of the time, however, writers notice only upon revision that some sections are thin and underwritten. As I've said, beginning writers almost always underwrite. So we have to become sensitized to areas of our stories where we do need more, sections that are meager, or missing something, or just plain missing.

Let's run through some common situations where more may be needed. Be on the lookout—we all succumb to them at one time or another.

SCENES IN WHICH CHARACTERS NEVER TALK, OR TALK IN INDIRECT DIALOGUE

In extreme form, a paragraph crying for more dialogue might look something like this:

> Alice's mother was adamant about her daughter not going out on a date with Rory, even though Alice was dying to. Her mother thought he was a piece of worthless trash, and told her so. Alice got upset, then angry, then hysterical, which only made her mother even more stubborn. She told Alice that if she went out with Rory, she needn't bother coming home. Alice said that the reason her mother hated Rory so much was that he reminded her of her husband, Alice's father, who'd left them when Alice was just four years old. When she heard that, Alice's mother slapped her. Alice screamed and swore at her and dashed out of the house.

People have emotions here. They act. They even talk, although entirely in indirect dialogue ("She told Alice that" kind of constructions—no direct quotes). But the scene seems weak and listless for one that is supposedly so emotionally charged. It seems like a key scene, yet it's not treated like one—it's summarized, sketched. It's thin soup. It's *less*. It needs More. Most of all, it needs direct dialogue. We need to *hear* Alice and her mother argue and swear and shout. So instead of "Her mother thought he was a piece of worthless trash, and told her so," we need something like this.

"Goddammit, Alice," her mother said with mounting fury, "he's just a piece of worthless trash! And you know it."

And instead of "Alice said that the reason her mother hated Rory so much was that he reminded her of her husband, Alice's father, who'd left them when Alice was just four years old," we need something like:

"I know what's really bugging you about Rory, Mom. It's 'cause he talks like Dad used to, right? He's got kind of a smart mouth like Dad, right? So you decided you'd hate him just like Dad."

Direct dialogue is always more dynamic than indirect dialogue. Indirect dialogue is useful when a quick summary of a conversation needs to be given, usually for informational as opposed to dramatic purpose. Thus, in a later scene, Alice might call up Rory and arrange to meet him for a surreptitious date. It would be tedious for us to hear her give a blow-by-blow recounting of the argument with her mother. Even though Rory hasn't heard it, we have. Getting Alice to the date with Rory is what's dramatically important—and what they will say there. So you might write her recounting of the argument in indirect dialogue:

"So what'd your old lady say?" Rory asked.

"That you were trash." Alice sighed. "And I'm not supposed to see you no more."

Rory laughed softly.

Alice told him how her mother had made fun of her, told her that she was just a *blob* of feeling. To Rory's amusement, she told him that she'd called her mother a bitch, and that when she'd repeated it, her mother had grounded her.

"Hey, sweetie," Rory said when she was done, "forget that old bag. Let's just get together, huh?"

For that matter, maybe this whole scene is no more than a bridge scene, a connector between the more critical ones of the argument and the subsequent meeting with Rory. Maybe it's best written *entirely* as indirect dialogue:

Alice called Rory right away. Much to Rory's amusement, she told him that her mother had called him trash, and that she was just a *blob* of feeling. She told him that she'd then called her mother a bitch, and that she'd been grounded. Rory laughed, and told her that he wanted to see her.

And we're off lickety-split to the more crucial scene.

SCENES IN WHICH CHARACTERS NEVER DO ANYTHING

This is an opposite kind of situation, in which characters may be talking a lot, or thinking a lot, but they never *do* anything. It might read like this:

> "Alice, you're not going to go out with Rory, and that's that!"
>
> "Mother, please—you don't know him! You—"
>
> "I said, that's *that*. I don't want to discuss this anymore."
>
> "That's just like you! Cutting things off. You just say something and I'm just supposed to do it. It—it doesn't matter what I feel. You don't have any respect for my feelings, and—"
>
> "Your feelings? That's all that's happening between your ears, Alice. You're just one big quivering mass of *feeling*. Over that trashy boy—"
>
> "He's *not* trash!"
>
> "Oh, I know all about him."
>
> "You're a bitch, mother!"
>
> "Why—you little—"
>
> "Bitch! Bitch! Bitch!"
>
> "That does it! You're not going out with Rory or anybody. For weeks. Ever!"

Etc., etc. The argument goes hot and heavy. It's certainly a lot more vivid than the scene in indirect dialogue. But something's wrong here too. After a while we feel we're reading a playscript, not a story. These characters only talk, they never do anything, and so they don't seem quite real. While they're arguing, do they stalk around the room? Slam a fist on the coffee table? Spread hands in exasperation? Twist their hair? Kick something? Break into tears? Shake a finger? Alice and her mother seem more like disembodied voices than flesh-and-blood people. What's missing is the flesh and the blood. We need more physicality, more *action*.

"Alice, you're not going to go out with Rory, and that's that!" Her mother made a hard chopping motion, one hand against the other.

"Mother, please—you don't know him! You—"

"I said, that's that!" Her mother turned her back to Alice, and crossed her arms. "I don't want to discuss this anymore."

Alice felt a hot churning in her stomach. . . .

Of course, you don't want to overdo it. Not every bit of dialogue needs an accompanying action. But without some, your characters will seem like ghosts. Which leads us to the next topic.

GHOST CHARACTERS

A problem related to the one above is characters who are never described, so that readers have trouble forming an imaginative picture of them. How old is Alice's mother? Is she tall or short? Does she have a raspy voice? A mole on her cheek? Are her eyes tired? Does she dress in tailored clothes, or fru-frus from the thrift shop? And what about Alice? Does she have acne? Blonde, brown or black hair? Dirty fingernails? A limp from a childhood accident? Surprisingly enough, character description, this very elementary aspect of writing craft, is often overlooked in early drafts. Why? Because we as writers *do* know what our characters look like, in our imaginations. So we take it for granted that readers do too. They don't. They can't "see" those characters until we give them voice, thoughts, actions—and a body. Your physical descriptions of a character may run to many paragraphs, like British writer Lawrence Durrell's often do. Here's a description of the old sailor Scobie in Durrell's novel *Justine*.

Youth is beardless, so is second childhood. Scobie tugs tenderly at the remains of a once handsome and bushy torpedo-beard—but very gently, caressingly, for fear of pulling it out altogether and leaving himself quite naked. He clings to life like a limpet, each year bringing its hardly visible sea-change. It is as if his body were being reduced, shrunk, by the passing of the winters; his cranium will soon be the size of a baby's. A year or two more and we will be able to squeeze it into a bottle and pickle it forever. The wrinkles become ever more heavily indented. Without his teeth his face is the face of an ancient ape; above the meagre beard his two cherry-red cheeks, known affectionately as "port" and "starboard," glow warm in all weathers.

Physically he has drawn heavily on the replacement department; in nineteen hundred a fall from the mizzen threw his jaw two points west by south-west, and smashed the frontal sinus. When he speaks his denture behaves like a moving staircase, travelling upwards and round inside his skull in a jerky spiral. His smile is capricious; it might appear from anywhere, like that of the Cheshire Cat. In eighty-four he made eyes at another man's wife (so he says) and lost one of them. No one except Clea is supposed to know about this, but the replacement in this case was rather a crude one. In repose it is not very noticeable, but the minute he becomes animated a disparity between his two eyes becomes obvious. There is also a small technical problem: his own eye is almost permanently bloodshot. . . .

And so on, for several more paragraphs. At the other extreme, a quick, vivid sentence or two might suffice to give a character body, as Joyce Carol Oates does so well. Here she describes the mother of Hope, the teenage protagonist of her short story "Capital Punishment":

The woman she remembers as her mother is thin, nervous, pretty, with pale heated skin, plucked eyebrows, a red lipsticked mouth, hennaed hair. She smells perfumy, but also of cigarettes; her breath smells sometimes of sweet red wine.

Some writer once said that you need at least three unique, vivid details to make even the most minor character seem real. Here, Oates gives us those three, and more, in two short sentences. Obviously the more extended Durrellian description is better suited to major characters and novelistic length, while Oates' more compressed description is better suited to the short story. But however you do it, you must describe your characters, with specific, vivid, sensory details. Otherwise they will remain ghosts, shadow puppets against the screen of the reader's imagination.

SCENES SET IN LIMBO

Another reason Alice and her mother in the earlier example seem so thin is because not only don't they do anything, nor have any physical characteristics, they also seem to be *nowhere*. Where are they arguing? By the swimming pool? In the living room? The kitchen? Is it morning, afternoon, evening? Winter? Spring? Shadows on the wall? Construction going on in the street, over which they have to shout? An Oriental rug on which Alice almost trips? Without a sense of setting, characters can seem ungrounded, floating in limbo.

Now as I've said before, I hate to write description. Here's a first draft section from "Piano Lessons," the story you read in the previous chapter, in which the narrator describes a typical lesson with Sister Benedict:

> . . . after a few moments, there would be another rustle of habit down the hall and I would wait, trying to guess which door Sister Benedict would come in, and then she would be there, nodding first to my father and then to me, never smiling. My father, embarrassed as if he suddenly didn't know what to do, would stand and say, "Well, here he is," and they'd both look at me, and I'd flush, and then my father would say, "I'll be back in an hour." Sister Benedict would watch as he left the room, her hands still folded, and then she'd turn to me, and we'd begin the music lesson.
>
> Sister Benedict and I would sit side by side on the piano bench. She uncovered the keys solemnly, with great ceremony: they also were a dirty cream color, like badly discolored teeth, or the cover of my music book. She smelled like wool that has stayed in a dresser drawer too long, and around her hung a faint aura of strong soap and something else, dry and harsh, like the smell of a seashell. She would wind the metronome and we would begin. I ran up and down whatever scale I had been practicing for her.

You'll note that several changes—chief among them the postponing of the appearance of the crucial metronome—were made somewhere between here and the final version. But what I want to draw your attention to right now is the fact that we get a good description of Sister Benedict, but nothing about the room they're in. And that's important for the atmosphere—*for the meaning even*—of this story. As you know, it's a story about a young boy feeling stifled by his world. In revision, I realized I had to insert a description of the music room not only to establish the setting, but also to help create that psychological atmosphere of suffocation.

> . . . Sister Benedict would watch as he left the room, her hands still folded, and then she'd turn to me, and we'd begin the music lesson.
>
> I was frightened of the music room, with its furniture that smelled of candlewax and alcohol and must. It was always too hot, the radiator pinging occasionally, and hissing as if it were a cat curled in the corner. The air was close, and I could never decide whether it were too sweet or too fetid. Sister Benedict and I would sit side by side on the piano bench. She uncovered the keys solemnly, with great ceremony. . . .

Now the room and the characters seem more grounded, more real. And more emotional resonance and dramatic meaning have been added to the scene.

A hint about setting. Some writers think that once they've described the room, the moors, the summer house, the Grand Bazaar, Sunset Boulevard, that's it, they're off the hook and nothing more need be said. Wrong. A writer has to stay aware—and make the reader stay aware—of the environment in which the characters are moving in order to sustain its reality in the reader's imagination. Settings are like unfixed photos, which fade unless freshened. If your characters are driving in a car along the Sunset Strip, you've got to keep interspersing concrete sensory details about the Strip, the traffic, the weather, the car they're in, whatever, in order to sustain the setting's believability. Never forget where your characters are and what's happening around them. A sentence or so every now and then might be enough to do it, but it's gotta be done.

A really good writer remembers *everything* that's been established about a scene, all the relevant details. He'll remember that a television was on in the room, even though no one was watching it, so that three pages later, in the middle of discussing restaurant choices with her husband, he can have a wife glance at the tube and have a fantasy about the sexy weatherman. A really good writer will remember that he described the conductor on the El as "tired-looking" when the youthful protagonist first got on board, so that two pages later, while that young man is wondering whether his girlfriend is cheating on him, the writer can have him look up and see that the conductor has now fallen asleep. And maybe that leads to the young man envying the conductor, since he himself hasn't been able to sleep since he began worrying about his girlfriend's faithfulness. The world you describe is alive and must stay alive in your imagination in order that it stay alive in the reader's.

This leads to a very important point: By richly and vividly describing your characters' world, and then by keeping track of what's been described, you provide yourself imaginative opportunities for character and conflict development. In effect, you're giving yourself and your characters props to work with. If the radiator in the room pings occasionally, you have the opportunity to show your character's nervousness by having him jump when it later pings sharply. If there's a sleepy conductor on the El, you provide yourself an opportunity to show your hero's insomnia and anxiety; if there's a sexy weatherman on the television, you provide an opportunity to show your heroine's boredom with her marriage. The more world, the more possibilities.

When describing your settings, try to avoid what I call the "Always-a-Robin" syndrome. The term comes from the following kind of description, which I've read over and over again in student writing:

> Jennifer woke up on a beautiful spring morning. The sun was
> shining brightly, and robins were singing. The breeze made the
> curtains softly part. Jennifer could smell fresh-mown grass.

For different scenes, there are always clichés. In spring morning scenes, for example, the sun is always shining brightly, the breeze always makes the curtains part, fresh-mown grass is always in the air, and a robin is always either singing or hopping on the lawn. These are clichés culled from the reading of a thousand stories, and not from fresh observation of a scene. The above description can be helped immeasurably—and very simply—by just inserting a few fresh, unique details to replace the tired generic ones:

> Jennifer woke up on a beautiful spring morning. The sun was
> half-hiding behind some wispy clouds, and doves were cooing
> under the eaves. The breeze made the venetian blind flap
> against the window. Jennifer could smell the newly blooming
> azaleas and dogwood.

It doesn't always have to be a robin, you see.

If you're sitting there revising and can't think of a fresh way to describe a spring morning, just step outside with your notebook and start making notes on what you see, hear and smell. Life will provide. Five minutes of observation will give you enough fresh details to go back inside and make that scene come alive. It isn't spring, you say? The dead of winter? Go outside anyway. You'll still see sun and clouds, see squirrels jumping from branch to branch, see an old lady walking her cocker spaniel, see and hear a man cursing and kicking his car's tires because he's locked himself out, hear a truck go by that makes the street shake, and so on. So take all those and put them in your spring morning.

CHARACTERS WITHOUT THOUGHTS

You could see this one coming, couldn't you? What makes fiction such an imaginatively powerful art form is that it uniquely allows us *to get inside characters' heads*. We can "hear" what they're thinking, which confirms or contradicts or raises doubts about what they're doing and saying aloud. It allows for a complexity of character that no other verbal medium—neither film, theater, nor television—allows. In all these we have to infer what characters are thinking through what they say and do (theater tries to overcome this limitation through the somewhat clumsy dramatic monologue: "To be or not to be . . ." and all that; film tries to do it through often equally clumsy voice-over narration). Indeed, as E.M. Forster so profoundly points out in *Aspects of the Novel*, one of the reasons we as readers seek out fiction is that it allows us to understand characters *completely*, in the round, in ways that we can never understand real people, even those nearest and dearest us. And part of that sense of completeness is "hearing" their thoughts.

Not to make use of this particular power of fiction is to severely limit yourself. Getting inside characters' heads more, letting us "listen in" on their thoughts, is a way of creating fuller, richer characters. Otherwise, they can seem opaque because they're missing that inner dimension of thought. We're seeing them entirely from the outside. Fiction allows us to go in. In the argument between Alice and her mother, we could do it like this:

> "Alice, you're not going to go out with Rory, and that's that!"
> "Mother, please—you don't know him! You—"
> "I said, that's *that*. I don't want to discuss this anymore."

That's just like her, Alice thought. Always cutting me off. It doesn't matter what I feel. "You just say something and I'm just supposed to do it," she said. "You don't have any respect for my feelings, and—"

"Your feelings? That's all that's happening between your ears, Alice. You're just one big mass of *feeling*. Over that trashy boy—"

"He's *not* trash!"

"Oh, I know all about him."

I can't stand it, Alice thought. I know I should keep my cool, but I can't, I just can't.

Note that direct thoughts, written in the first person and in the present of the character's consciousness, are usually more dramatic than indirect or third-person thoughts. Thus:

That's just like her, Alice thought. Always cutting me off.

and

I can't stand it, Alice thought. I know should keep my cool . . .

are more vivid than

That was just like her, Alice thought. She was always cutting her off.

and

Alice thought she couldn't stand it. She knew she should keep her cool.

Summing Up

To sum up: Look at your scenes with these questions in mind: (1) Do my characters need to talk more? (2) Do more? (3) Think more? (4) Be described more? (5) Exist in a vivid setting? If a scene is too one-sided in any direction—dialogue, thought, action—it may be a sign that it needs more of something else, more action in a talk-heavy scene, for example. Now maybe that's not necessary. Maybe in that particular scene, your characters don't need to do much. Maybe that's the whole point of the scene. The important thing is to know exactly what you're doing, exactly what you need and the options at your disposal. To everything there is a season, a time to cut and a time to add.

CRUCIAL AND NONCRUCIAL SCENES, AND WHAT THEY NEED

For the most part, we've been talking about scenes that are grossly out of balance. These, of course, are the easiest ones to spot on revision. But as you develop skill and sensitivity as a writer, your scenes may show a proper balance between talking, doing and thinking, or if they feature one over the other, it's done with knowledge and artistic intent. Yet some scenes still need something "more" that is harder to define. What is that "more"?

A story has critical scenes and noncritical scenes, in the sense that they're transitional, bridge, summary, whatever. An embittered boyfriend may be mulling whether to go disrupt his former girlfriend's wedding reception. He decides to do it. He drives over to the hotel, storms into the reception, overturns the table with the wedding presents, and while everyone is aghast, screaming, and trying to restrain him, smashes the wedding cake with his fists. Now, the scene in which he's mulling what to do and the scene at the reception are without doubt important. The drive over there probably isn't. It's a bridge scene, whereas the other two are (da-dah!): *Scenes of Crucial Conflict.* They are the scenes in which something important relating to the characters' conflict or conflicts is happening. Things are getting worse, things are getting better, things are remaining miserably the same, whatever. But important things are going on.

Now: A sine qua non about scenes of crucial conflict is that they *must* be richly evoked. They must be as imaginatively "thick" as possible. Less is *really* less in these scenes. Bridge scenes, however, can be summarized. In Anton Chekhov's short story "The Lady With the Pet Dog," the following bridge scene comes between the lovers' meeting again at the theater, when Anna pledges to meet Gurov in Moscow and thus reopen their affair, and a scene months later in Moscow, when they despair of ever getting free of their "intolerable fetters":

> And Anna Sergeyevna began coming to see him in Moscow. Once every two or three months she left S— telling her husband that she was going to consult a doctor about a woman's ailment from which she was suffering—and her husband did and did not believe her. When she arrived in Moscow she would

stop at the Slyanksy Bazar Hotel, and at once send a man in a red cap to Gurov. Gurov came to see her, and no one in Moscow knew of it.

It wasn't necessary, Chekhov obviously decided, to show all—or even a few—of their rendezvous in Moscow. These could be summarized in this bridge scene. What *was* important—and richly dramatized—is the scene before (their decision to renew the affair), and the scene after (their despair that they will ever be more than occasional lovers).

But more about bridge scenes later in this chapter. Here, we're concerned with crucial scenes, the ones that are dramatically necessary to show or advance the conflict. Decide what they are, then ask yourself several key questions about them:

1. Are there other aspects to the character(s) that I can show here, which I haven't yet seen? Can I make my characters even more rich and complex in this scene?

2. Are there other aspects to the conflict(s) that I can show here?

3. Are there ways I can advance the story dramatically, i.e., Get On With It, in this scene that I haven't yet realized?

What you're trying to do, obviously, is not only to richly render your critical scenes, in ways I suggested in the first part of this chapter, but also to get the most possible dramatic mileage from them.

Some examples may make all this clearer. In "Bagpipes," the story you read in chapter two, you recall the scene in which the narrator's girlfriend, Kate, while making love to a record of animal sounds, bites him. In the first draft, that's where the scene ended:

> She touched my lip with her finger. "Look," she said, almost wonderingly. And smiled. "Blood."

And the story went on from that point with a new scene. Of course, this is a crucial scene in the story, since it dramatizes the narrator's unsatisfactory relationship with Kate after he and his wife have split. Yet upon re-vision, it seemed incomplete somehow. Something more was needed to show not just Kate's freakiness, but also *his* desperation. This is his story, after all, not hers. And so I added more:

> She touched my lip with her finger. "Look," she said, almost wonderingly. And smiled. "Blood."

> One time we made love to the sound of humpback whales. "I feel like I'm underwater," I joked, and started making mock drowning, choking sounds. "Help," I said. "They're after me, the whales."
>
> "They're not going to hurt you," she said. "Whales are friendly."

This addition to the scene gives more texture to their relationship, showing its humorous (albeit desperate) side, not just its darker, almost sadomasochistic one. More importantly, it shows the narrator's conflicted feelings, his desperation, which he doesn't yet fully understand or recognize. There was more to *character* here than I had first written. Also, this added section provided a connective bridge to the whale-watching scene with his former wife that follows.

Another example. "Fireflies" is about the conflict between two sisters, one of whom, Alice, is selfish and free-spirited—and her father's favorite—while the other, Helen, the narrator, is more withdrawn and reclusive. She's elected to stay on the family farm to be close to the father, who's suffered a debilitating stroke and is in a nearby nursing home. In a crucial scene, the sisters argue about what Helen should do with her life. In the first draft it read as follows:

> "Why do you do this?" I [Helen] ask.
> "Do what?"
> "You come home and you criticize me. You tell me I'm not living right. What do you want me to do? Just get up, leave the place, move to San Francisco?"
> She's silent.
> "What am I going to do? What do I know how to do? You tell me."

Upon re-vision, I felt something more was needed in this argument. Leaving for Helen would mean leaving her father, to whom she feels bound in a kind of desperate love. She would probably bring this up here, not only because it concerns her, but also to dramatize her own martyrdom versus her sister's selfishness. So I extended the scene:

> " . . . What do you want me to do? Just get up, sell the place, move to San Francisco?" A pause. "Leave Poppa?"
> "There's nothing you can do for him. What do you do—just go and sit? What good's that?"

"I couldn't just leave him."

"What good are you doing for him staying here?"

"He looks forward to the visits."

"Bullshit—he doesn't even know you're there."

"That's not so. He's not dead you know. You may think he is, but he's not."

"I don't think he's dead."

"Well, you talk like you do."

She's silent.

Their father is behind everything in the sisters' relationship. Sure of his love, Alice has abandoned him; jealous and resentful of her sister, and forever seeking her father's love, Helen has chosen a joyless devotion to him, denying her own emotional needs. More, I saw, could be done to dramatize their *conflict* here and so deepen our understanding of what it's all about.

In another short story, "Summer People," a young man, Frank, and his father are closing the family summer home for the season and also for the last time, since it's been sold. While they do this, the tension between them builds. Behind much of it is Frank's guilt and resentment over what he perceives to be his father's disapproval of his life. At one point, they're putting up storm windows. Frank suggests that his father thinks him a failure because of his divorce. The scene in an early draft went like this:

"I want to ask you something," Frank said. "You think it's my fault that Jena and me split, don't you?"

"I wouldn't know." He turned over a shutter and pointed: The number "5" was marked in grease pencil on the underside. "I've got a system. See—this one goes to window number 5."

Frank stared. "What the hell is window number 5?"

Upon re-vision, I felt something more was needed here. Frank's divorce is a sore spot for both men. Earlier in the story, they skirted around Jena before, the topic almost too touchy to discuss. Here, they do it again—and drop it again. But Frank's resentment and guilt have been festering all afternoon. It was time for him to explode a bit, time to bring the conflict more into the open. So I interpolated the following section (in italics).

"I want to ask you something," Frank said. "You think it's my fault that Jena and me split, don't you?"

"I wouldn't know."

"But you think it, don't you? You think I'm to blame."

"What does it matter?" His father stood up. "It's over, like you said."

"Your darling Jena wasn't so spotless either," Frank said. "I could tell you stories about her."

"Let's go get the storm windows," his father said.

Frank pursued him across the lawn to the cellar, and followed him down. His father was turning over storm shutters. . . .

And so on. The conflict between Frank and his father is dramatically escalated and deepened by this addition. It dramatically advances the story. Instead of their continuing to step gingerly around the sore spots—which would result in the story spinning its wheels—the conflict escalates. The emotional stakes have been raised for Frank and his father. They, and the story, have to move into new territory now.

What I've been trying to suggest through these examples is that sometimes "more" has to be added to scenes of crucial conflict in order to more fully show character, or conflict, or to move the story along. Of course, all these go together like bread and butter, oil and lube, hand in glove. When you show more conflict, you reveal character more, and you probably move the story along.

So—you add not only to make the reader see and hear more vividly, but also to more richly dramatize what the story's about in the first place. Of course, this presumes that you know what it's about, which you might not, even after writing the first draft or two. But as you begin to chop away what *isn't* the story, it may become more obvious what it *is,* and what scenes need to be expanded, or even created out of whole cloth, in order to make it the richest possible imaginative experience.

DRAMATIZING SCENES THAT "TELL" MORE THAN "SHOW"

I've been saving one aspect of Adding What's Essential for last, because it's so important. We all know—it's one of the first things taught in every fiction-writing workshop and every fiction-writing book—that it's usually better to "show" rather than "tell." Among other things, showing is dramatizing characters and conflict rather than talking about them. There's a big difference in dramatic punch between "Jason was nervous about calling Greta" and "Jason's fingers shook as he dialed Greta's number." "Telling" is the province of various kinds of nonfiction writing, such as the psychological case study. If we want to be told about obsession, for example, we can read a psychology book:

> [Obsession is] contents of consciousness which, when they occur, are accompanied by the experience of subjective compulsion, and which cannot be got rid of . . . the contents of consciousness which preoccupy the obsessional neurotic are concerned with ideas of harm, contamination, sex, and sin. . . .

If, however, we want to see it dramatized so that it becomes vivid and terrifying to us in a way a case study may never be, we read fictions such as Edgar Allan Poe's "The Tell-Tale Heart":

> It is impossible to say how first the idea entered my brain; but, once conceived, it haunted me day and night. Object there was none. Passion there was none. I loved the old man. He had never wronged me. He had never given me insult. For his gold I had no desire. I think it was his eye! yes, it was this! He had the eye of a vulture—a pale blue eye, with a film over it. Whenever it fell upon me, my blood ran cold; and so by degrees—very gradually—I made up my mind to take the life of the old man, and thus rid myself of the eye forever.

We're not dealing with bloodless abstractions here, but with an old man, a filmy eye, a very real murderous intent. We're being shown obsession, not told about it.

When we're revising our stories, we should always ask ourselves if we're dramatizing what should be dramatized, or could be dramatized, or if we're taking the lazy and less imaginatively effective way, and telling about our characters and their conflicts. The beginning of a story about a young man on the road could be written like this:

> Driving along the interstate, he felt free. He owned the world. He thought about his girlfriend Stacy, and what a phony she was. He was glad to be leaving her.

Here, we're *told* what he's feeling in summary form. The language is abstract, vague. Now let's try to *dramatize* his feelings in rich detail:

> He slapped the steering wheel in time to Jimi Hendrix' chords. "This is my life!" he yelled to a passing interstate sign. He took a deep breath of sweet, hot, tarry air and turned the music even louder. He thought of his girlfriend Stacy. She said she loved him, but he remembered how she was always glancing at other people when she talked to him, and how she held his arm extra tight only when her friends were around to see. Phony, Jack thought. "To hell with her," he muttered, and gunned the car.

His feelings are being shown—dramatized—through vivid, specific details: Jimi Hendrix' chords, a slapped steering wheel, sweet, tarry air, Stacy's glances at other people, the way she held his arm and so on.

You've got to take the time to show, really show. As you might guess, you must especially do this in your Crucial Scenes. An example to make this even clearer: My short story "Stargazers" concerns a father who has mental problems and the anxiety they cause his daughter, the story's narrator, and her younger brother. In the first draft, the opening went like this:

> I don't know when it was that I first understood that my father was a strange man and a remote one, but it was sometime around the fall of my tenth year. He had always been a quiet man, and my younger brother Jason, who was six then, and I always were circumspect around him, as if he were an island shrouded in clouds that demanded care in navigation when one came close. In the summer of that year, he had grown stranger and sadder somehow, and I didn't understand why, and it bothered me. Not that he had ever been a particularly cheery man. He never really did things with Jason and me, except for occasionally tossing a baseball mechanically back and forth, something which he always suggested, but which he always seemed to do as a chore, so that both he and I quickly lost interest. But in that summer he seemed to become quieter and sadder. . . .

Now there's nothing overtly wrong with this, aside from the need to straighten up the prose. It's all perfectly straightforward. There's even a nice image here—the father as an island. But on re-vision, I realized that I was *telling* about the father and his problems more than *showing* them. So in a subsequent draft I changed the opening:

> Late one summer night in my tenth year, when I was fast asleep, my father woke me. "What," I asked sleepily, and for a moment thought that it was time for school, before I saw that it was still dark and before I remembered that it was summer, and there was no school. My father put his fingers to his lips, then raised his other hand. He had on a baseball mitt.
>
> "Get your glove, Marcy," he said. "Let's play catch."
>
> "Now?" I said.
>
> "Yes, now."
>
> "But it's night." Next to my bed, my little brother Jason was still asleep, back turned toward us.
>
> "I know it's night," my father said. I'd never heard him whisper like this in our house. "Come on."
>
> "Where's Mom?"
>
> "Asleep," he said. He sounded annoyed, as if I should know this. "Shh—"
>
> So I got up, stumbling and tired and a little disturbed, but not wanting to argue. Strangely, I didn't want to waken my mother or Jason.

This is close to how the scene appears in the published story. The important thing is that now the father's "craziness" and the daughter's anxiety are being dramatized instead of talked about. The baseball scene mentioned in the first draft is now going to be shown us, and through it, even more of the father's disturbed mental state. And the image of the father as island, neat as it was, had to be sacrificed for the better cause ("Kill your darlings," remember?). Maybe I'll use it in another story sometime.

MORE ABOUT BRIDGE SCENES

Not every scene needs full dramatization, of course. As we discussed earlier in this chapter, bridge scenes don't. They may be summarized. Just as you must ask yourself what your Crucial Scenes are, you must ask yourself what your bridge scenes are. Some writers have a problem deciding that and wind up dramatizing *everything*. Every scene seems to have equal weight, which makes it hard to get any kind of real dramatic momentum going. For example: For three pages a man debates whether to rob a Kentucky Fried Chicken. He decides to do it, jumps in his car, and drives over there. For another three pages, almost every store and street and sight along his way is detailed for us. Then he arrives at KFC and robs it for another three pages. The problem is, those three pages of drive, while they may be full of beautiful description, have impeded the dramatic momentum of the story. Just when it's getting tense, there's a long time out for some leisurely sight-seeing. The drive over is ripe for condensation, perhaps to a single paragraph, and on to the more important scene of the robbery. Keep the crucial scenes closely linked. Either eliminate non-crucial scenes (ask yourself, Can I do without this scene entirely?) or make them bridge scenes.

A potential bridge scene is one in which the conflict, whether interior or exterior or both, *is not being significantly advanced, yet the scene serves to impart necessary information or to link two other crucial scenes.* Bridge scenes are especially helpful in

1. Condensing a broad swatch of time (as in the section of "The Lady With the Pet Dog" we looked at).
2. Condensing a broad swatch of space (as in our robber driving to KFC).
3. Condensing a series of actions. (Example: A man in suburban Connecticut lies in bed, reluctant to get up. He's terribly anxious about the meeting he has today at the office. He has dire fantasies. Finally, he gets up, gets dressed, has breakfast with his wife and kids, reads the newspaper, and drives off to work. On the way, he fantasizes turning onto the expressway, leaving home and job behind, and driving to Florida. Here, his actions between his fantasies in bed and his leaving for work are ripe for becoming condensed into a bridge scene.)

But always remember that your Crucial Scenes—the ones that significantly advance the conflict—*do* need rich dramatic development. Watch out for skimping on them. Ask yourself if you're telling and summarizing rather than dramatizing them. And if you are dramatizing, are you doing it richly enough?

CHAPTER SEVEN

REARRANGING
THE PLOT

R emember those puzzles in the magazines we read as kids in which a series of pictures depicting a story were jumbled up? You know, the first of four out-of-order frames showed a family on a beach, the second showed them in their house packing for a trip, the third showed them driving in the car, and the fourth showed them loading it. And we were supposed to put them back in order. (Actually, in a more advanced version, didn't questions like this show up later on SAT tests?) Well, a similar process of unscrambling goes on in revising fiction. Sometimes the elements/events/scenes of early drafts are jumbled up, in the wrong order. We may know it as we're writing the first draft . . . and then again, we might not know until we start revising. It's something to watch out for. If, while you're writing the first draft, you realize a scene is missing that should have come earlier, or that something earlier is needed in the scene you're writing, just write the scene or addition to scene *right then,* while you're thinking of it. Flag it some way, of course, so that when you're revising, you can see that it's supposed to go before. As I mentioned earlier, I usually do this by typing "Put before," with maybe a note as to just *where* before it belongs—if I know yet. Then I write the out-of-order scene. When I've finished it, I type "Back to," alerting me when I'm revising that I'm back to the story as I left it. And back I merrily go. These out-of-order scenes present no problem, of course, when you're revising. You've flagged them, and you probably know fairly well by now where they belong. In your next draft, in they go in the right spot and everything's hunky-dory.

It's interesting—I never write scenes that I know will come later. Some early scenes wind up later, of course, upon revision. But I don't knowingly write a future scene earlier. I suppose it's possible, and some writers may do it—they just can't wait, I guess. But I prefer to write as sequentially as possible. Just as we experience life more or less sequentially, so too it's easier to experience imaginative life that way. No need to get to the future ahead of time. And besides, maybe in the course of getting there, that future will have necessarily changed. Why write it too soon then, when you might have to change it anyway?

In revising, you always have to assume that some of the events of the story (by events I mean either whole scenes or sections of a scene) will be out of order. And often you won't be aware of it until you start revising. Story events can be out of order in different ways.

CHRONOLOGICALLY OUT OF ORDER

You realize to your horror that Audrey's husband has said on page four that he has no intention of going to the Baumgartens' party, but on page ten you have a scene in which Mrs. Baumgarten calls Audrey to invite her to the party. These mix-ups are the easiest to spot and deal with. Just put them in the right order. This is no problem if your story proceeds more or less in straight time. If it doesn't, that is, if it has a lot of flashbacks, or loops back and forth in time, then you may have to juggle and puzzle and think a little more.

Time-out for Another Disquisition About Flashbacks.

As I've said in an earlier chapter, I'm not against them, but I think they should always be questioned, especially lengthy ones. Besides being "time-outs" (like this one), which leave the "present" story— presumably the important one—hanging, another big drawback is that writers tend to overrely upon them to fill in "backstory," i.e., what's happened before the present story begins. Often this can be done more effectively in the main story, without flashbacks. Rather than a flashback in which we see what a jerk Charlie's brother was when they were kids, which is the source of tension between them today, you could have Charlie—in the main story, no flashback—tell his wife about his brother's holding his face under the mud until he choked. Or he could remind his brother about it. Through dialogue, we'd see that the brother, at least to Charlie, was a jerk.

One easy way to fix chronology flashback problems is of course to get rid of the flashbacks. Often the information they present isn't that important anyway. But if it is, consider eliminating flashbacks by (a) thinking of ways to incorporate the information into the dramatic "present" of the story, as in the example above; and/or (b) shortening them—for example, changing them from full-fledged scenes to a sentence or two. It's amazing how many can be radically condensed.

End of time-out. Back to the main story.

As I've said, it's usually pretty easy to spot scenes that are chronologically out of order and fix them, so I won't spend much time with this. Sometimes, however, things can get a bit subtle. Here's an example from my short story "Camel," in which the narrator is describing the rides at an amusement park:

> And there were rides: the Bug, its cars whipping over its rail with a scratching sound, like sandpaper blocks . . . and the Merry-Go-Round with its mirrors that bounced sunlight against skin so that it seemed we were riding our horses through a haze of trembling silver motes . . . and the Whip, which whooshed and whizzed so that standing near it I could feel its metallic rush of air. *At the end of the rides parents and children and teenagers clutching one another would get off, and others watching them would cheer, as if they'd come back from a long and dangerous voyage, and were now different, transformed . . .* And the Hell-Hole, a small dark tunnel in which you rode in a small car, which looked so innocent on the outside, but within which whole worlds of danger and wonder were waiting. Looking at its black maw and clutching my mother's hand, I felt I glimpsed something of the power and temptation of Darkness.

Sometimes out-of-order events can occur within a single paragraph. The section in italics, describing the reactions of people getting off the rides, seems out of place chronologically, since right after that the narrator details yet another ride. It seemed more logical—and stronger dramatically—that his observation about the people getting off the rides would come at the end of the description of those rides. I shifted that sentence to the end of the paragraph, and it was much better.

PSYCHOLOGICALLY OUT OF ORDER

Rearrangement isn't done only to get the chronology straight. Some-times events may be psychologically out of order. These are harder to spot. Here, you realize upon revision that a character would do or think or feel or say *x* before *y*, whereas right now *y* comes before *x*. For example, Barbara, suspicious of her husband's infidelity, wouldn't start making inquiries of her friends before she stewed about it a while, telling herself she was imagining things. But right now you have her calling her friends before she stews. Or Aunt Clara wouldn't berate her niece about her child-rearing practices quite so vocifer-ously before she sees little Jason playing with the dead bird. Always be asking yourself, Would so-and-so do or think or feel this *now?* Or earlier? Or later? Sometimes in our eagerness to tell the story we stumble all over the development of our characters' conflicts.

An example: In my story "Feral Cats," a man visits his terminally ill mother at the family summer house to which she's run off. When Frank gets out of his car, he's accosted by a vicious wild dog, which his mother shoos away. They then go into the house, where they talk about the dog, and Frank notices his mother's frailty. In the first draft, the scene read like this (sections later rearranged in italics):

> "Hush up! Get away, damn you!" My mother appeared on the porch of the summer house. She was waving a baseball bat. It looked much too heavy for her.
>
> "Stay back, Mom," I yelled, but she came slowly down the steps, hunched a bit as if favoring one side. "Mom—" I cried. The dog turned and looked at them, then amazingly trotted off, around the side of the house, into the woods.
>
> *I embraced my mother, kissed her lightly on the cheek. She wore a red kerchief around her hair, or what was left of it, and blue jeans. I squeezed her arm—it felt like a little girl's. Behind us, there was a deep growl of thunder. We walked back to the house.*
>
> "That's my old baseball bat," I said.
>
> "Is it? I just found it . . ." Her voice trailed away.
>
> "Where'd the dog come from?" I asked as we walked back up the porch.
>
> "I don't know," she sighed. "He was just hanging around when I came up here last week. Probably left here by one of

the summer people. It's just amazing what they throw away."

"God, he's an ugly one," I said.

"Isn't he, though?"

It was much cooler in the house. I smelled the familiar smell of pine and mildew and something else. Childhood. Every summer I'd ever had. Memory.

My mother tried to raise the window to put the bat back in and seemed to be having difficulty. I went to help.

"No!" she snapped peevishly. "I can do it."

I pushed it up anyway, put the bat inside to prop it up. She was panting a bit. "I could've done it," she said. She looked out the window. "I wish that damn dog would go away."

"You seem to scare him," I said. "More than I did, that's for sure."

She shook her head. "I'm not sure about that. I don't think I scare him at all. He hangs around here because of the cats, you know."

"The cats?"

She nodded. "We've got a whole colony of feral cats living under the back porch. Ones that've been abandoned here over the years."

"That's incredible they're still here." I remembered when we spotted the first ones—I must have been twelve. Over twenty years ago.

"It's funny," she said. "There never seem to be more than ten or so. They must die off or get killed. The winter must do them in something fierce. But that damn dog has been getting to them." She sighed, and rubbed her hands, as if they ached. She looked at me. "You look good."

"So do you," I lied. *She looked much frailer than when I saw her last, after the operation, her step more hesitant, considered, as if she was thinking more about where to go and how to get there. She seemed to be conserving energy in little ways, her movements smaller. When she walked she was slightly hunched, leaning to one side, as if some support had given way. . . .*

Upon revision, it seemed more logical that Frank would notice his mother's frailty (the last section in italics), when he *first* embraced her, before they go into the house. After all, he's supposedly shocked by how much she's changed, right? It seems absurd that he'd have such a delayed reaction. I mean, is he dense or what? Similarly, it seems more realistic that he'd comment about his mother's scaring away the dog (the first section in italics), and she'd tell him about the cats, when they're outside, when it's fresh on both their minds. So I shifted these sections. The scene now read like this (again, shifted sections in italics):

"Hush up! Get away, damn you!" My mother appeared on the porch of the summer house. She was waving a baseball bat. It looked much too heavy for her.

"Stay back, Mom," I yelled, but she came slowly down the steps, hunched a bit as if favoring one side. "Mom—" I cried. The dog turned and looked at them, then amazingly trotted off, around the side of the house, into the woods.

I embraced my mother, kissed her lightly on the cheek. She wore a red kerchief around her hair, or what was left of it, and blue jeans. I squeezed her arm—it felt like a little girl's. *She looked much frailer than when I saw her last, after the operation, her step more hesitant, considered, as if she was thinking more about where to go and how to get there. She seemed to be conserving energy in little ways, her movements smaller. When she walked she was slightly hunched, leaning to one side, as if some support had given way. . . .*
Behind us, there was a deep growl of thunder. We walked back to the house.

"That's my old baseball bat," I said.

"Is it? I just found it . . ." Her voice trailed away.

"Where'd the dog come from?" I asked as we walked back up the porch.

"I don't know," she sighed. "He was just hanging around when I came up here last week. Probably left here by one of the summer people. It's just amazing what they throw away."

"God, he's an ugly one," I said.

"Isn't he, though?"

"You seem to scare him," I said. "More than I did, that's for sure."

She shook her head. "I'm not sure about that. I don't think I scare him at all. He hangs around here because of the cats, you know."

"The cats?"

She nodded. "We've got a whole colony of feral cats living under the back porch. Ones that've been abandoned here over the years."

"That's incredible they're still here." I remembered when we spotted the first ones—I must have been twelve. Over twenty years ago.

"It's funny," she said. "There never seem to be more than ten or so. They must die off or get killed. The winter must do them in something fierce. But that damn dog has been getting to them."

It was much cooler in the house. I smelled the familiar smell of pine and mildew and something else. Childhood. Every summer I'd ever had. Memory.

My mother tried to raise the window to put the bat back in and seemed to be having difficulty. I went to help.

"No!" she snapped peevishly. "I can do it."

I pushed it up anyway, put the bat inside to prop it up. She was panting a bit. "I could've done it," she said. She looked out the window. "I wish that damn dog would go away."

She sighed, and rubbed her hands, as if they ached. She looked at me. "You look good."

"So do you," I lied.

A whole lot better.

In "Glory," you remember, a mother worries about her son's being tormented by a school bully. Yet in the first draft, it wasn't until page *twenty* that I wrote the following scene, in which, days after first learning about the bully, she imagines how he looks:

> I catch myself at odd moments during the day thinking about Duane Miller, trying to form a face, construct a body. I imagine him as a kid with a harsh, raspy voice, like that freaky kid in the TV commercials a few years ago. He's not lean and strong— no, he's stocky, almost a little bit fat, his face pudgy and soft, with eyes that are sunk far back in his head, like raisins in cookie dough. There is no color to those eyes, and they are unpitying. He's big, of course, much bigger than most kids his age, and he carries his bigness like a club, swaggering almost . . .
>
> I hate him.
>
> Duane Miller grins.

It's hard to believe, especially since she's been so obsessed by his bullying her son in the nineteen previous pages, that the mother wouldn't have visualized Duane Miller sooner. This scene comes too late, psychologically, and needs to be put much sooner, which I did in the next draft.

One more example: In my story "In the Night" a man is wakened by a phone call from his emotionally disturbed girlfriend, who is at a pay phone at a gas station on a lonely country road, too scared to drive further. They talk, and he tries to calm her and reason with her. After many pages of dialogue—and on page fifteen of a twenty-three-page first draft—he says the following:

> "Look—" I have an inspiration—"do you want me to call the state police? I can have them look for—"
> "No!" her cry is sharp, pained. "No. I don't want that!"
> "Why, Allie? They'd—"
> "No! I'd be so ashamed . . ."

Upon revision, it seemed incredible that he wouldn't have thought this sooner—indeed, isn't it one of the first things anyone would think of if he received a phone call from a girlfriend lost in the middle of the night on a country road? Call the cops! Get help! But he only thinks of it later, and not because he's thick. It's because I was. Upon revision, I put this section much sooner—it became one of the first things he said to Allie to try to help her.

Interesting things can happen to characters psychologically when you rearrange story elements. They can become totally different, sometimes with just the shifting of a few sentences. Look at this paragraph from a story by the young writer, Tony D'Souza. Rem, a young man on the Grand Tour, is sitting at an outdoor café watching the waitresses and patrons:

> They were all men outside, sitting alone at tables. The man at the table next to Rem drank martinis with two speared olives in them. Across from the man, a place was set. Rem expected a woman to arrive and sit there. When the waiting girl came to the man, he leaned across the table, grabbed her wrist with one hand, pointed to the clouds with the other and asked her, "How about this weather?" Then he pointed his finger at her and said, "You will come with me?" A gust blew a leaf into the man's curly gray hair. The leaf, browned, looked like a sugar almond, like a praline, Rem thought. On the back of this man's

head, it looked like a label. The man did not realize it was stuck there. In one more week the patio would close because of the cold and the mess made by fallen dead leaves. After the leaf stuck in the man's hair, Rem fingered his own to check. He did not want to be caught unaware, to be embarrassed like that. When the man again asked his question of his waiting girl, Rem laughed quietly, thinking the old man ridiculous and sad. The other men turned to see the drunk make a fool of himself.

A little Hemingwayesque café incident. Rem comes across here as a bit smug, intolerant and condescending. But look what happens if we juggle a few sentences (in italics) around:

They were all men outside, sitting alone at tables. The man at the table next to Rem drank martinis with two speared olives in them. Across from the man, a place was set. Rem expected a woman to arrive and sit there. When the waiting girl came to the man, he leaned across the table, grabbed her wrist with one hand, pointed to the clouds with the other and asked her, "How about this weather?" Then he pointed his finger at her and said, "You will come with me?" *When the man again asked his question of his waiting girl, Rem laughed quietly, thinking the old man ridiculous and sad. The other men turned to see the drunk make a fool of himself.* A gust blew a leaf into the man's curly gray hair. The leaf, browned, looked like a sugar almond, like a praline, Rem thought. On the back of this man's head, it looked like a label. The man did not realize it was stuck there. After the leaf stuck in the man's hair, Rem fingered his own to check. He did not want to be caught unaware, to be embarrassed like that. *In one more week the patio would close because of the cold and the mess made by fallen dead leaves.*

By simply shifting the order of sentences, by putting his laughing at the old man *before* he fingers his own hair, Rem now comes off more sympathetically, someone whose initial scorn of the old man is replaced by a nascent identification with him, a dawning realization that mortality will come to him also. Also, in the second version, ending with the line "In one more week the patio would close because of the cold and the mess made by fallen dead leaves" gives it much more atmospheric weight. It becomes less a physical description than a foreboding of mortality, Rem's as well as the old man's, and so the whole tone of the scene shifts.

Re-visions. Small rearrangements, but large shifts in character and atmosphere. Which version is right? It depends which Rem you want, what you want his character to be, which ultimately depends upon what your story is really about. It's a lot of fun to do this kind of shifting around to see what changes occur psychologically and atmospherically. Try shifting not only whole scenes, but portions of scenes, even sentences within one paragraph. They might result in shifts in character that never occurred to you, which take the story into exciting new areas.

DRAMATICALLY OUT OF ORDER

Another reason for rearranging story events is to make the dramatic pacing more effective or more powerful. When we're writing first drafts, we often have a tendency to proceed in too predictable, too lockstep a fashion. First this happens, then this, then this, according to the plan we've worked out in our Revision Before Writing. But sometimes events proceed with a clockwork precision that upon revision *after* writing seems a little too well ordered, structured, pat. Life is messier than all that, more random, and our stories should reflect that. (I don't mean that stories should be messy and chaotic. No, no. Just that they should artfully *depict* life's chaos and randomness. Big difference.) Let's look at an example of what I mean.

In "Fireflies," a story we've already looked at in the previous chapter, the two sisters, Helen the recluse and Alice the sophisticate, are having an argument about their respective lifestyles:

> I sit and wait for her to say something else. I've learned to wait with her. She wants me to ask her about herself, but I won't. I'll wait.
>
> "Why do you stay here?" she asks.
>
> "It doesn't cost me anything. It's our house. I like it."
>
> "I couldn't stand it," she says. "It gives me the creeps just being here." She tosses her cigarette on the grass.
>
> "I wish you wouldn't do that," I say.
>
> "What? The cigarette? Don't worry—it's biodegradable."
>
> "I don't like the lawn littered."

"Well, sorry." After a pause: "Do you want me to go get it? Is that what you want?"

"That's OK," I say.

"Jesus." She shakes her head. She wraps her arms around her shoulders. "I always get the heebie-jeebies back here, I don't know why."

"Why?" I ask.

"I just told you—I don't know why."

I count in my head. "Our family's lived here seventy-nine years. Grandpa built it when Poppa was five or six. So he's told me."

"And you've been here all that time—all your life," my sister says. She shakes her head.

"I was in college for two years," I remind her. "And then I was in Des Moines for a year."

"Good God," she says. "I forgot about that."

"It was pretty forgettable."

"What happened?"

"Nothing," I say. "It just didn't suit me."

"And then you came back here. Good God."

"It's home," I say.

"It's nowhere!" She makes a sweep with her arm to include the lawn, the copse of woods that leads down to the spring that divides our property on the east from the next farm. "Jesus, what do you do all day? How do you meet anybody?"

"Every time you come," I say, "you tell me the same thing. It gets old."

As it goes, okay . . . but there's something a little too staged about this argument. Its rising conflict rises a little too neatly. Its construction is too contrived; we sense a Writer At Work. In life, things are messier, more guarded, more circuitous. People say something that's hurtful or provocative, then they regret it, and back off. Or they get nervous and try to "make nice." Upon revision, I felt that the lockstep progression of this argument should be broken up a bit. So I took another scene—of the two women trying to turn cartwheels on the lawn as they'd done when they were kids—and inserted it here, right in the middle of the argument. In the next draft, the scene went like this (inserted scene in italics).

I sit and wait for her to say something else. I've learned to wait with her. She wants me to ask her about herself, but I won't. I'll wait.

"Why do you stay here?" she asks.

"It doesn't cost me anything. It's our house. I like it."

"I couldn't stand it," she says. "It gives me the creeps just being here." She tosses her cigarette on the grass.

"I wish you wouldn't do that," I say.

"What? The cigarette? Don't worry—it's biodegradable."

"I don't like the lawn littered."

"Well, sorry." After a pause: "Do you want me to go get it? Is that what you want?"

"That's OK," I say.

"Jesus." She shakes her head. She wraps her arms around her shoulders. *"Let's turn cartwheels," she tells me.*

I look at her to see if she's kidding. She's grinning. For a moment she looks like the sister I remember, the young one dancing on the lawn, the one who rode on the school bus with me but insisted on sitting in separate seats.

"I can't," I say, but she's already off the porch down on the wet grass. She stands almost exactly where I'd seen her ghost before. "C'mon, come on," she calls.

I shake my head, but I come down. I recently mowed the grass, and it feels squeaky. My sister faces me, her hips thrust out slightly, her arms swinging loosely, warming up.

"I can't do this," I say. "Something's going to tear. I'll break a leg."

"Oh don't be silly," she says.

"I forget how to do them . . ."

She shakes her head mischievously. "You never forget. Here, I'll go first."

She raises her arms, as if invoking an ancient god, and seems to meditate for a moment, like divers and gymnasts do on TV. Then she bends over and throws her arms to the ground and does it, she turns a cartwheel. "See?" she says. "Not hard at all."

After trying to do cartwheels, they go back. And the argument from the first draft picks up again:

Reluctantly, she follows me up the lawn. We sit back down on the porch. Thunder rumbles over the fields behind the barn.

We're silent for awhile, then she says, "I always get the heebie-jeebies back here. I don't know why."

"Why?" I ask.

"I just told you—I don't know why . . ."

And so on. The interpolated scene adds a bit of levity and also makes for a more realistically paced, less lockstep argument. Psychologically, it's truer. And it's also more dramatically effective since it now ironically underscores just how tense things are between the sisters, measured by how much they want to ignore it, and how impossible it is for them to do so.

Another example of unrealistic, "stagey" plot development comes from "Glory." Here, the mother decides that her son should have boxing lessons to protect himself from the school bully. But this isn't so easy to arrange. In an early draft, she made a series of frustrating phone calls to (1) her boyfriend; (2) the YMCA; and (3) a gym to ask about lessons. (In the first draft, there were *four* phone calls, but that was obvious overkill, and out went one right away.) Still, three phone calls in a row, bam, bam, bam? Upon reflection, this seemed a little too mechanical. Call up about boxing, get rejected, call up about boxing, get rejected. . . . The dramatic pacing slowed down with one similar scene after another. Yet each call seemed important. So on the next draft I intercut the phone calls she makes with one she *receives* from her former husband, in which they talk about things other than boxing lessons. Not only did it break up the clickety-clack rhythm of her making boxing lesson phone calls, it also allowed us to see other frustrations in her life.

Sometimes we rearrange the events of a scene for better dramatic structure. In "Turk," the eleven-year-old narrator, his twelve-year-old friend Jonquil, his mother, and her boyfriend Turk are on the beach. As originally written, the scene went like this:

"My God," Jonquil hisses. "Look up there!"

My mother has taken off her top now, and lies bare-breasted on the beach towel. She's never done that before, and I look away, embarrassed. "Jesus," Jonquil says.

"If it bothers you, Jonquil," I say, "you don't gotta look." But I can't look either, and I stare out to a sea so flat and bright that it's almost black. But I force myself to look back, maybe she'll have put her top on, I think, and now Turk's sitting beside her, rubbing sun tan oil on her stomach in little circles, like he was polishing something very soft and fine.

"Someone could *see*," Jonquil says, and I say to her, "Nobody but you, Jonquil." Just the same I look up and down the beach, but nobody's there. I wish there was, so I could say, "Somebody's coming."

"Hey, Jonquil," Turk calls out, "why don't you take off your top too? Let's see those little boobies of yours."

"Shut up, Turk!" she yells. "Why don't you just take off yours!" He laughs and stands up and rolls down his swimsuit an inch or so. Mom sits up now, hands crossed in front of her legs, and shades her eyes. She waves to us. Turk cackles.

"I'm going for a walk," Jonquil whispers to me. I start to follow, but she waves me off. "You don't have to follow me everywhere!" she says. She walks briskly down the beach, her long arms swinging like some wild bird. Every now and then she kicks some wet sand, hard, then sweeps into the water and back again in wide half-loops. I follow, and catch up with her, and we walk.

"Look," I say pointing to something on the sand the surf just rolled in. "A baby shark's mouth."

Jonquil bends over and studies it, pokes it with her toe. "That's not a shark's mouth," she says. "That's just an old grapefruit that's been in the sea."

I gaze at the gaping hole in the circular object and decide she's right. How could I have been so stupid?

Upon revision, it seemed to me that the scene's dramatic high point comes when Jonquil sees Daryl's mother with her top off, followed by Turk's embarrassing her. It's the real climax of the scene. It's here that the simmering sexuality rises to a pitch. But as written, this is dissipated by their walking off, and further deflated by the comic discovery of the "baby shark's mouth." So in the next draft I rearranged the events (in italics):

She walks briskly down the beach, her long arms swinging like some wild bird. Every now and then she kicks some wet sand, hard, then sweeps into the water and back again in wide half-loops.

"Look," I say pointing to something on the sand the surf just rolled in. "A baby shark's mouth."

Jonquil bends over and studies it, pokes it with her toe. "That's not a shark's mouth," she says. "That's just an old grapefruit that's been in the sea."

I gaze at the gaping hole in the circular object and decide she's right. How could I have been so stupid?

"My God," Jonquil hisses. "Look up there!"

My mother has taken off her top now, and lies bare-breasted on the beach towel. She's never done that before, and I look away, embarrassed. "Jesus," Jonquil says.

"If it bothers you, Jonquil," I say, "you don't gotta look." But I can't look either, and I stare out to a sea so flat and bright that it's almost black. But I force myself to look back, maybe she'll have put her top on, I think, and now Turk's sitting beside her, rubbing sun tan oil on her stomach in little circles, like he was polishing something very soft and fine.

"Someone could *see*," Jonquil says, and I say to her, "Nobody but you, Jonquil." Just the same I look up and down the beach, but nobody's there. I wish there was, so I could say, "Somebody's coming."

"Hey, Jonquil," Turk calls out, "why don't you take off your top too? Let's see those little boobies of yours."

"Shut up, Turk!" she yells. "Why don't you just take off yours!" He laughs and stands up and rolls down his swimsuit an inch or so. Mom sits up now, hands crossed in front of her legs, and shades her eyes. She waves to us. Turk cackles.

"I'm going for a walk," Jonquil whispers to me. I start to follow, but she waves me off. "You don't have to follow me everywhere!" she says.

The scene now ends strongly instead of just drifting away. A simple shifting around—and voilà! More punch to the page.

Another example. In "Tombs" a married couple, Frank and Jena, are in Greece, where they come across an archaeological site of ancient Minoan tombs. They are alone except for a man who offers his services as a guide, even though he doesn't speak English. As the tour progresses, the tensions between Frank and his wife become more apparent. The "guide" starts to flirt with Jena, and Frank becomes increasingly jealous. In one scene they are sharing some *raki*, a local moonshine, and she decides to take a picture:

"Come on," Jena said. "We've got to get a picture." She picked up the camera and stood up. "Will you—" she pointed to the guide—"take a picture of—" she pointed to herself and Frank—"us?"

The guide nodded. Jena set the f-stop. "Here." She mimed focusing the camera, pressing the shutter. "Press this." The guide held the camera gingerly, as if it might break. "Come on," she said to Frank. "There. With those tombs in the background."

Frank and Jena walked some twenty yards away, turned and faced the camera. Frank put his arm around Jena's shoulder and she moved closer, but kept her arms by her side. The guide mumbled something, held the camera up. Frank tried to smile, but the muscles of his mouth felt frozen. The shutter clicked. Jena pulled away, and they walked back to the table. The guide was looking at the camera, as if expecting it to do something. He seemed reluctant to hand it back.

"Here," Jena said. "Let me get a picture of you." She pointed to the guide and raised the camera. He shook his head and made a small gesture of protest. "No, no," Jena said, touching his arm. She pointed to the spot where Frank and she had stood. "Go on." The guide walked over to it, put his hands on his hips and stared at them in a pose of exaggerated, almost pompous, solemnity. She snapped the picture. The guide started to walk back, but then Jena said, "Wait. I want a picture with him. Stay there." She walked over to the guide, now standing with his hands on his hips, almost swaggering. "Take a picture of us together," she said to Frank.

Frank looked through the viewfinder. "A little closer together," he said. He motioned with his hand. Jena moved a little closer to the guide, who stood stiffly. "Raise your hat, Jena." She tipped up her sun hat. "Closer," Frank said. "Get closer." Through the viewfinder he could see her eyes widen for a moment. She opened her mouth as if to say something, but didn't. She pursed her lips and moved closer. She looped her arm through the guide's and held it. He looked startled, and glanced at Frank.

"Smile," Frank said. "Just smile. Both of you." He snapped

the picture. "I've got to do it again," he said. "Neither of you were smiling." Again he raised the camera to his eyes and looked through it.

"Hurry up, Frank," Jena snapped.

"Smile," he said. "I want this to be good." He pulled his own lips upward in a rictus of a smile. "Don't you want this to be good?"

Tensely, Jena and the guide smiled. He snapped the picture. "OK," he said. "Got it."

Jena stalked back to the table. She put the camera back in her purse and sat down, not looking at him. "That was a good picture," Frank said. "You'll like that one, Jena."

"Shut up."

The cicadas were loud, the high-pitched whining like many small voices screaming at once. Jena put her hands over her ears. "Very loud," she said to the guide. He nodded, laughed. He rose and looked up into the tree which shaded them, studying it intently. What could he be looking at? Frank wondered, and then the man reached up, snatched at the bottom of a leaf. He uncupped his hand slightly and showed them. Inside his cupped hands was a thick black insect, like a stubby grasshopper. Frank felt foolish: He had never realized somehow that cicadas were so close. You could just reach out and touch them, he thought.

The guide held the cicada up and pressed his cupped hands to his ear, like a conch shell. He listened, smiled. He held it to Jena's ear.

"You can hear him," she said with delight. "Frank—you can hear him. It's amazing—one single cicada!"

The guide held his fist to Frank's ear. His skin was coarse, hardened and cracked. His hands smelled of sweat, earth, tobacco. Frank listened, but heard nothing. He shook his head. "It's stopped singing," he said. The guide listened again, and shrugged.

"Don't kill it," Jena said suddenly. They both looked at her. "Don't kill it," she repeated. Whether he understood or not, the guide opened his fist. The cicada fell onto the ground. It stood unsteadily for a moment, then flew away, back into the trees.

"I thought he was going to kill it," Jena said.

When I was revising, it seemed better that the cicadas should come *before* the picture-taking. Why? For one thing, it seems more logical they'd simply notice the cicadas sooner. And in the scene as written Jena seems to have strangely stopped being irritated at Frank. In this sense, the sections are out of order chronologically. But there were also more subtle reasons of dramatic pacing. First, it seemed like the picture-taking carried more dramatic "weight" than the cicada-plucking. It shows Frank's jealousy, which has been building, and Jena's disgust with him, which has also been building. It's the more powerful part of the scene. Better to end with it. Second, the cicada-plucking really foreshadows Frank's increasing isolation from the guide and Jena (he can't "hear" what they can), which comes to a climax in the picture-taking scene. So, better to shift things around and put cicada-plucking first, then the picture-taking. Now events build with more logic and more dramatic force.

COMPLEX DRAMATIC SHIFTS

So far we've been looking at relatively simple rearrangements of scenes or events within a scene. One shift, a scene or sentence or paragraph, and that's been it. But sometimes these rearrangements can become quite complicated: You may have to juggle around many elements to make a more coherent or dramatically effective story. In "Trips," a family is in a car on vacation and having a very tense time. In the first draft, the scene read as follows:

> We're quarreling, about what, I don't know, I can no longer remember. It's happened again, I think, what we were determined wouldn't happen. We'd started this trip with such high hopes. We need to get away, we decided, this trip will do us good.
>
> In the back seat the boys are squabbling about something, about who colored in the other's book.
>
> Can't you get them settled? I ask, and you glare at me. Suddenly I'm leaning over the back of the seat, slapping at one of my sons, striking his leg, his knee, the bone hurting my hand. He yells, more surprised than hurt.
>
> Don't hit them, you tell me.
>
> I don't want to hear any more arguing, I tell my sons. Do you understand?

They say nothing.

Or else I'm going to stop this car and give it to both of you.

You're so overbearing, you say. Everything has to be physical.

Here, I tell the oldest boy, why don't you count license plates?

That's stupid, he says.

Hey, Dad? says my other son. Can you turn on the radio?

I don't want to turn on the radio, I say. Let's have a little peace and quiet, OK?

But you reach over and turn on the radio. A heavy metal band pounds out leaden chords.

Hey, Twisted Sister, my son says. The other boy begins bouncing in his seat.

We're not listening to that, I say.

You're so rigid, you say.

No, I'm not. I just don't want to hear that crap. I turn the dial.

I'm tired already, and the trip has just started.

You rummage in the ice chest. Here, you tell the boys, have a candy bar.

They shouldn't be eating candy now, I tell her. We're going to stop for lunch soon.

I thought we were eating along the way.

She's right, I think. That's what we'd planned.

I'll have a sandwich, I say.

You hand me a tuna fish sandwich. The bread tastes stale. A thin splotch of blue-green mold mottles the crust.

This goddam bread has mold on it, I say. Just look at it. I hand it to you.

So? you say.

What do you mean, so? It's mold.

So don't eat it. Just take it off.

The bread's rotting. That's what you're feeding me and the kids?

Stop it, you say.

I throw the sandwich out the window. Droppings of tuna fish splatter the back windows.

You got tuna fish on the windows, Dad, my older boy says.

I turn the radio on again, flip the dial. And there's a ball game on. I stop. From somewhere, the announcer tells me, someone is 3-and-2, and there's a man on base.

Here, I say, let's listen to this.

I don't want to hear any ball game, the younger boy says, and the older one just sighs dramatically.

This is America, I say. This is the great American game.

I feel badly now that we've never gone to any ball games, that I've never played catch with them. They were never interested, but still—it's something I should've done.

Can't we listen to something else, Dad, my older boy gently asks. And suddenly it seems very important that we do listen to this ball game, there is something here that will disappear if not attended to, and I say, No, we listen to this.

They sigh.

You know, you say, I'm tired of you.

I say nothing.

If you're going to be this way the whole trip, why don't we just forget it, you say.

I brake, and pull the car off the side of the road, onto the emergency strip.

What are you doing, you ask.

Why don't you just get out here? I say.

You stare.

I lean across and open the door on your side. You flinch.

Well, go on. Get out.

I push you.

Stop it, you say harshly.

Daddy, my son says.

I push harder. Get out, I say, my voice rising.

You bastard. You strike me on the arm with your fist. I reach for your hand, and we fumble, me trying to push you out, you flailing away at me. Stop it, stop it, my older son cries, and the younger bawls.

Stop it, I say. Your movements become smaller, tireder, and then you stop. You stare straight ahead. A tractor-trailer rolls by with a gush and a whoosh, making our car tremble. I reach over and close the door. The motor throbs.

Be quiet, I say to the boys. It's OK, it's over.

And I think how different trips have become, how they're no longer taken with any sense of expectation or excitement, but rather from a sense of duty, with little anticipation and even fewer hopes. Everything has already been seen, it seems, there are no more destinations that beckon. There are no more billboards advertising strange wonders and sights, there are no more small towns with wooden-floored stores and Nehi in bottles and strange exhibits kept in the back of gas stations. There are no more towns even; everything has become an exit that promises nothing beyond its name.

Upon revision, it seemed that much needed rearranging. First, the rumination that the scene ends with ("And I think how different trips have become . . . .") seems to belong much earlier, with the narrator's opening musings about the trip. Second, his almost immediately slapping his sons when they're squabbling seems to come too quickly— it's much too premature a reaction, more appropriate as a climax to a slower-building, smoldering tension. Having it here, followed by the relatively calm discussion that follows, diffuses its impact. So it should come later. Third, his wife's saying she's "tired of him" might more appropriately be her reaction to his slapping the kids, rather than just coming out of the blue in a moment of calm, as it does now. Fourth, the discussion about the ball game seems better coming earlier, as part of the developing tension, rather than coming as late as it does, when it seems more like an afterthought, the scene just drifting away, like smoke. When all these shifts (in italics) were made, the scene read as follows:

We're quarreling, about what, I don't know, I can no longer remember. It's happened again, I think, what we were determined wouldn't happen. We'd started this trip with such high hopes. We need to get away, we decided, this trip will do us good. *And I think how different trips have become, how they're no longer taken with any sense of expectation or excitement, but rather from a sense of duty, with little anticipation and even fewer hopes. Everything has already been seen, it seems, there are no more destinations that beckon. There are no more billboards advertising strange wonders and sights, there are no more small towns with wooden-floored stores and Nehi in bottles and strange exhibits kept in the back of gas stations. There are no more towns even; everything has become an exit that promises nothing beyond its name.*

In the back seat the boys are squabbling about something, about who colored in the other's book.

Can't you get them settled? I ask, and you glare at me.

Here, I tell the oldest boy, why don't you count license plates?

That's stupid, he says.

Hey, Dad? says my other son. Can you turn on the radio?

I don't want to turn on the radio, I say. Let's have a little peace and quiet, OK?

But you reach over and turn on the radio. A heavy metal band pounds out leaden chords.

Hey, Twisted Sister, my son says. The other boy begins bouncing in his seat.

We're not listening to that, I say.

You're so rigid, you say.

No, I'm not. I just don't want to hear that crap. I turn the dial. *And there's a ball game on. I stop. From somewhere, the announcer tells me, someone is 3-and-2, and there's a man on base.*

Here, I say, let's listen to this.

I don't want to hear any ball game, the younger boy says, and the older one just sighs dramatically.

This is America, I say. This is the great American game.

I feel badly now that we've never gone to any ball games, that I've never played catch with them. They were never interested, but still—it's something I should've done.

Can't we listen to something else, Dad, my older boy gently asks. And suddenly it seems very important that we do listen to this ball game, there is something here that will disappear if not attended to, and I say, No, we listen to this.

They sigh.

I'm tired already, and the trip has just started.

You rummage in the ice chest. Here, you tell the boys, have a candy bar.

They shouldn't be eating candy now, I tell her. We're going to stop for lunch soon.

I thought we were eating along the way.

She's right, I think. That's what we'd planned.

I'll have a sandwich, I say.

You hand me a tuna fish sandwich. The bread tastes stale.

A thin splotch of blue-green mold mottles the crust.

This goddam bread has mold on it, I say. Just look at it. I hand it to you.

So? you say.

What do you mean, so? It's mold.

So don't eat it. Just take it off.

The bread's rotting. That's what you're feeding me and the kids?

Stop it, you say.

I throw the sandwich out the window. Droppings of tuna fish splatter the back windows.

You got tuna fish on the windows, Dad, my older boy says.

Suddenly I'm leaning over the back of the seat, slapping at one of my sons, striking his leg, his knee, the bone hurting my hand. He yells, more surprised than hurt.

Don't hit them, you tell me.

I don't want to hear any more arguing, I tell my sons. Do you understand?

They say nothing.

Or else I'm going to stop this car and give it to both of you.

You're so overbearing, you say. Everything has to be physical.

You know, you say, I'm tired of you.

I say nothing.

If you're going to be this way the whole trip, why don't we just forget it, you say.

I brake, and pull the car off the side of the road, onto the emergency strip.

What are you doing, you ask.

Why don't you just get out here? I say.

You stare.

I lean across and open the door on your side. You flinch.

Well, go on. Get out.

I push you.

Stop it, you say harshly.

Daddy, my son says.

I push harder. Get out, I say, my voice rising.

You bastard. You strike me on the arm with your fist. I reach for your hand, and we fumble, me trying to push you out, you flailing away at me. Stop it, stop it, my older son cries, and the younger bawls.

> *Stop it, I say. Your movements become smaller, tireder, and*
> *then you stop. You stare straight ahead. A tractor-trailer rolls by*
> *with a gush and a whoosh, making our car tremble. I reach over*
> *and close the door. The motor throbs.*
> *Be quiet, I say to the boys. It's OK. It's over.*

Better. Not only does the scene now seem more attuned psychologically to how the characters would actually think and act, but it also
develops dramatically in a much stronger way. And now it ends on a
dramatically resonant note, rather than with the weaker philosophic
musing of the first draft.

SCENES OR STORY ELEMENTS OUT OF ORDER IN TERMS OF MEANING

There's another way—and a very important one to understand—in
which scenes, sections of scenes or story elements can be out of order.
And that's in terms of the dramatic development and meaning of the
story. For example, let's look at this passage from an early draft of
"Piano Lessons," part of which I already quoted in chapter six:

> Sister Benedict and I would sit side by side on the piano
> bench. She uncovered the keys solemnly, with great ceremony:
> They also were a dirty cream color, like badly discolored teeth,
> or the cover of my music book. She smelled like wool that has
> stayed in a dresser drawer too long, and around her hung a
> faint aura of strong soap and something else, dry and harsh,
> like the smell of a seashell. She would wind the metronome
> and we would begin. I ran up and down whatever scale I had
> been practicing for her. I hated the metronome. It clicked back
> and forth like a tongue making a shaming sound, as if it knew
> that I could never keep up. Because the truth was this: I had
> no sense of rhythm, couldn't keep the beat at all. The metro-
> nome was always gaining on me, and I couldn't keep up, as if
> it were racing onward, and I struggled just to keep up, but it
> was already ahead, endlessly marking time, marking time.
> "Keep up," Sister Benedict would murmur.

As you know from having read "Piano Lessons," this scene with the
metronome, here presented as something happening from the very
first piano lesson, was later moved to a more dramatically climactic

moment in the story. In the final version, Sister Benedict brings in the metronome much later, to help the boy keep time, and the frustration of trying to keep up with it becomes the trigger for his breakdown. Upon re-vision, I saw that the metronome had more dramatic possibilities than I'd first considered, and it had the most if it were introduced later rather than sooner. As you revise and re-vise, the meaning of your story will become clearer. Be on the lookout then for scenes, sections of scenes or story elements, such as the metronome, that might help make that meaning clearer—and the story dramatically stronger—by being shifted around. Play with these possibilities even: List your scenes, or put them on index cards or slips of paper, and shuffle them around. Imagine your story in that order. Of course, some scenes will resist shuffling because of chronological or dramatic logic. But you'll find that several could come here, could come there. Which way is dramatically stronger? Which way best helps dramatize the story's meaning? Which way helps create a new meaning you'd never before considered?

SUMMING UP

Obviously all of these ways events can be out of order—chronologically, psychologically and dramatically—are closely related. If scenes are out of order chronologically, chances are good the dramatic pacing will be off too. Or the psychology of the characters will be muddled. If scenes are out of order psychologically, chances are they'll be dramatically weak also. And so on. Straighten up the dramatic pacing and you straighten up psychology. Straighten up psychology and you straighten up dramatic pacing. In fiction, unlike real life, everything is truly connected. Casting a critical eye on the arrangement of your scenes—and the arrangement of the events and elements within each scene—can not only be a lot of fun (it's like playing with those flip books for kids in which you can interchange and mix up people's heads and bodies), but can also make your story stronger. So mix 'n match, and see what happens. It can yield very surprising and wonderful results for your story.

CHAPTER EIGHT

REVISING ENDINGS

Everything must come to an end, stories too, and a fiction writer hopes his end with a bang and not a whimper. By "bang" I don't mean anything overwrought or melodramatic. A story needn't have corpses littered over the stage, as in *Hamlet*, although that *was* a hell of an ending—but only after it had been carefully set up through a brilliant unfolding of character and motivation. What I mean by "bang" is emotional punch, and often that's best achieved through endings that are subtle yet emotionally illuminative and powerful. No other area of a story seems to be harder for writers (openings are a close second, for reasons we've already discussed). Chekhov thought that endings, as well as openings, were where authors did "most of their lying." Hemingway labored mightily over the ending to *A Farewell to Arms*, in which the protagonist, Frederic Henry, stoically, perhaps numbly, walks off into the rain after the death in childbirth of his wife and baby. When asked what the problem was, Hemingway replied, "Getting the words right."

We can infer much from Hemingway's revision efforts—and his provocative comment. Endings must be very important. They are worth sweating over. And every word must count. Why is this so? Why do endings arouse such anxiety, such aesthetic sweat? And what exactly does that mean, "getting the words right"?

Let's first consider what a good ending should do.

WHAT A GOOD ENDING SHOULD DO

A good ending must satisfactorily resolve the conflicts dramatized in the story. These conflicts may be resolved tragically, comically or even indeterminately, but they must be resolved. "Tragically" and "comically" are obvious, but how can a story be resolved "indeterminately," you ask? Consider the following story: A young man can't decide whether or not to marry his girlfriend. We see the pressures on him—the girlfriend's insistence, his mother's opposition, his father's indifference and lack of help. He sways one way, then another. In frustration, he has a one-night stand with a woman he meets in a bar, with whom he impetuously, unrealistically, falls in love. He tells her about his dilemma with his girlfriend. They fantasize running off to New York or Paris. But in the morning, he finds he can't do it, nor can he even face the young woman to tell her. While she's still sleeping, he leaves and returns home, where he's once more faced with the same pressure to decide whether or not to marry. And he still doesn't know what to do. End of story.

In one sense, nothing has changed for this guy. He's still trying to decide. The ending is indeterminate. Yet assuming it's been well dramatized, nothing is left hanging either, since we understand the story is about his being trapped in and doomed to indecision and noncommitment. The events of the story and its ending fully dramatize this, and we feel aesthetically and emotionally satisfied.

Maybe a better way then of saying what endings should do is that *they should fully dramatize the consequences of characters' conflicts.* In Katherine Anne Porter's phrase, they must be "right and true." We talk in writing workshops about endings being "earned." This simply means that they must represent the fully imagined and dramatically appropriate consequences to characters' conflicts. If they don't—and all weak endings fail in this, to some degree—we as readers feel cheated.

Endings must be unexpected, yet believable. Flannery O'Connor gave one of the best definitions of what a good ending should do in her collection of essays on fiction writing, *Mystery and Manners.* They must be both "totally right and totally unexpected," she said. (She was actually talking about significant dramatic "gesture," but with just a little imaginative extension it applies to endings as well.) Now think about that for a moment. Between those two propositions, many endings founder. Some endings are unexpected, but not "right," i.e, believable. In our example story above, a little green Martian could land and swoop up the hero and take him to

Mars where he enjoys a life of Martian wine, women and song. Totally unexpected, yes, but outrageously unbelievable. We'd fling that story into the fire, followed by the author, if possible. Or less outrageously, he could see a little girl on the street being pushed in a stroller by her mother, be suddenly overcome with paternal feelings, and dash home to propose to his girlfriend. More believable, but not much so. From everything we've seen of him so far, he just ain't that kind of guy. We don't buy it for a second, not without something more to account for his sudden conversion. Into the flames with that story too.

On the other hand, we might have a story where the ending *is* totally believable—in fact, we believed we saw it coming on page two, deepened our suspicions on page five, were certain on page seven, were dead certain by page eleven, and indeed, had our initial belief confirmed when the ending finally arrived on page twenty-two. It's believable, but not unexpected. It presents no delight. In stories, we don't want to know a mile away how it's going to end. We don't know what's going to happen in life; if we did, it would be predictable, but boring. Who'd want to lead that kind of life? Similarly, who wants to read that kind of story?

Endings must resonate. After all, they're the last thing one reads in a story. They should have a powerful impact upon the reader, so that the story echoes in the imagination after the last sentence is read, the book closed, and the dishes done. A good ending leads us back into the story, to ponder it (note I said "ponder" as in "mull," not "ponder" as in "puzzle over"). Oedipus blinds himself, and we ponder the curiosity that drives men to seek knowledge that they possibly shouldn't have. Gatsby is killed, his dreams come to nothing, and we ponder the futility and illusions of romantic love. In fantasy-writer Ursula K. LeGuin's story "Sur," we ponder male vanity and vainglory when a team of women discover the South Pole before Amundsen but decide never to tell anyone, leaving "no footprints, even."

INEFFECTIVE ENDINGS

Whew! you say. Endings have to do all that? No wonder we labor over them.

There are certain common ways in which endings fail to do what they're supposed to do, fail to be "right and true." I'll spend the rest of this chapter discussing them. You may remember the Akira

Kurosawa film *Rashomon,* in which a woman's rape is told from the point of view of four different characters, the story radically changing each time? Well, I'm going to take a pedagogical *Rashomon* approach to illustrate. I'll present several possible endings to a hypothetical story in order to illustrate ways in which endings can go wrong.

Let's assume this story concerns Sheila, a young woman who is pregnant. During her pregnancy, she's taken a drug that has recently been shown to cause birth defects. Concerned, she's gone to her health clinic for a sonogram and is anxiously awaiting the results. She's conflicted over what to do if the fetus is deformed. Her husband, an overbearing and insensitive man who browbeats her—and worse— has demanded, if the fetus is deformed, that she get an immediate abortion, the same day, if possible. Although he wants a child, as does Sheila, no way does he want a handicapped child. She's a meek woman, fearful of opposing him, and isn't sure herself whether she wants a handicapped child. Yet this is her longed-for baby, flesh of her flesh, and she can't bear the thought of ending its life. The story could end this way:

Ending #1: Message Endings
[She has been told by the doctor the fetus is indeed deformed.]

> She lay on the cold examination table. The nurse came in and asked her if she'd like to get dressed now. Sheila nodded, swung her legs over the table, and on uncertain feet—her legs felt as heavy as her thoughts—she stood and reached for the laces on the hospital gown. It seemed she didn't have the strength to pull them apart. She started crying, heavy leaden sobs that wouldn't stop.
>
> "Oh my," the nurse said. "Here—sit down again." She helped Sheila sit on the table.
>
> "I—I don't know what to do," Sheila cried. Everything poured out—the sonogram results, the deformed fetus, her husband's injunction. The nurse listened attentively, her gray eyes cool and kindly.
>
> "Do you really want to go through with the abortion?" she asked.
>
> "I don't know," Sheila murmured.
>
> "Listen," the nurse said, her voice dropping to a half-whisper.

"Maybe I'm talking out of turn . . . but don't these kind of children have as much right to life as any of us? They have souls just like we do, don't they? To have an abortion, even in these circumstances, well, it's not right. I know it's not fashionable to say so, for a nurse even, and I'd probably get fired if anyone here heard me say all this. But certain people I feel I have to tell what I think, and I have a feeling you're one of them."

"But it'll be so hard—"

"There are good programs these days to help parents through the stress of having a . . . different child. You can get help from many agencies. I can put you in touch with some of them. Marvelous things can be done today with rehabilitative help and prosthetics. A child like yours could lead a happy, productive life."

"Do you really think so?" Sheila asked.

"I know so," the nurse said. She put her hand on Sheila's arm. "You see, I have a child like this myself. She was born blind. It was rough, I admit, but she graduated college and is going to law school in the fall."

Sheila felt hope bloom in her breast. Perhaps there was a way that she and Jack could deal with this after all.

All right, it's a bit exaggerated for effect, but in workshop stories I've seen this type of ending over and over again. It's the *Message Ending*. All of a sudden, we feel that the character's conflict has been abandoned for a Paid Political Announcement. We're no longer in a short story, we're at a sermon. We feel the writer has an agenda that she's pushing, and that the whole story, no matter how convincing until this point, has existed not to serve the characters, but the agenda. The ending is reminiscent of those nineteenth-century temperance novels like *Ten Nights in a Bar-Room*, in which good men were inevitably victimized by drink (until rehabilitated, of course), their families were all-suffering, bartenders were all evil, and temperance crusaders all good. Characters were Just One Thing, cardboard cutouts who existed to make a Point in a preordained melodrama. If fiction is not anything, it is not propaganda. Fiction exists in freedom, in three dimensions, not the mono-dimensionality of characters who are either spokesmen for or foils against a particular point of view. We read fiction for its promise of a free, full and fair examination of human character in conflict. If we want ideology, we'll read political screeds.

As Samuel Goldwyn once said, "If you want to send a message, use Western Union." Don't use a story.

Ending #2: Deus Ex Machina Endings

So—we go back to the drawing board and try again:

> She lay on the cold examination table. The nurse came in and asked her if she'd like to get dressed now. Sheila nodded, swung her legs over the table, and on uncertain feet—her legs felt as heavy as her thoughts—she stood and reached for the laces on the hospital gown. It seemed she didn't have the strength to pull them apart. She started crying, heavy leaden sobs that wouldn't stop.
>
> "Oh my," the nurse said. "Here—sit down again." She helped Sheila sit on the table.
>
> "I—I don't know what to do," Sheila cried. Everything poured out—the sonogram results, the deformed fetus, her husband's injunction. The nurse listened attentively, her gray eyes cool and kindly.
>
> "Do you really want to go through with the abortion?" she asked.
>
> "I don't know," Sheila murmured.
>
> The door of the examination room opened and Dr. Miller came in, holding a manila folder. He was smiling, something he hadn't been doing just a few minutes ago. How can he be smiling? Sheila thought angrily.
>
> "Mrs. Thompson," he said. "I don't know whether to cry or apologize or laugh or what. There's been a mix-up. I want to say these things never happen, but they do, I guess, and we've done it." He pulled a sheaf of sonograms from the manila folder and jammed one up into the light box. "We somehow mislabeled the sonograms. Well, not exactly mislabeled." He tapped one of the sonograms. "There was a woman with your same last name that had a sonogram done on the same day, and they just got mixed around. The abnormal fetus is hers, unfortunately. Yours—" he pointed to the other sonogram on the light box—"is this one. It's just fine."
>
> Sheila felt relief flood her heart like warm honey.

You may think I'm exaggerating again, but I can't tell you how many times in writing workshops I've seen variants of this ending. The problem, of course, is that it's a *Deus Ex Machina Ending*. A deus ex machina, Latin for "God from the machine," was literally that—an actor in ancient Greek drama playing the part of Zeus or some other Olympian deity who at the play's climactic moment—say just before the two armies were about to fight, or someone's head was about to be cut off—descended from the sky in a basket to stop the action, make a speech, reconcile the warring parties, and in general tidily resolve everything. The problem, of course, is that characters' conflicts have not been given the chance to play out realistically to their conclusion. Instead they've been conveniently solved by some outside person, agency or fortune coming from nowhere. A mother and daughter are arguing about her lackadaisical attitude toward school, they get in the car, the argument escalates—and they're hit by a semi and killed. End of argument. Or an Iowa family is struggling to save their farm, it's put on the auction block, and on the morning of the auction, the wife gets a letter informing her that a long-lost relative has died and left her enough money to save the farm. End of problem. Deus ex machina endings are artificial and imposed endings, always unrealistic and always unsatisfying. Think of it: Presumably in the course of a story we've become deeply involved in our characters' conflicts. Real human problems have been posed. We want to see how they will work out on their own. In the above story, Sheila is conflicted over how to deal with the problems an abnormal fetus will pose for her and her husband. We empathize. We want to see what will happen in this very human situation. By having it all be a mix-up, no problem at all, that real dilemma is conveniently and unrealistically dodged and avoided. In effect, the writer is avoiding responsibility for working out the problems of his own story.

There are all kinds of deus ex machina endings, some obvious, some not, and you have to be alert to sniffing them out. Having your character(s) rescued—or ruined—by some outside agency or person. Or by a stroke of luck. Or by an accident or natural catastrophe. Or by some convenient and hitherto unknown piece of information, e.g., Isabel is not Archie's sister after all, so they can marry. Avoid them all.

Ending #3: Trick Endings

We try again.

> She lay on the cold examination table. The nurse came in and asked her if she'd like to get dressed now. Sheila nodded, swung her legs over the table, and on uncertain feet—her legs felt as heavy as her thoughts—she stood and reached for the laces on the hospital gown. It seemed she didn't have the strength to pull them apart. She started crying, heavy leaden sobs that wouldn't stop.
>
> "Oh my," the nurse said. "Here—sit down again." She helped Sheila sit on the table.
>
> "I—I don't know what to do," Sheila cried. Everything poured out—the sonogram results, the deformed fetus, her husband's injunction. The nurse listened attentively, her gray eyes cool and kindly.
>
> "Do you really want to go through with the abortion?" she asked.
>
> "I don't know," Sheila murmured.
>
> The door of the examination room opened and Dr. Miller came in. He smiled thinly. "Well, Sheila," he said. "Are you ready?"
>
> She felt her heart race, almost in a panic. No, she wailed silently, I'm not ready, I'm not . . .
>
> Sheila sat bolt upright in bed, the ghost of a silent scream on her lips. She sat there, breathing hard, until the darkness, the soft mattress beneath her—not the hard examination table at all—and the soft breathing of Jack beside her comforted her: she'd been dreaming. She patted her tummy, and told herself again the baby was fine. The sonograms had proved it just last week. It was just another one of those nightmares. She had to get a grip on her anxiety.

This, friends, is the *Trick Ending*. It's really a kind of deus ex machina ending, one in which the outside intervention that conveniently solves everything is some variant of we-haven't-been-told-the-straight-story-to-begin-with-but-now-it-can-be-revealed. At least in the regular deus ex machina ending, vital information hasn't been withheld and the whole fictive world of the story revealed to be something else; in the trick ending, it has. It's really all been a dream. Or a movie. Or a fantasy someone has been having. Or a lab experiment. Or a television show being analyzed by Martians. Or the narrator has really been dead. Or unborn. Or a dog. Whatever it is, the trick is supposed to astonish us with its cleverness. Usually it makes us want to slap the writer upside the head. Clever like that can get you shot.

Trick endings don't work for the same reason that deus ex machina endings don't work: They dodge truly and realistically resolving the conflicts of the story. What's worse, they also break faith with the reader. He's taken the fictive world's "reality" in good faith, and now it's revealed to have been something else all the time. We expect the writer to deal squarely with us. We don't like to be fooled. The only way a trick ending can work is if the "trick" has been adequately prepared for, so that when it's unveiled, we feel that yes, of course, that was always a possibility, and it makes sense. It may be unexpected, but it's believable, and it satisfactorily and delightfully resolves the story's conflicts. A trick ending like this is hard to pull off. I can think of only a few that work—Jorge Luis Borges' story "The Wizard Postponed" comes to mind. (O. Henry stories—despite popular belief—don't feature trick endings. His endings, albeit unexpected, arise straight from the character and conflict as we've seen them. Surprising, but no tricks.) The Borges story takes place in the Middle Ages, and concerns a dean (a low-level religious functionary) of Santiago who comes to study the art of magic with Don Illán, a famed magician of Toledo. Don Illán is happy to see the dean, but expresses worry that, although seemingly a man of good character, the dean might become ungrateful if he were taught everything Don Illán knows. Power corrupts, etc. The dean swears no. And so they begin the study of magic, which is interrupted, however, by messengers arriving with news that the bishop of Santiago is dead, and that the dean has been elected to replace him. Don Illán is overjoyed for his student and asks for a small favor, which the dean, now bishop, refuses. Don Illán accompanies the dean back to Santiago. Over the years, good fortune continues to come to his former student, culminating in the dean's becoming pope. Along the way, however, he continually and ever more ungratefully snubs Don Illán. And then comes the ending.

Now I hate to spoil the Borges story for you by analyzing why the trick ending works—thus divulging that ending—but pedagogical duty demands I must. So go read the story right now, before you read any further here! You'll find it in the collection titled *A Universal History of Infamy*. I warned you!

Back again? Great story, right? So why does the trick ending work?

Because we've been told up front that the wizard is a magician and that he is concerned about the dean's character. When it is revealed that everything the dean has experienced after that has been a test of that character, not reality at all, we are amazed and delighted. Borges has kept faith with us: Yes, the deception could have happened, because after all the wizard is a mighty magician. And yes, he has truly tested the dean's character, as well he might. We have been "tricked" just as the dean was, even though both of us were given necessary information right from the start to let us know what we were getting into.

Ending #4: Smoky Endings

Back to the drawing board:

> She lay on the cold examination table. The nurse came in and asked her if she'd like to get dressed now. Sheila nodded, swung her legs over the table, and on uncertain feet—her legs felt as heavy as her thoughts—she stood and reached for the laces on the hospital gown. It seemed she didn't have the strength to pull them apart. She started crying, heavy leaden sobs that wouldn't stop.
>
> "Oh my," the nurse said. "Here—sit down again." She helped Sheila sit on the table.
>
> "I—I don't know what to do," Sheila cried. Everything poured out—the sonogram results, the deformed fetus, her husband's injunction. The nurse listened attentively, her gray eyes cool and kindly.
>
> "Do you really want to go through with the abortion?" she asked.
>
> "I don't know," Sheila murmured.
>
> "I'll leave you alone for a few minutes," the nurse said. She opened the door and went out.
>
> I just want to sleep, Sheila thought. She lay down on the table. Images roiled through her mind of buying a changing table at the Thrift Shop and the crib mobile that played "Red Sails in the Sunset."

Jack will be so upset, Sheila thought. He'll blame me somehow.

I'm just so tired, she thought. I could close my eyes right here and go to sleep for a thousand years.

This is an example of the *Smoky Ending*. Like smoke, it just . . . drifts . . . away. It's unsatisfying not because it's implausible but because it's not really an ending at all. Remember—endings have to fully dramatize the consequences of conflicts established in the story. That usually occurs during the climax of the conflict, which is part of the ending. Here, the conflicts have been avoided simply by just . . . ending. No climax. Some beginning writers may think this very arty. After all, they say, aren't we showing the irresolvability of Sheila's conflict? But that's not what we're doing. We're just showing her going to sleep.

But isn't that just like life? you ask. Sometimes we can't decide. Sometimes we just go to sleep. Well, fiction isn't life. It represents life, but one in which consequences of character and conflict can be fully imagined, fully examined, fully developed in a way that reality doesn't allow us. We turn to fiction, in E.M. Forster's words, because there "we can know people perfectly, and, apart from the general pleasure of reading, we can find here a compensation for their dimness in life."

It's almost a rule of thumb: If a reader of your story feels it "just drifted away" or "ended too soon," it's probably because there's been no satisfactory climax to the conflict. The story has simply ended.

Ending #5: Confusing Endings
And so again:

She lay on the cold examination table. The nurse came in and asked her if she'd like to get dressed now. Sheila nodded, swung her legs over the table, and on uncertain feet—her legs felt as heavy as her thoughts—she stood and reached for the laces on the hospital gown. It seemed she didn't have the strength to pull them apart. She started crying, heavy leaden sobs that wouldn't stop.

"Oh my," the nurse said. "Here—sit down again." She helped Sheila sit on the table.

"I—I don't know what to do," Sheila cried. Everything poured out—the sonogram results, the deformed fetus, her husband's injunction. The nurse listened attentively, her gray eyes cool and kindly.

"Do you really want to go through with the abortion?" she asked.

"I don't know," Sheila murmured.

"I'll leave you alone for a few minutes," the nurse said. She opened the door and went out.

I just want to sleep, Sheila thought. She lay down on the table. Images roiled through her mind of buying a changing table at the Thrift Shop and the crib mobile that played "Red Sails in the Sunset."

Jack will be so upset, Sheila thought. He'll blame me somehow.

The door opened again. It wasn't the nurse, but Dr. Moore. "Nurse tells me you're not certain what to do," he said.

Sheila nodded.

The doctor pulled up a chair close to her. He took her hand. "I know it's hard," he said. "I see it all the time." And he bowed his head and started to cry. Sheila was amazed. She felt her heart go out to him. She reached over and stroked his bent-over head. His hair felt exactly like her little brother's did when she'd held him to comb it. He'd fallen and broken his leg once and they had to take him to a hospital, and she'd been worried sick.

Dr. Moore sighed deeply and rose. "I've got something I want to show you," he said. He rose and went over to the medicine cabinet and pulled out an instrument which Sheila had never seen before. "Do you know what this is?" he asked.

Sheila shook her head.

He began banging the instrument against the side of the cabinet, leaving deep dents with each blow. Sheila closed her eyes, and when she opened them again, the nurse had come in. "Doctor," she said, "there's another patient waiting."

Huh? Say what? We don't have the slightest idea what's going on here. Why is the doctor crying? What is the instrument he's showing her and why? What's the relationship of Sheila's memories of her brother to all this? As the King said in *The King and I*, "Is a puzzlement." This is a *Confusing Ending*. More questions are raised than are resolved, and one of the purposes of an ending is to resolve. Confusing endings aren't believable because they introduce elements into the imaginative world which don't "fit." It's like seeing an ostrich being chased by a polar bear in the middle of Halsted Street. If we see this, we're going to want an explanation. If it happens in a story, we had better be dramatically *shown* one. Here, the enigmatic (the doctor's behavior) and the heretofore unshown (her feelings about her brother) are presented, and that's that. Beginning writers often like these kind of endings because they think—again—that they're arty. Deep, significant things are being hinted at. But all that's really happening is that the reader's totally bewildered. A confusing ending usually means the writer is bewildered too, and is trying to pass off this bewilderment as profundity. Uh-uh. Fools nobody.

Sometimes a writer will tell me, "But this is a confused character. I'm just showing her confusion." No, no, no. Think for a moment: Obviously you can't write a boring story to show a boring character. You have to write a *fascinating* story about a boring character. Just so you can't write a confusing story to show a confused character. Your job is to show us a *confused*—not a confusing—character. There's a big difference. A confused character may be confused to herself and others *in the story,* but to us, from our more godlike perspective, she's understandable.

What's the difference, you might ask, between a Confusing Ending and one that legitimately presents a certain ambiguity, a tension between possibilities? I think it's this: In the latter ending, we can put our finger on the tension, the possibilities. We can say, Either this or that. We know what the possibilities are because they've been sufficiently shown to us. In a Confusing Ending, we have no idea what they may be, and have to start searching for them. Could be almost anything, we feel. A confusing ending makes you think you've missed something; a resonant ambiguous ending, however, leaves you pondering, but satisfied.

If several friendly readers tell you that they were confused by your ending and had to "go back and reread" the story to try to understand what happened, you are, believe me, in Big Trouble. In real life, you won't find readers, agents or editors who will take the trouble to go back and reread. A story gets one reading, one chance to stand on its little legs and sing. If it's confusing on the first reading, it won't get a second one. The only true desire to reread comes from the pleasure and emotional power we've felt from the story *on the first read,* which makes us want to experience it again. Not puzzle over. Fiction is not a philosophic treatise, or an economics text, where you often need to go back and review the argument. It's an unfolding, impelling, compelling drama that should carry you to an ending that's both powerful and satisfying.

Ending #6: Unearned Endings

We try again:

> She lay on the cold examination table. The nurse came in and asked her if she'd like to get dressed now. Sheila nodded, swung her legs over the table, and on uncertain feet—her legs felt as heavy as her thoughts—she stood and reached for the laces on the hospital gown. It seemed she didn't have the strength to pull them apart. She started crying, heavy leaden sobs that wouldn't stop.
>
> "Oh my," the nurse said. "Here—sit down again." She helped Sheila sit on the table.
>
> "I—I don't know what to do," Sheila cried. Everything poured out—the sonogram results, the deformed fetus, her husband's injunction. The nurse listened attentively, her gray eyes cool and kindly.
>
> "Do you really want to go through with the abortion?" she asked.
>
> "I don't know," Sheila murmured. "There's no way Jack will be able to handle a deformed child. And he'll blame me, I know he will." She started sobbing harder.
>
> "Listen," the nurse said. "I'm sure it's not as bad as that. I'm sure something will work out—"
>
> "No, it won't," Sheila wailed. "Oh God, it won't. You don't know Jack . . ."
>
> "So you want to go through with the abortion?"
>
> "I—I don't know," she murmured.
>
> "I'll leave you alone for a few minutes," the nurse said kindly. She opened the door and went out.
>
> I just want to sleep, Sheila thought. She lay down on the table. Images roiled through her mind of buying a changing table at the Thrift Shop and the crib mobile that played "Red Sails in the Sunset."

She wanted to escape from everything, she wanted to sleep for a thousand years.

Suddenly she felt new strength. Who was Jack, after all, to dictate her life and the life of her unborn child? If he couldn't live with a deformed child, then let him leave, let him divorce her. She and the baby would survive. She didn't yet know how, but they would. She would go home, and show Jack the sonogram, and tell him everything that had been told her. And then she'd tell him she wasn't going to have the abortion. She felt a warmth like strength suffuse her body. She couldn't wait to do all this.

The nurse came back in. "How's it going?" she asked.

Sheila's voice was firm and strong. "Do you have a phone?" she said. "I want to call my husband. And then I'm going home."

The problem here is that this is an *Unearned Ending*. As I mentioned earlier, we often talk about endings being "earned,", i.e., flowing logically, dramatically and emotionally from the characters and conflicts that have been developed in the story. They're not the products of spontaneous generation. They have to come from somewhere, not from nowhere. If a character changes at the end, it has to be a change resulting from aspects of that character and her conflict shown and/or developed earlier in the story. Unearned climaxes are "not believable," not simply "unbelievable"—there's a difference. A deus ex machina ending is just plain unbelievable, but an unearned ending has the *potential* to be believable. After all, Sheila *could* change the way she does in the above ending—but that change is simply not prepared for and shown. Some critical dramatic development is missing. If Sheila decides she will confront her husband and have the baby, we have to see where that comes from. What has happened there in the examining room that has led to this change of consciousness? Why now, as opposed to earlier? Has there been potential for strength in her character all along? Have we seen that? To have her just change isn't enough. Remember what Flannery O'Connor said? Unexpected, *and* believable.

Unearned climaxes are sins of omission, not commission. They happen for several reasons:

1. The writer doesn't really know how to get from the conflict to the desired ending, and so is trying to "fudge" it.

2. The writer knows, but is trying to be too subtle, and has left too much out.

3. The writer has the wrong ending, and the conflict should really lead to another one.

4. The writer is lazy and doesn't want to take the time to really show where the ending comes from.

GETTING TO THE GOOD ENDINGS

It should be obvious by now that if your ending fails, your whole story fails. Because the ending is where everything is being resolved. If the resolution of character and conflict fail here, then those characters and conflicts will be perceived as flawed to begin with. A corollary is that almost all failed endings result from not having fully imagined and teased out the depths of your characters and the implications of their conflicts. Bad endings may be imperfect resolutions of good conflicts, or perfect resolutions of badly developed conflicts. Getting to the good ending means getting to the one that most fully, faithfully and surprisingly resolves the story's conflict. All other endings are the writer trying to impose something on what's not there, trying to resolve things artificially rather than organically.

I know what you're thinking. What then *would* be a good ending to Sheila's story? The answer is, I don't know, because the full story hasn't been written, and so the conflict hasn't yet been fully dramatized. If I—or any of you—were to do that, maybe it would become obvious what the proper ending should be. Or maybe not. Maybe we'd get to the end and be stuck. Maybe we'd have to work through several unsatisfactory endings. Based on what little we've sketched out, however, I can suggest several possible endings I might explore, if I were writing this story. All of them potentially meet the criteria for good endings noted at the beginning of this chapter:

1. Sheila, awaiting the sonogram, learns that the fetus is *not* deformed. Yet she has become so angered at her husband's injunctions and insensitivities—we've seen that anger simmering through the story—that she decides to spite him by having an abortion anyway. That leads to a further choice for the writer: She doesn't tell her husband about this, in keeping with her passive character. It's her secret, from which she takes a grim satisfaction. Or, she does tell

him. The decision to abort and to tell him allows her to assert herself to him.

2. Or another possibility: The fetus *is* deformed, and she decides to abort it because she realizes she's a weak, nonassertive woman, and that the child will need help and strength that she just can't give. In this case she has a deep insight into the limitations of her character and decides to abort the child out of a kind of love. Or maybe we see it's just a rationalization on her part. Out of that same weakness, she's deceived herself in a most horrible way. Again, you as writer have a choice how to present it. Which Sheila is yours?

These may not be the best endings, of course. But I think they could arise naturally from the characters and conflict as we've seen them, and so are believable, yet also unexpected. A suggestion: Good endings often come from exploring the darker, or "opposite," aspect of a character's character—a re-vision, a re-seeing, of that character and her conflict. Seeing our characters as Just One Thing, in Just One Way, is seeing them one-dimensionally—and it leads to one-dimensional endings. In noted short-story writer R.V. Casill's "The Father," a man, guilt-ridden over having caused his young son to lose his hand in an accident, feels he deserves a punishment that never comes. Over the years it pretty much drives him crazy, and eventually leads him to kill his beloved grandson, his son's son, perversely reasoning that for this terrible act, he will at last suffer his deserved and long-postponed punishment. The astonishment over the ending, why it works so well, is that we see how love turns to violence, and how remorse for one act leads to one of even greater barbarity. It's unexpected. And yet it's totally believable. Yes, we feel: The father's guilt, his desire for punishment, could lead to this.

In our story, Sheila's darker side might be her potential to kill what she loves out of an even greater hate for her husband; her "opposite" side might be her capability to act strongly and decisively, even if it's misguided.

Another example of getting to the good ending: Here's the first draft ending to "Piano Lessons." You might want to contrast it with the published version you read in chapter five:

> "That's it." [his father tells him] "No more nuns. No more piano lessons."

I rested my head against the cold window and no longer felt flushed. I was just tired, warmly tired, as if I were already in bed. I closed my eyes and thought again about the nuns throwing snowballs, the black of their habits almost luminescent now in memory. I imagined Sister Benedict among them, slugging and dodging snowballs herself—she could have been there, I knew, if I hadn't upset her. And suddenly I realized that perhaps she had been afraid of me as much as I had been afraid of her, both of us speechless, unable to speak to one another, or speak at all, trapped within the music room, with only the stilted language of scales and chords, primitively known and poorly learned, repetition and mistake, to guide us. I wished the nuns had never stopped their snowball fight. I imagined Sister Benedict laughing with them, hooting in delight, and I smiled, and wished she would never stop laughing, that the snowball fight would never stop, that the snow would never stop falling, that my father would never stop driving me home, that my life—all my eternal life—would never stop, and I knew with a shiver approaching wonder that the world from this point on would be far stranger and more terrible and more wondrous than anything I've ever imagined before.

There are several problems with this ending, one of which I'll discuss in the next section. But the major problem is that this ending makes the story seem to be about the young boy realizing a sympathetic bond between himself and Sister Benedict. Now that's a nice ending and a noble one. But upon re-vision I saw that this was not what the story was about. It wasn't about his relationship with Sister Benedict so much as his seeing that life could be more wondrous than his father's pessimistic outlook would allow. Ergo, I had to take out most of the stuff about Sister Benedict in the final paragraph so that the ending would dramatize this and not something else.

EXPLANATORY ENDINGS

One last word about endings. Let's say you do have an ending that works well dramatically. In our example, let's say that Sheila has decided to have an abortion, even though the fetus is normal, as a way of spiting her husband. And we end the story like this.

She imagined herself going home after it was over. There wouldn't be any pain, they told her, but maybe she'd have to rest for a little while. And then she'd get up and make dinner, Jack's favorite, macaroni and cheese, broccoli, rice pudding for dessert. She'd be making it when he came home. If he asked her how things went at the clinic—if he even remembered to ask—she'd say, Fine. Fine, he'd say, what does fine mean? And she knew that even at that moment, stirring the rice so that it wouldn't lump up, that she could lie and tell him the fetus was deformed, or tell him it was just fine. It's a boy, she could tell him, a perfect little boy. Later, she'd have to make some excuse for the end of her pregnancy, for the "miscarriage." It could happen sometime when he hit her, because she knew he would, sometime. Maybe she'd egg him on a bit to make it happen. He'd hit her and she'd fall, and start gasping, and clutch her stomach, and gag, and tell him something was wrong, bad wrong. Is it the baby? he'd say. It's not the baby? And she'd nod. And she'd look at him with feigned pain and accusation: If anything's wrong, she'd tell him, I'll never forgive you.

She hated him enough to do that. He would feel that it was his fault they lost the baby, and then he'd feel guilty. It would be her way of punishing him. It would be something she could hold over him, a power almost.

Sheila lay back on the cold examination table, and smiled.

This ending has some punch, but its power is diluted by the penultimate paragraph. Why? Because it's an *Explanatory Ending,* in which the writer tries to tell us—*even if it's already been satisfactorily shown*—what the ending means. An Explanatory Ending stems from insecurity. The writer is worried that somehow the ending hasn't been satisfactorily dramatized, and so the reader won't get it. More is needed, the writer anxiously thinks: a last page, a couple of paragraphs, even a sentence or two, to explain. No. If the dramatic gesture of the ending hasn't shown us what the story's about, then you can't fix it through a tacked-on explanation. You fix it only through making the dramatic events of the story, or its ending, clearer or stronger.

Sometimes that requires a lot of revision. Sometimes it's as simple as lopping off the paragraphs or sentences that make it an Explanatory Ending and letting the story end back before you started explaining things. As a matter of fact, it's a good policy in revising your endings to see if they might not more effectively end earlier. Often the true ending, the one with the most punch and resonance, happened a paragraph or two before. Ask yourself, Could I do without the last sentence? The last paragraph? The last page? The last chapter? Thus, my recommendation for fixing our example Explanatory Ending is simply to lop off the penultimate paragraph. Maybe the last one too. Read it now. Maybe not perfect, but better, right? We are now simply *shown* what the omitted paragraph tried to *tell* us.

Here's the final paragraph again of the first draft ending to "Piano Lessons":

> I rested my head against the cold window and no longer felt flushed. I was just tired, warmly tired, as if I were already in bed. I closed my eyes and thought again about the nuns throwing snowballs, the black of their habits almost luminescent now in memory. I imagined Sister Benedict among them, slugging and dodging snowballs herself—she could have been there, I knew, if I hadn't upset her. *And suddenly I realized that perhaps she had been afraid of me as much as I had been afraid of her, both of us speechless, unable to speak to one another, or speak at all, trapped within the music room, with only the stilted language of scales and chords, primitively known and poorly learned, repetition and mistake, to guide us.* I wished the nuns had never stopped their snowball fight. I imagined Sister Benedict laughing with them, hooting in delight, and I smiled, and wished she would never stop laughing, that the snowball fight would never stop, that the snow would never stop falling, that my father would never stop driving me home, that my life—all my eternal life—would never stop, and I knew with a shiver approaching wonder that the world from this point on would be far stranger and more terrible and more wondrous than anything I've ever imagined before.

On the very next draft, before I made any other changes in the ending, I took out the section in italics, because I could see that it was trying to explain what the story (as I then conceived it) was about. So out it went.

As the old Billie Holiday song advises, "Don't explain." Good advice for both love and stories.

THE IMPORTANCE OF LAST PARAGRAPHS AND LAST SENTENCES

Vigorous, precise prose is extremely important at the end of a story, in the last paragraph and especially the last sentences. This is because these are the last words the reader will "hear" in the story. They are the words that will linger and resonate in her imagination. They *can't* be mushy, or imprecise, or weak. I often struggle mightily with them. My story "Waiting for the Night Flight" provides an example. It ends with the narrator, a lonely salesman, sitting in the airport. He's just had an encounter with two pro basketball players and an unsatisfactory phone conversation with his former wife. Now he's waiting for his flight and musing. In the published version, the last paragraph went like this:

> I sit and close my eyes, and imagine Fuzzy and Magic flying over Los Angeles now, as well they might be. I remember how the city looked from above, all the lights spread out and shining like oil through the valleys and hills and canyons, each one of them a home where someone lived. And I think how Marian, probably asleep now, would have a light on to scare away burglars, and so she'd be one of those lights that Magic and Fuzzy could see. If she were awake and looked out her window at just the right moment, she could see them too, moving through the night. I think how they might see each other, and be that close, and yet not know each other is there. The thought makes me shiver. It's like seeing a face on a passing bus and wondering if it's someone you used to know, a long time ago; or like hearing a phone ring in someone's home, maybe your home, and you don't know, you really don't know, if anyone's ever going to be there to answer it ever again.

It was that last sentence that gave me conniption fits. I don't know how many times I reworked it. In the first draft it went like this:

> It was like the space between waves of the surf, or the space when the phone is ringing and you don't know if someone's going to answer or not.

The prose certainly doesn't have much punch, and the image of space between waves has no connotation of missed connections, missed communications. Another draft went like this.

It was like the space between waves of the surf, or hearing the phone ringing in someone's home, maybe your home, and you don't know, you really don't know, if anyone's going to be there to answer it ever again.

Here, the prose is getting punchier, with the addition of "maybe your home," the repetition of "you really don't know," and the more dramatically effective cadence of "if anyone's going to be there to answer it ever again." But there's still the problem of the "waves" image. So I kept trying different possibilities:

It's like holding your ear to a seashell and thinking you hear something far away . . . *(Better, but lengthy, and a little strained for the idea of "missed" communications.)*

It was like standing on a sand bar and feeling the sand slip away . . . *(Better still, but not quite resonating with people "missing" one another.)*

It was like somebody called your name while you were walking and you turned around and couldn't see who it was . . . *(Already this one was getting a little too convoluted, wordy and farfetched.)*

It was like standing on the shore and waving to someone passing on a boat . . . *(This one is even worse than the one before! And it has a holiday atmosphere, not a brooding one.)*

It was like listening to a voice from the other side of the moon . . . *(Evocative, but farfetched.)*

It was like watching a face at the window of a passing train . . . *(Ah! Not quite it, but we're beginning to get somewhere . . .)*

And so on, until I finally hit upon the images (the passing face on the bus, the phone ringing in the empty house) that seemed to (a) carry the required connotation, (b) not be strained, and (c) not be wordy. But not until I felt I had ransacked the entire physical world for similes and driven myself twenty ways to despair! It was important though, and worth the search. That sentence—its rhythm and its imagery—had to be *exactly* right, because these were the last words, the last images that would resonate in the reader's mind. In a very real sense, last sentences carry the story. If they're flat, if they're vague, if they're anticlimactic, even if the story has been terrific, the reader will feel let down. So make them as powerful as possible. And in the next chapter, we'll examine ways to give your sentences, whether at the end or elsewhere, just that power and punch.

CHAPTER NINE

REVISING YOUR PROSE FOR POWER AND PUNCH

You've got the main dramatic elements of your story—character, conflict, plot, pacing—under control. It's working. You like it. You feel you're nearing the end of your revision efforts. Now it's time to tidy and polish and make it absolutely perfect. We come to that part of revision that many beginning writers assume to be the whole; namely, stylistics, or fine-tuning your prose for power and punch. Under this rubric fall all sorts of rules/quasi-rules/thoughts/suggestions about making your prose read fluidly and forcefully, so that it helps create that "vivid, continuous imaginative dream" John Gardner deems fiction to be. As I've tried to suggest by saving this chapter for later, you should be concerned with stylistics only *after* you've addressed the first concerns in revision—getting the story and characters straight, arranging events in proper sequence, expanding what needs expansion and deleting what needs deletion, and so on. Only then are you ready to dot your *i*'s and cross your *t*'s and make your prose sing.

Before we go into specifics, consider for a moment what you're doing when you "fine-tune" your prose. You're really removing the sense of a "writer" from the work, so that the only thing of which a reader is aware is the imaginative world of the story. You're removing any stylistic "glitches" or infelicities that could interfere with this and make your reader uncomfortably aware that these are *only* words on paper and not a living imaginative reality. "Glitches"—like those you see on television when there's interference—is a good metaphor here. The occasional glitch is not going to interfere with your involvement in a show. But if there's a lot of them, you start to become distracted. You start noticing glitches more than show. If there are too many, you just can't see the show anymore. You give up and turn the channel. Just so in reading a story. One or two stylistic glitches or infelicities are not going to bother a reader. He can still stay imaginatively involved in the story. But the more that occur, the more a reader notices them, and the less he's involved. The imaginative illusion—the vivid, continuous imaginative dream—is broken, and the reader becomes all too aware that there's a *writer* there, and not a very skilled one. Remember *The Wizard of Oz*, when the curtain is pulled back to reveal a little old man at the controls of Oz? We writers, like the Wizard, usually want to keep that curtain closed. If we do want to part it and show the writer/wizard at work, as in certain kinds of metafiction, we want to do so on our terms, with full skill and control. We don't want to ruin the illusion through easily remedied stylistic glitches.

So what are these stylistic glitches? How do we best fine-tune our prose?

First of all, I'm assuming that you're perfectly capable of making the obvious revisions of grammar, capitalization and punctuation. Those are the province of grammar books, not this one. And I'm assuming you will correct any misspelled words. That's what a spell checker, or a good dictionary, is for. What follows is something else: a laundry list, culled from years of teaching fiction writing as well as revising my own work, of the more common stylistic "glitches." They pop up over and over again. Watch out for them. Without exception they are to be carefully considered, if not outright avoided. Trust me.

KAPLAN'S LAUNDRY LIST OF STYLISTIC GLITCHES

Abstract or imprecise language. The more specific and concrete your language is, the more powerful. Note the difference between

> He picked up something heavy and hit James on the face.
> James cried out, and fell.

and

> He snatched up a rock and smashed it against James' nose.
> James groaned, and sank to his knees.

"Snatched" is both more concrete and more exact than the vague "picked up," just as "smashed," "groaned," and "sank to his knees" are more specific and vivid than the words they replace. And "nose" is much more exact than the vaguer "face."

Unnecessary words and phrases, especially unnecessary adjectives. Sometimes called overwriting. It's ironic. Beginning writers are taught to write exactly and vividly—what I noted above—but then sometimes they go overboard and start describing things too minutely and too vividly. Every noun starts to have a modifier, maybe two or three. Unwittingly, the writer is drawing attention to herself: Look, Ma, I'm really *writing!* Consider the following (words suggested for deletion italicized):

> The morning sun's *silent rays* burned Julia's skin as she walked from the grassy, *open* field into the deeply *forested* woods. Immediately the late spring air felt cooler. She sat down on a *gray* rock, took off her *Cordura nylon* backpack, pulled open the *sticky Velcro* fastener from a side pocket, and took out a *plastic* bottle of soda water. She opened *the blue screw-type top,* and drank *thirstily.* Her *green and gold speckled* kerchief felt sticky *against her sweaty skin,* so she loosened it. Crows cackled wickedly from somewhere in the dark woods. A *small* ladybug with one wing torn off was crawling on the rock's *rough surface* . . .

Here, every noun and verb seems to have an adjective or adverb attached to it. We feel there's a writer *really writing.* What the writer should be doing is making you forget that. Eliminating about half the adjectives and adverbs here will help a lot. The trick is to decide which ones are essential and which are fluff. Do we need to know that it's the sun's rays burning her? Isn't that what usually burns? Do we need to know the field is open and the woods forested? Aren't they usually? And aren't most ladybugs small and most Velcro fasteners sticky? For that matter, do we really need to know that it's a Velcro fastener, or that the backpack is made from Cordura nylon, or that the bottle top is a screw-type, or that the rock is gray and her kerchief green and gold? Are all of these details really advancing the story or slowing it down?

On the other hand, it does seem important to know that it's late spring—this situates us in time. And it's important to know that her kerchief feels sticky, the ladybug has one wing torn off, the crows' cackling is wicked, and the woods are dark. These descriptive details are unique and add important sensory information *and* emotional atmosphere to the scene. When an adjective or adverb or descriptive phrase is doing both, it's essential and should be kept. If not, consider deleting it. If we eliminate the nonessential words, we have:

> The morning sun burned Julia's skin as she walked from the grassy field into the deep woods. Immediately the late spring air felt cooler. She sat down on a rock, took off her backpack, pulled open the fastener from a side pocket, and took out a bottle of soda water. She opened it and drank. Her kerchief felt sticky, so she loosened it. Crows cackled wickedly from somewhere in the dark woods. A ladybug with one wing torn off was crawling on the rock . . .

Now we can see the scene, not the writer.

Kaplan's Law of Words: Any words that aren't working for you are working against you. So weed them out. If a word—yes, any single word—isn't adding something we don't know *and need to know,* it's adding nothing. Worse, it's distracting. It's slowing down the prose. Too much, and the reader—consciously or unconsciously—feels she is plodding through thick prosey muck.

Words and phrases of unnecessary specificity. We touched on this somewhat in the section above. Sometimes we belabor the obvious, as in the following:

> Elwood turned off the ignition, opened the *driver's side* door, picked up the gun *with his left hand,* got out, and walked up the *concrete* sidewalk to the house. He pushed the doorbell *with his finger,* and waited. He pressed his *right* ear against the door. Hearing no one come *from inside the house,* Elwood pushed open the *front* door.

The words in italics are all unnecessarily specific. If you're driving, what other door will you open to get out but the driver's side door? Does it really matter whether Elwood picks up the gun with his left or right hand? For that matter, how else do you pick up something than with your hand? And what else do you push a doorbell with but your finger? If Elwood's going to push it with his nose, surely the writer would tell us this! Why bother us with the obvious? Similarly, if we're not told differently—that it's made out of pebbles or alabaster—we probably assume the sidewalk's concrete. Most are. And what other door would Elwood be walking toward, with a sidewalk and doorbell and all, but the front one, unless we're told differently? Where else would he be listening for people coming than from "inside the house"? And is it really important to know that it's his right ear, not his left, that he's pressing against the door? Too many of these unnecessary words, and the prose starts to slow . . . down . . . and readers feel as if they're again slogging through verbal molasses.

This issue is important enough to warrant a few more examples. Examine the following sentences, all of which contain words or phrases of unnecessary specificity:

A small frown appeared on her face. *(Where else do frowns appear?)*

He squinted his eyes. *(With what else do you squint?)*

She shrugged her shoulders. *(With what else do you shrug?)*

The child nodded her head. *(With what else do you nod?)*

After he pulled up the chair, he sat down on the seat. *(Where else?)*

He held the bird in his hand. *(Unless he's holding it with something like fire tongs, he's probably using his hand.)*

An unknown stranger appeared at the door. *(Are there any known strangers?)*

Their voices echoed back and forth through the canyon. *(That's what an echo does: it goes back and forth.)*

When he was alone again, he muttered to himself, "I'll get even." *(If it's established that a character is alone, do you need to say that he muttered/spoke/whispered/yelled "to himself"? Who else is there?)*

"P-please . . . c-c-come in," she stammered with difficulty. *(Are there any easy stammers?)*

"Come into my parlor," the spider whispered in a soft voice. *(Whispers are by definition soft.)*

That's right, she thought to herself. *(Who else do you think to, unless you're telepathic?)*

The horsemen disappeared from sight. *(How else?)*

A black and white penguin was trundling across the snow. *(Are there penguins that aren't black and white?)*

"I'm through with you!" Joyce yelled. "You—"
"Don't say that," Kevin interrupted. *(We've just seen him interrupt—why tell us too?)*

"I'm through with you!" Joyce yelled.
"You can't say that," Kevin said to her. *(If it's been established Joyce is the only one he's talking to, then "to her" is superfluous.)*

Weasel words. There are some unnecessary words that aren't ones of undue specificity or overdescription; they're more outrightly unnecessary. They're the written equivalent to the "uhs" and "wells" and "you knows" in conversation—space fillers. They convey no useful information and add to the sense of mushy, imprecise prose. I call them "weasel words." They seem innocent enough, but should *always* be regarded with suspicion. The following list includes some of the most common ones:

about	exactly	simply
actually	finally	somehow
almost	here	somewhat
almost like	just	somewhat like
already	just then	sort of
appears	kind of	suddenly
approximately	nearly	then
basically	now	there
close to	practically	truly
even	really	utterly
eventually	seems	

How do these work as "weasel words"? Consider the following paragraph.

The man was *there* in the bushes, waiting. When Joan was *just* three feet away, he *kind of* tensed, *then* leaped out and grabbed her. Joan struggled, but *it seemed* he was *just* too strong for her, and *finally* they fell down. She *actually* screamed, and *even* scratched his face.

All the italicized words aren't necessary. They create mushy prose. They show a writer insecure about what he's describing. Take them out, and see how much more vigorous the writing becomes:

The man was in the bushes, waiting. When Joan was three feet away, he tensed, leaped out, and grabbed her. Joan struggled, but he was too strong for her, and they fell down. She screamed, and scratched his face.

Overusing adverbs. As in the following example:

She slammed the phone down *forcefully* and muttered, "Damn." She *quickly* jumped to her feet and strode over to the china cabinet. She *hurriedly* riffled through the papers in the top drawer.

An adverb well chosen is a wondrous thing. But too many in a row (because of the "-ly" ending that most adverbs have) create a singsong, clickety-clack effect that draws attention to itself. Also, many adverbs are unnecessary because they're already denoted or connoted by the verbs they modify. How else do you slam a phone down but "forcefully"? How else do you jump to your feet but "quickly"? How else do you riffle but "hurriedly"? And so on. Why belabor the obvious? Take them out. Remember—words that aren't working for you are working against you.

Overuse of the conditional or past perfect verb tense. We're talking here about "would" and "had" verb constructions, as in the following:

Every morning that summer, John *would get* up around six. He *would smell* the bacon and pancakes his mother *would be making* in the kitchen, and his stomach *would give* a little hungry flip. He *would jump* out of bed and *would rush* to the bathroom. The tile floor *would be* cool against his bare feet. He *would wash* his face quickly.

Or in the past perfect tense:

> Every morning that summer, John *had gotten* up around six. He *had smelled* the bacon and pancakes his mother *had made* in the kitchen, and his stomach *had given* a little hungry flip. He *had jumped* out of bed and *had rushed* to the bathroom. The tile floor *had been* cool against his bare feet. He *had washed* his face quickly.

Again, as in overusing adverbs, the "would" and "had" constructions start to grate. How do you solve this? Very simply. Introduce the conditional or past perfect tense at the beginning of the passage, then slip into the simple past. It works, and makes for less intrusive, more graceful prose:

> Every morning that summer, John had gotten up around six. He smelled the bacon and pancakes his mother was making in the kitchen, and his stomach gave a little hungry flip. He jumped out of bed and rushed to the bathroom. The tile floor was cool against his bare feet. He quickly washed his face.

Strict grammatical tense agreement is a wonderful thing, but agreeable prose is even better.

Overusing participial phrases. One of the most common errors in beginning writing. They are often overused with verbal tags, as in the following:

> "This is a really boring movie," Susanna said, *fidgeting* in her seat.
> "You said it," Bob agreed, *handing* her the popcorn. *Considering* for a moment, Susanna took a big handful.
> "I really shouldn't be eating this stuff," she said, her voice *dropping.*

I don't know what it is about dialogue tags, but participial phrases just seem to fly to them, like bees to honey. Again, the "-ing" construction creates that self-conscious, clickety-clack rhythm. What to do? Transform some of the participial phrases into sentences in their own right. So:

> Susanna fidgeted in her seat. "This is a really boring movie."
> "You said it." Bob handed her the bag of popcorn. Susanna

REVISING YOUR PROSE FOR POWER AND PUNCH

considered for a moment, then took a big handful.

"I really shouldn't be eating this stuff," she said, her voice dropping.

Keeping *one* participial phrase is fine. But get two or more close together, and they start to draw attention to themselves.

Illogical use of "as" or "while" adverbial constructions. Consider the following examples:

"Hey Jim! How about another for this guy, and give me a Tequila Sunrise." While she said this, Anna leaned forward and dropped one leg to the floor.

Jennifer's head shot up as she looked above her.

"Damned lighter," Jack said as the dash lighter dropped onto the floor.

The problem with "as" and "while" constructions is often one of logic. It's unlikely someone would be able to notice a lighter falling and say "Damned lighter" in the half-second it takes one to drop. And how could Jennifer already be looking up at the same time her head shoots up? And isn't it unlikely that Anna would be giving that long drink order, all the while dropping to one knee? It would have to be a slow-motion drop!

The solution, of course, is to turn each into the discrete actions they really are. Thus:

"Hey, Jim!" Anna leaned forward and dropped one leg to the floor. "How about another for this guy, and give me a Tequila Sunrise."

Jennifer's head shot up. She looked above her.

The dash lighter dropped onto the floor. "Damned lighter," Jack said.

Run-on prepositional phrases. As in:

He hardly moved except to puff on his cigar which burned judiciously *in* the ashtray *next to* a red glass lantern *with* a small fluttering candle *in front of* him.

Clickety-clack, clickety-clack. The prepositional phrases all in a row create a monotonous rhythm and at the same time make the geography of the scene almost impossible to visualize. The solution, of course, is to eliminate or replace phrases that aren't important, or to rearrange phrases so they don't all fall in a row, or to think of simple words to replace prepositional phrases, or to break the sentence up into several smaller sentences:

> He hardly moved except to puff on his cigar which burned judiciously in the ashtray. In front of him, a small candle fluttered in a red glass lantern.

Repetitious words or phrases. Another case of the unnecessary, as in the following:

> By the time Gabe arrived at Ellsworth's apartment with Angela, his girlfriend, *there* were several other friends *there*. Now that the master of ceremonies was *there,* the party was all set and the tradition would continue. *There* was the strangest feeling in the air that night.

Or:

> Jay instinctively headed for the *back* seat of Sarah's car. He always sat in *back* on long road trips. This was his time to sit *back* and gaze out at the landscape.

The solution for both of these is either elimination of some of the repetitious words or substitution of other words for them. Thus:

> By the time Gabe arrived at Ellsworth's apartment with Angela, his girlfriend, several other friends were there. Now that the master of ceremonies had arrived, the party was all set and the tradition would continue. The strangest feeling was in the air that night.

> Jay instinctively headed for the back seat of Sarah's car. He always sat there on long road trips. This was his time to sit and gaze out at the landscape.

Tortured, convoluted phrasing. Brevity is the soul of wit, and often of writing too. Sometimes less *is* more. Consider the difference between "Jesus felt tears falling from his eyes" and "Jesus wept." Or between "You no longer are going to be working here" and "You're fired." Or between "I feel a strong affection for you" and "I love you."

Tortured phraseology is used by bureaucrats, but it has little place in fiction, except for effect (a character who speaks or thinks in bureau-cratese, for example). Short, pungent, concrete and specific are key here. So instead of:

> The place turned out to be a laundromat.

> She launched herself forward at him.

> He raised himself from the chair and came to stand by the bar.

Say more simply:

> The place was a laundromat.

> She jumped at him.

> He rose from the chair and stood by the bar.

Weak sentence structure. Powerful prose is created sentence by sentence, not paragraph by paragraph or page by page. When revising, you should make sure each sentence is written in the most powerful way possible. Keep in mind that the most important part of the sentence is its end—that's what echoes in the reader's mind. Ending sentences with prepositional, adverbial or participial phrases is often weak. Look at these:

> Chris and Aaron high-fived outside on the back patio.

> George knocked after a moment's hesitation.

> Annette saw the accident as she was looking out the window.

> "I hate you," Julia said while picking at her nails.

These sentences end weakly, without punch, with subordinate phrases or clauses. The power words in the first two sentences are the verbs "high-fived" and "knocked." The prepositional phrases are but modifiers to those verbs; putting them at the end weakens the sentences' force. The power word in the third sentence is the noun "accident"; in the last one, it's the statement "I hate you." Look how much more forceful each becomes when these power words or phrases end the following sentences.

> Outside on the back patio, Chris and Aaron high-fived.
>
> After a moment's hesitation, George knocked.
>
> As she was looking out the window, Annette saw the accident.
>
> Julia picked at her fingernails and said, "I hate you."

Too picky, you say? Not at all. Anything, no matter how small, affects the imaginative illusion and emotional power of a story. It's all held together, like the strands of a spider's web, by each individual word and sentence. Weaken one strand, and the whole intricate lacelike pattern can start swaying dangerously. Weaken two, and the beauty of the design may collapse.

If you're having trouble developing a good inner ear for sentence strength, the best thing you can do is read your sentences aloud as if they were individual lines of poetry. This will give you a better feel for each sentence's rhythm and dynamism.

Dialogue tag problems. Here's a snatch of dialogue between Mary and her friend Jeanette:

> "Did you see that dress that Jezebel was wearing?" asked Mary, disbelievingly.
> "Did I ever! It looked like some penguin outfit. A very fat, black penguin!" said Jeanette.
> "I'm surprised her mother let her out of the house like that," said Mary, reaching for another blueberry muffin.
> "Well, the way her mother dresses . . . ," replied Jeanette. "I don't know."
> "Yeah," said Mary, nibbling on her muffin. "I guess you're right."

This dialogue needs polishing. First, there are only two people here, Mary and Jeanette. Why do we need to keep identifying them with verbal tags? We can keep them straight. Don't overuse tags— use as few as you can get away with. A second problem is the dangling verbal tag in the second paragraph. It's only after three sentences that we finally see who's speaking, which is way too long to wait for this information. It seems like an afterthought to boot. Don't tack on tags at the end of a string of sentences, or God forbid, a lengthy paragraph. Put them near the beginning, even if you have to break up a sentence.

A third problem is the overuse of participial phrases, which I've discussed before. Either get rid of them, or (better yet) condense a verbal tag and a participial phrase together into a separate sentence, thus solving two problems at once.

Doing all these, our revised dialogue might look like this:

> "Did you see that dress that Jezebel was wearing?" Mary asked in disbelief.
>
> "Did I ever," said Jeanette. "It looked like some penguin outfit. A very fat, black penguin!"
>
> "I'm surprised her mother let her out of the house like that." Mary reached for another blueberry muffin.
>
> "Well, the way her mother dresses . . . I don't know."
>
> "Yeah." Mary nibbled at the muffin. "I guess you're right."

Impossible, overinflated, hyperbolic imagery. In prose a good simile, metaphor or personification adds texture and emotional layering to its referent. A bad image only calls undue attention to itself and to a writer straining to be "literary." Worse, it almost always produces an unintentionally comic effect:

> Doubt overwhelmed him, like a plane circling an airport in a storm which grew louder and stronger, until the thunder and lightning drowned out the sound of the engines and no planes could land.

> The smells hit him like a swarm of wasps, buzzing and vengeful, ready to fly into his nose and sting him.

The first example is ludicrous. Homer could get away with extended similes, but they were carefully constructed and always came from the same world as their referent. They sustained their logic. But this simile just breaks down. We get lost somewhere in the storm. And the imaginative connection between a nonsubstantial thought and very physical airplanes, with fuselages, wings, engines and so on is strained at best. The second example has some potential, even though it's straining a bit to connect the sound of wasps with smells. But it falls off the deep end when it also asks the reader to think of smells as something visual and kinesthetic too ("ready to fly into his nose and sting"). Better would have been to keep the image simple, and confined to only one sensory paradox: "The smells hit him like a swarm of wasps." Short, sweet and punchy.

Unnecessary phrases of realization and discernment. Look at the following constructions, quite common in unpolished writing:

> *He saw that* there were three men running over the hill.

> *He discovered* he was not alone in the room.

> *Barbara realized* a sound was coming from the closet.

> *Tammy noticed that* the man had long, dirty blond hair.

> *He could see that* George hadn't shaved in days. *He also saw that* he was whispering to himself.

> *It seemed* she was lost.

Most sentences of this ilk can be strengthened simply by eliminating the phrase of discernment (in italics above). It's often not needed, especially if the point of view has already been established. And the sentence automatically becomes punchier:

> Three men were running over the hill.

> He was not alone in the room.

> A sound was coming from the closet.

> The man had long, dirty blond hair.

> George hadn't shaved in days and was whispering to himself.

> She was lost.

Overuse of the passive voice. I know, this isn't news. It's something all creative writing instructors and texts emphasize. We all know that "He heard gunshots" is stronger than "Gunshots were heard by him," and that "She threw off the covers" is stronger than "The covers were thrown off." But there are also two *hidden* passive constructions that are often overused, but overlooked: "there are/were/is/was" constructions and self-reflexive constructions. Look at these examples:

> There was a hush that fell over the party.

> There were two men stumbling down the street.

John found himself trembling.

She thought of herself as a strong person.

These are not as strong as:

A hush fell over the party.

Two men were stumbling down the street.

John trembled.

She thought she was a strong person.

or even better:

I'm a strong person, she thought.

Unnecessary telling. Consider the following paragraph:

Fascinated, Sarah watched Mrs. McQuade take the book in her hands, open it, remove the bookmark, and smooth the pages. The teacher adjusted her glasses. Her every movement seemed precise and pure, Sarah thought. Mrs. McQuade began reading the poem by Byron, and Sarah was lulled again by the teacher's soft warm burr of a voice. She wasn't listening to the words at all. She was just listening to their sound, and watching the way Mrs. McQuade's thin, delicate finger traced the lines on the page, the way her eyebrows rose and fell, the slight quiver to her nostril as if the words gave off a fragrance. *She was completely hypnotized by the teacher.*

We've already seen very vividly that Sarah is entranced by her teacher. We don't need to be told, as in the italicized sentence. Similarly:

If he tries to call me again, Jean thought, I'll tell him to kiss off. She imagined him saying he was sorry and how this would be the last time he'd ever cheat on her, but this time she wouldn't give in. "Kiss off," she'd tell him, or "Go cheat on her, I've had enough." *Jean was fantasizing.* If he comes to the door, she thought, I'll slam it in his face. He could stand and talk to it. In fact, he probably would. And she'd just slip out the back door and down the stairs.

We *see* Jean's fantasies; we don't need to be told that's what she's doing. In both cases, take out the unnecessary explanatory sentences.

Monotonous sentence rhythm. We've already seen an example of this with the overuse of participial phrases. Monotonous sentence rhythm happens when one or both of two things happens: Sentences are always of the same length without a specific aesthetic reason, and/ or sentences are always constructed in a similar way. Often the two occur together, like Tweedledum and Tweedledee. An example:

> Dan looked at his watch. It said three o'clock. He looked down the street. The street was empty and silent. A neon sign was blinking over a bar. Dan rubbed his chin. A man walked out of the bar. Dan sighed.

The prose sets up that old clickety-clack monotony because the sentences are all of similar length—here, short—and because they're all similarly constructed: subject/verb/object or adjective/adjectival clause. That example is fairly obvious, but here's one with the same problems, a bit more disguised:

> Pulling back the sleeve of his sweater, Dan looked at his watch. It said three o'clock. When he looked down the street, Dan saw it was empty and silent. Blinking over a bar was a neon sign. As Dan was rubbing his chin, a man walked out of the bar. Dan sighed.

Here, we see more variety in sentence length, but too many too close together feature the same construction: They begin with a participial or adverbial phrase or clause. And again monotony creeps over the prose.

Okay—quiz time. Let's put what we've learned to work. Here's a sentence ready for polishing. What's wrong with it, and how can it be revised?

> He saw that there were two men just dashing quickly across the field, screaming "Fire!" in loud voices.

We examine. We read aloud. We consider. We realize "He saw that . . ." is an unnecessary phrase of discernment. "There were" is a hidden passive. "Just" is a weasel word. "Quickly" is unnecessarily specific ("dashing" denotes moving quickly), as is the phrase "in loud voices" (how else do you scream?). Also, that prepositional phrase makes the sentence end weakly. A revised sentence might read like this: Two men were dashing across the field screaming "Fire!"

Punchier, right? But too easy, you say? Let's look at a more extended example, a section from a story by a student, Michele Kwiatkowksi, before revision and after. In the draft below, I've indicated by underline and interlinear comment the particular stylistic glitch involved.

```
St. Nicholas Church was just like Mary remembered.

She walked up the concrete steps to the huge, oak
                                    repetition
doors and reached for the brass handle. The handle

was cold, sending a chill up Mary's arm. She pulled
        repetition    unnecessary word
on the handle of the solid, heavy door and couldn't

weasel word
even crack it open a couple of inches. Mary pushed
                            unnecessary specificity
the sleeves of her sweater up toward her forearm
        convoluted phrasing            convoluted
exposing a melted patch of flesh. She caught sight of
    repetition                unnecessary specificity
the burn scar and quickly pulled the one sleeve back
unnecessary specificity
down to her wrist. Mary used both hands to open the
                        convoluted phrasing
door, just as she did when she was a little girl. The
            repetition
weight of the church doors always seemed oppressively
unnecessary specificity
heavy to her, sometimes making her feel as though she
    convoluted phrasing
weren't really welcome. She stepped inside the
                    unnecessary word
vestibule and let the heavy doors shut behind her.
```

repetition   *unnecessary word*
The doors shut out the outside world with one great

                      repetition
thump, and entombed her in her childhood church.

unnecessary phrase of realization
Mary discovered this old church had not changed. It

weak sentence structure
still had two marble basins filled with holy water on

run-on prepositional phrases; unnecessary phrases
each side of the double doors leading from the

vestibule to the inside of the church. The basins

                 unnecessary words
stood like sentinels guarding royalty. You were not

      unnecessary words   *unnecessary word*
to pass their post without their blessing first. She

            repetition   *overusing adverbs*
walked toward the double doors slowly peering into

      weak sentence structure   *overusing adverbs*
the church nervously. She stopped momentarily at one

      repetition   *unnecessary specificity*
of the marble basins and gently dipped her middle

finger into the cool, calm water and blessed herself

weak sentence structure; unnecessary phrase
before entering the church.

Behind the stylistic glitches, there's good, strong prose here. If we correct the glitches, we have a paragraph that could read:

> St. Nicholas Church was just like Mary remembered. She walked up the concrete steps to the huge, oak doors and reached for the brass handle. It was cold, sending a chill up Mary's arm. She pulled on the heavy door and couldn't crack it open a couple of inches. Mary pushed up the sleeves of her sweater, exposing a scar from a burn. She looked at it and

quickly pulled the sleeve back down. Mary used both hands to open the doors, just as she did as a little girl. Their weight always seemed oppressively heavy, sometimes making her feel unwelcome. She stepped inside the vestibule and let the doors shut behind her. They shut out the world with one great thump, and entombed her there. The old church had not changed. Two marble basins filled with holy water stood like sentinels on either side of the double doors. You were not to pass without their blessing. She walked toward the doors, nervously peering into the church. She stopped at one of the basins and gently dipped her finger into the cool, calm water and blessed herself.

Better, right? You see how it works? Cut away everything that isn't the strong prose. Say exactly what you mean, and no more. Polish, polish, polish.

THE KEY CONCEPTS

This discussion of stylistic glitches is by no means complete. I've described several that pop up frequently. There are many others. The important point is that you grasp a few crucial concepts behind all of this fine-tuning:

1. Don't worry about fine-tuning your prose until you've got the bigger problems of your story under control. You can't polish a silver bowl until it's been smelted and cast. Just so with a story. Of course, you can't help doing some fine-tuning at the same time you're solving the other, bigger problems. That's natural. But don't make it your focus in early revisions. You'll start seeing trees instead of the forest. Map out the forest first, then start trimming trees.

2. When you're fine-tuning, every sentence, every word, counts. Everything has an effect. Words and sentences are the building blocks of your fictional universe. They're either working for you or against you. A weasel word here, a passive construction there, and you've got a limp, mushy sentence. A few of those sentences, and you've got a limp, mushy paragraph. Enough of those paragraphs, and you've got a limp, mushy story—and a disinterested reader. Just as you are what you eat, your story *is* what you write. If you think that's a tautology, think about it again.

3. So, when you're fine-tuning, go over your prose with the idea of making *each and every* sentence as strong as possible.

4. Go over it again.

5. Go over it again. A story is finished only when it's perfect, each and every word. Don't be in a hurry. Don't "finish" it before it really is finished. Remember what I said in an earlier chapter about the editor who complained that he saw too many early drafts? Unpolished prose is a sure sign of an early draft.

6. Most importantly, start becoming aware of your own particular stylistic quirks and glitches, so that you can watch out for them upon revision. You may be prone to overusing the passive voice, for example, or to overusing adverbs. If so, you must become especially sensitive to these infelicities and watch out for them. Every writer has stylistic weaknesses, and it's no shame to indulge them in early drafts. But only bad writers live with them through the final draft.

CHAPTER TEN

PUTTING IT ALL TOGETHER, GETTING HELP, BEING STUCK, GIVING UP

The problems I've been discussing in this book will concern you and occupy your imagination through successive drafts of your story or novel. Of course, some will present more of a problem than others; some may not be problems at all. You hope, of course, that as you move from draft to draft, you'll see your story more clearly, solutions will appear, and the story will become more focused, more emotionally resonant and powerful. Things will get better, in other words. (If they're not getting better, then the last half of this chapter is for you.) And that's the revision process: write, read it over, make revisions, new draft, read it over, make more revisions, etc. As I mentioned earlier, I like to print out a draft, mark it up by hand with all kinds of cross-outs and notes and shiftings around, then retype it into the computer, print out the new draft, then start the whole process all over again. You might like to work differently. You might like to cut up your story with scissors and rearrange pages and paragraphs like a puzzle. Or you might like to revise directly onto the computer rather than by hand. Or you might like to work in nonsequential sections— first the middle, then the end, then the beginning, for example. Whatever works for you and gets you most quickly, expeditiously and felicitously to journey's end, the Perfect Story, is just fine. Part of becoming a skilled writer is discovering what revision methods work best for you. Not that it will make revision any less imaginatively difficult— but it will save you time in struggling for a methodology, a way of working, which can preoccupy beginning writers.

PUTTING IT ALL TOGETHER

Let me show you how the revision process worked from draft to draft with the opening page of my story "Summer People." As you remember from a previous chapter, it's a story about a father and son closing down the family summer house for the last time after it's been sold. They've had a difficult relationship, and the tensions between them simmer and boil and finally explode during the course of the day. As we go from draft to draft with this one page, we'll see several of the concepts I've been discussing in this book at work. Here is the unedited first-draft opening paragraph of the story:

Draft #1

They had come to the lake, not at the beginning, but at the end of the season, and they had come after all the other vacationers in their summer places had left for the season, and even some of the people who minded the stores, the motorboats had gone and the fisherman with them, and the occasional waterskier, although that was rare, since the lake was pretty far north and so tended to get mostly regulars as opposed to people from the city, fishermen and families who tended to stay for a month at least, of the season. There used to be an amusement park on the far side of the lake, the opposite shore where they were, and Frank had gone to it when he was a child, the first few summers they had come to the cottage, but it had closed for lack of business when the new recreation area at the dam project had opened up forty miles away and the interstate had been completed. He still remembered his disappointment upon hearing that the park was closed, and hadn't believed it until his father had taken him there and he had stared through the cyclone fencing that had been been hurriedly strung around the park.

Well. The first and most obvious thing we can say about this writing is that it's almost gibberish. Sentences run on and on and on, language is often murky and elliptical. If this were handed to me by one of my students as a finished story, I would be in despair. It's terrible writing.

But I'm not worried about any of that at this point. It's only a first draft, and remember what I said about them? The most important thing about first drafts is just getting the story out and down on paper.

I don't worry about anything else—whether the plot structure is coherent, whether characters are fully rounded, whether the writing is bad. I know I'm going to have lots of opportunity, in subsequent drafts, to make it make sense and sound good. It's in re-vision and in revision, I hope, that I'll become a Good Writer.

In the next draft, we can see some big changes:

Draft #2

They drove up to the lake and pulled into the small patch of dead grass that served as a parking area for their cabin. It was still early morning and a milky haze—the ghost of an earlier fog—hung over the lake. Trees—blue pine and spruce, oak and hemlock—loomed grayish-green in the haze. Some cantilevered slightly as if trying to rake the water. For a moment, Frank felt nineteen years roll away, and he was ten years old on a summer morning much like this one, when he'd wake to find the woods and the lake transformed to ghosts, and yet he'd still run to the dock and dive into the misty waters, and it was as if he were diving once more into his dreams, and re-entering the world of sleep. Even in late August the water was cold, fed as it was not only by streams and run-off, but by an underground source that had never been pinpointed.

"They think it might be the size of a river, running underground, somewhere out there," Mr. Kremins, the man who took care of their cabin in the winter, had told him. "Sometimes at night, if you hear what sounds like a million leaves rustling out there, why that's just the sound of the river coming to the surface."

Frank smiled. To think he'd once taken that seriously. . . .

The prose is a little bit tighter, although stylistic infelicities still abound, and there's one beauty of a run-on sentence ("For a moment . . . world of sleep."). But again, I'm not terribly concerned about polishing the prose at this point. I *am* concerned, however, with making the story start quicker. Rather than talking about the lake, I'm now describing it concretely—showing it—and trying to get the main characters on stage sooner. Now Frank is right there, looking at the water (although his father isn't). And something else: The amusement park has disappeared. This amusement park and what it meant to Frank as a child occupied two pages in the first draft. Upon revision, it seemed to me that (a) it was an unnecessary flashback that slowed down the opening of the *present* story, and (b) a tangent, having little to do with the story at all. Even though I'd done all of my Revision Before Writing, on the first draft I was still trying to figure out which elements of the story were important and which were not. I had to write the amusement park sequence in the first draft to follow it out. It was actually not a bad sequence, but it was not essential and slowed the story down. So I took it out. Right away though (I'm a slow learner!) I've added another flashback, as Frank stands there lakeside and contemplates things! In the passages that follow the section quoted above, he thinks about his father and the communication problems they've had:

> His father had called and asked if he would come back to help this year, "since it's the last year," he said, "and I want to do a good job." Frank had resisted. He was uncomfortable with his father, and had been for some years. They had argued violently while he was in college, and in exasperation and frustration he had put distance between himself and his father, and called that understanding. Being with his father was painful to Frank, and so he had chosen to stay apart, and had made his visits home—when his mother was alive—as brief as possible, and tried as much as possible not to be left in the same room alone with his father. The silences were painful when they were; but even more painful was the small talk, and then the small irritations, and finally the arguments, the raised voices, and his mother finally coming in, her face tense, anxious, to try to make peace.

I could see upon revision that not only was I deep in a flashback that interrupted the forward flow of the story, I was also *talking about* Frank's communication problems with his father rather than dramatizing them. Something had to change here.

I've also added a new scene and character, Mr. Kremins, with his cracker-barrel observation about the underground source of the lake. In this draft he was a character who popped in and out of the story, offering homespun observations and folksy wisdom. As it turned out, when I revised further I decided he was just a Big Bore, and so he too was cut in the next draft, which now went like this.

Draft #3

Frank and his father drove up to the lake at the end of the season, after the summer people—including those who had rented the house—had returned to their real homes, taking with them their grills and motorboats and folding chairs and waterskis. It was an early morning in late September and a milky haze—the ghost of an earlier fog—hung over the water. The blue pines and spruce loomed grayish green in the watery air, the ones nearest the bank cantilevered slightly as if trying to rake the water. His father pulled into the area of dead grass and packed dirt which served as a parking area.

"We're here," he announced, and Frank nodded.

"How does it feel to be back?" his father asked, and Frank shrugged.

"About the same," he replied.

While his father unlocked the basement to find the tools they needed, Frank walked to the dock, hands in his pockets, and stared into the haze. Waves lapped the pilings; an oily scum of decaying leaves and algae formed a thin yellow ring along the bank. He lay down on the dock and dipped his hand into the black water.

The prose is getting tighter now, and beginning to sound a little more fluid and graceful, a little more like English. You'll note I went back and pulled the opening sentence from Draft #1 to use here (much revised, of course). But I'm still mainly concerned with story pacing. I'm getting to the action even more quickly. Now, instead of Frank being at the lake and immediately meditating upon the past, with his father offstage, I have Frank and his father pulling into the drive and talking. Mr. Kremins is gone too. After three drafts, I've finally realized (slow learner again) that the story *is* about Frank and his father. Mr. Kremins, the underground source of the lake (pretty heavy-handed symbolism too, and thus deserving of the ax), the amusement park—all were not essential to that story. They were tangents. And if it's about Frank and his father and the difficulties they have in communicating, why not get them both *there* already, and get them talking, or not talking, as the case might be. In other words, let's introduce the characters and their problems and Get On With It. Which is what I'm trying to do in the brief snippet of dialogue they have after pulling into the drive. I'm now trying to dramatize what needs to be dramatized—to show the difficulties they have in communicating, rather than have Frank just meditate about it. In the next draft, this will become even stronger.

Draft #4

Frank and his father drove up to the lake at the end of the season, after the summer people—including those who had rented the house—had returned to their real homes, taking with them their grills and motorboats and folding chairs and waterskis, leaving behind the lake which seemed to dream in the fall light. A milky haze—the ghost of an earlier fog—hung over the water, and the trees—blue pines and spruce, oak and sycamore—loomed grayish-green in the watery air. His father pulled onto a patch of dead grass and dirt which served as a parking area.

"Well, we're here," he announced, and Frank nodded. It had been eleven years since Frank had last been here. In that time he'd graduated college, spent a year in Europe, moved to a job in another state, married Jena, and now was separated from her.

While his father unlocked the basement to find the tools they needed, Frank walked to the dock, hands in his pockets, and stared into the haze. The lake seemed larger than he remembered. Waves lapped the pilings; an oily scum of decaying leaves and algae formed a thin yellow ring along the bank. He lay on the dock and dipped his hand into the ashen water.

Revisions are becoming less ones of wholesale addition and cutting, and more ones of fine-tuning. Vague words like "area" and "said" are replaced by more vivid and specific ones such as "patch" and "announced." Sentences don't run on, and are less syntactically complex (for example, all that business about the trees cantilevering over the water is cut). Some dialogue is cut too. Now all Frank's father says is the obvious, "We're here," to which Frank doesn't even reply. The story, after all, is about how they can't talk. So why not *see* them not really talking? It's more effective dramatization. However, even though I've cut a lot, I've added a section summarizing the last eleven years in Frank's life. I just can't seem to get rid of that desire for flashback (slow learner still). But in the next draft I did cut this section not only because its backstory summary seemed too obvious, but also because it was *telling* about Frank's past rather than *showing* it. In the final story, all this information is conveyed at appropriate points through Frank's thoughts or through dialogue with his father. Shown, in other words, not told.

You see the process at work, draft through draft? At first I'm interested just in getting the story out. Then I start to work on major problems such as getting to the story quicker, cutting unnecessary flashbacks and tangents, adding what's essential (descriptions of the lake), and showing conflict rather than talking about it (the little dialogue Frank and his father have). Note that all the revisions didn't come at once, on the second draft. Only through doing one revision do you see more clearly what problems are still there for the next revision. Note also that sometimes things you think are good revisions (like the addition of Mr. Kremins in one draft) turn out to be wrong. And it's only on the fourth draft that I really begin to fine-tune the prose. Now imagine the whole story undergoing the same process we've been discussing for this one page. The story—and this page—went through four more drafts after this one, although many of the major problems had already been solved. I knew what the story was about and what it wasn't about and what the scenes would be, so changes became more and more slight rearrangements of events within scenes, small additions and deletions to them, more fine-tunings of prose. Here's the page as it appears in the published story:

Published Version

Frank and his father drove up to the lake at the end of the season, long after the summer people—including those who had rented the house—had returned to their real homes, taking with them their grills and motorboats and deck chairs and water skis. It was an early October morning. A milky haze—the ghost of an earlier fog—hung over the lake, and the trees loomed grayish green, half-water, half-air. His father parked on the dead grass behind the summer house. Geese honked from somewhere within the haze.

"We're here," his father announced.

Neither of them moved to get out. Frank sipped the coffee,

already lukewarm, that they'd bought in the country store down at the turnoff. His father rolled down the window and breathed deeply.

"Chilly," he noted.

It's a long ways from the mishmash of Draft #1, right?

Your reader never sees that mishmash, nor all the other digressions, tangents, extraneous scenes and characters, turgid passages and just plain boring ones that you've revised in all those drafts between the first one and the final story.

GETTING HELP

At some point in the revision process—after draft three, or five or fifteen—you're going to want somebody to read what you've written. You *need* somebody to read what you've written. Maybe you think the story is finished and just fine and dandy and ready to be read by an admiring world. You want corroboration. Or you may know that it has a few problems. One scene isn't working right, one character is a bit fuzzy, and you're hoping another reader can give you some help. You want advice. Or you may be *really* stuck: The story's an utter mess, and you don't have a clue what to do with it anymore. You want someone not only to give you insight, but also consolation and inspiration.

Writers need readers, and not just after publication. Revision is *re-vision,* remember—seeing again. Another reader gives you another vision, another way of seeing your story.

Who are these readers? Where do you find them?

Let me first tell you who they aren't.

They probably aren't your girlfriend or boyfriend or best friend, or husband, wife, daughter, son, mother, father or kissing cousin. If they don't have some familiarity with and sophistication in fiction writing, these people are best left unbothered. Even if they do, they're probably best left unbothered. Why? Because they're just too close to you to be of much help. Thick blood often makes thickheaded readers. They love you, presumably, and so are more likely to proclaim your genius than to proclaim your story a mess. You don't need your genius proclaimed, you need an honest analysis of your story's strengths and weaknesses. Let your darlings read your work after it's published—it's best that way.

Another reader you don't want is someone who just isn't simpatico with your work. She may be a good writer herself, but her own sensibilities and style and passions and preferences are out of sync with yours, and she just can't put those aside. If, for example, you're an experimental writer for whom character and plot are less important than wit and style, you may get a less than sympathetic reading from a writer of psychological realism. Or if you're a writer of great irony, you may get an unhelpful reading from an unabashed sentimentalist. And so on. This reader may not be sensitive to the particular problems you face: A writer who's never written a mystery, for example, might not be so aware of the intricacies of red herrings in plot construction, which is exactly where the problem in your story may lie. I'm not saying that writers of widely diverging styles, subjects and fictive persuasions can't be excellent readers of one another's work. But it may be more of an effort.

A third reader you don't need is someone who just can't read well, i.e., who can't give clear, helpful and thoughtful comments. There are *lots* of wonderful writers who are lousy readers of other people's work. They know what to do with their own work, but they can't discern or articulate the problems in someone else's. Or they can, but can't offer solutions. Even if your reader is a Famous Writer, if he can't help you with what you're trying to do, fame don't mean a thing.

So whom *do* you need for a reader? You need a reader who can do four things:

1. Understand what you're trying to do in your story;
2. Have enough imagination, knowledge and insight to help you;
3. Be willing to tell you what seems wrong, even if it hurts;
4. Offer criticism in a positive, constructive manner that doesn't set your teeth on edge or send you into the Slough of Despond. This means that your readers more than likely will be writers themselves, either master writers, or teachers of writing, or discerning fellow writers. They could also be people associated with writing who understand its aims, techniques and problems, people such as editors or agents.

A word about your reader's style of giving you feedback. Admittedly, this is highly personal. Some people like their readers to be drill sergeants. Others want shrinks. Most of us fall somewhere in between. However your reader frames his criticism, most important is that it be honest. You don't need people to tell you how wonderful you are. You need readers who will tell you what's wrong and how you might possibly fix it. All else is *sansara*, illusion. It will get you nowhere. You may feel a warm glow, but you won't become a better writer. Which do you want?

Wanting praise is understandable, of course. Writing is such a solitary, lonely business. We sit in small rooms, stare at silent walls and blank paper, and either babble to ourselves or rock catatonically. Schizophrenics do this too. And writing's gratifications are so deferred. It takes time to mull something over before writing it, then time to write it, time to revise it . . . and revise it . . . and revise it. . . . More than likely, it takes more time to get it accepted for publication. And even more time before it appears in print. And another long time before your readers find you. If you want quick fixes of adoration, it's probably easier and quicker to try to become a rock star. No wonder we want our poor first readers to praise our work, to affirm that it's all been worth it and that what we've written isn't solipsistic maundering, but a moving, powerful fictional experience. But it might not be. And so back to reality—and revision.

FINDING GOOD READERS

It's important to be able to distinguish a potentially good reader from a potentially bad one. When you're just beginning to write, this is often hard to do. You may not yet have enough understanding of craft to be able to distinguish good from bad advice. Someone may be very sympathetic with your work, but have no idea what its problems might be or how to solve them. Someone else may have a lot of bad ideas, yet sound persuasive. You think, Aha, he must have a point, when maybe he doesn't. That's again why it's so helpful at the beginning to participate in a writing class or workshop—you'll get a wide variety of readers' comments and so begin to learn to distinguish wheat from chaff. You must learn to discern what advice is relevant and helpful, no matter how harsh it is to hear, and what's just noise, static and irrelevance. (Remember—unwarranted praise is just noise too.) Criticism is relevant if it shows understanding of your story's characters and their problems. It's relevant if it tells you what you suspected, but didn't want to hear. Yes, the story *is* dull in the middle third; yes, Aunt Gertrude *is* a thumping bore. It's relevant if it leads to an Aha! on your part, as in, "Aha! She's right! If I take out the scene where they fall in the fountain, it *does* move faster, with no loss to the characterization." It's often relevant if it's specific and offers ways to fix problems. It's relevant if it energizes you—no matter how harsh it's been—and makes you want to get back to the legal pad or typewriter or word processor and *revise!*

Other difficulties in finding good readers may be attributable to your own ego. You might not like to hear that your story doesn't work, and so you label your reader insensitive and dumb, and turn him off, when he might have a point. (Much of the way you find a good reader is by being a good listener. And by being a good reader yourself.) Conversely, someone else may praise you to the skies, and you think him a *brilliant* reader, yet he can't see the obvious problems in your work. You need the former reader, not the latter. You've got to develop a tough, hard-nosed attitude toward your work. Like children, stories should be conceived in love and wonder, then raised with love *and* discipline. As with a child, you don't want to spoil your stories. They need fair and honest discipline if they're going to grow up to be the best they can be.

I've always thought that a writer ideally needs just two good readers—a "line" reader and a "concept" reader. They usually aren't the same person. A concept reader focuses on the Big Picture. She can tell you what is and isn't working overall in your story. She can make suggestions for scene shifts, for adding or dropping characters, for changing middles and ends and beginnings. Concept readers Think Big. They don't sweat the small stuff, such as whether this word is better than that word, or whether this sentence could be phrased more felicitously, or whether the rifle a character shoots should be a .30-.30 or a .30-.08, or just what the difference is between an egret and a heron, and do you really mean the latter when you said the former. That stuff is important though, and that's where line readers excel. They revel in stylistics, detail, minutiae. They go over your work like a hound dog on the trail of a raccoon, word by word, line by line. They do what a good copy editor at a publishing house does. You're lucky if you have a reader like this. They are pearls of great price, and rare as hen's teeth. So—if you have a good concept reader, look for a good line reader, and vice versa. You are *really* lucky if you have both. Then you've got the best of both worlds.

BEING STUCK

No revision ever goes smoothly. We work in fits and starts, and sometimes everything just comes to a halt and we're stuck. Now, there are different levels of stuckness. There's being temporarily stuck, when we just need a little time away from our story. Or when we need a good reader to give us a fresh perspective. But sometimes, alas, we're *stuck*. When you've taken time off, you've consulted your good readers, you've mulled and cogitated and revised and still nothing is happening with your story—then you may be stuck. I'm not talking about Writer's Block, about which more fuss is made than necessary. (To me, Writer's Block always boils down to two possibilities: Your imaginative well is dry, in which case stop for a while and get out and jump back into life to fill it up again . . . or you're just reluctant to sit down and Do It—either from lack of organization or plain laziness— and Writer's Block is merely a romantic moniker to legitimize this. The solution then is to put your butt to the chair and Get On With It.)

How do you know when you're really stuck? Here are some of the telltale signs:

1. You feel each succeeding draft of your story is like the draft before, with only minor variations. You are spinning your writerly wheels.

2. After trying change after change, you suspect that draft fifteen is almost exactly like draft three. Rereading confirms this. You are spinning your wheels again, only in a larger radius.

3. You are so bored by your characters and all of their creations that a trip to your story is like a visit with your most dreaded relatives.

4. Your story starts to seem thinner and thinner, smaller and smaller, instead of increasingly rich, juicy, complex and mysterious.

5. Some Big Thing is wrong. The characters, no matter how much you change them, don't seem to belong in the same story. Or something about their problems seems hokey, false, contrived, unrealistic, sentimental, boring—whatever.

6. You've sought the advice of your Good Readers, and it is of no avail. Their comments make no sense, or they contradict each other, or they have no clue themselves why your story is such a mess.

What to do when you're stuck? The first and best thing, of course, is to put the damn thing aside again, probably for a long while. How long is "a while"? Maybe a month, six months, a year or two. Who knows? Time, as it does with all wounds, often heals old stale ways of looking at a story, and distance *can* make the imagination grow fonder. There's no rush in this business. There are other stories to work on, after all. Let this one gestate and percolate in the primal imaginative soup. Go back either when you feel reenergized, or when you feel you have a new slant on it. But don't go back if you don't want to. I've set aside stories for a year or more, then gone back and finished them. I have others that have gone through umpteen drafts and years later still sit in my files, unfinished. Some of these I'll get back to: There's something about them that still intrigues and moves me, and I'm just waiting for inspiration. Others I'll never finish, and just as well. They were probably misconceived to begin with. Some stories need to die naturally, after all, rather than being beaten to death. Putting them aside helps with that. This is part of re-vision too: Sometimes "re-seeing" is simply seeing that the story wasn't very good to begin with and deserves to be put out of its misery. Not that the time and effort have been wasted—I'm a firm believer that *nothing* is wasted in writing. You learn something from the stillborn stories and novels as much as from the successful ones. Maybe more.

Something else you can do when you're stuck: Put the story aside and read some writers you admire. Often reading someone whose work you love will inspire you to go back to your own. Sometimes rereading fine writing shakes your imagination so that suddenly you can see what's wrong with your story. You can almost make this master reading prescriptive: If you're having trouble with minor characters, for example, read Dickens, who is a master at creating vivid, vibrant minor characters. Trouble with omniscient narrators? Read Tolstoy, a master of that point of view. Trouble with language and style? Read poetry. In fact, problems aside, to grow in your writing, you *must* constantly be reading master writers. The great writers. If you don't know who they are, get an anthology of English and

American literature and read those authors. Read anthologies of both classic and contemporary short story writers. Reading good writers is the way we absorb, almost by imaginative osmosis, models of effective writing. Consider: you can't write beyond what you haven't read. Can't be done. There's no way that you will write a novel as powerful as *The Scarlet Letter* if all you've read is pulp romances. Even if you *want* to write pulp romances, reading *The Scarlet Letter* and other master works will help you write better ones.

Still stuck? Be consoled. Being stuck is always a sign that the true story has not yet revealed itself, and you should wait for that revelation. As a character in Ann Beattie's story "You Know What" says, "I believe that sometimes you have to be patient and listen for a long time before you hear the true story. People talk quite a lot, but you often have to wait for their true stories." Being stuck prevents you from writing facile, half-baked work. Among other things, it's your artistic conscience speaking, if only you listen. Be patient. Be of good hope. All things (well, most things) come to him who waits.

I'll close with an example from my own work. Remember the story "Feral Cats," whose opening pages we examined in chapter seven? As you recall, it is a story about a man visiting a dying mother who is having difficulty accepting her impending death and so has run off to the family's summer house. Well, here are the opening pages of "Feral Cats" from the first draft (tidied up a bit stylistically. Note that it was first titled "Lidian.").

Lidian

I hadn't seen Lidian for seven years when I pulled into the driveway of the small farmhouse where she was now living. It was evening in the flatlands of eastern North Carolina . . . I had driven through one small town after another—Henna, Justice, Peace Grove, Gilead—towns that weren't even towns really but a store or a crossroads. Tobacco had just been harvested on either side of the small white farmhouse in front of me. It had a tin roof and a noticeable sag to the porch, like a farmer's belly. Paint was peeling in great scabs, and broken panes in the windows were filled in with paper. . . .

I got out of the car and saw a huge dog, black, yet mottled with grayish patches, coming toward me. It looked like a cross between a shepherd and some other breed, and it was ugly, one lip seeming to curl in a permanent snarl. It carried its head forward, alert, tail down, as if it was about to attack. It snarled and I got back in the car . . . Lidian appeared on the porch.

She clapped her hands smartly. "Get out of here, you damn thing," she yelled. The dog looked at her. "Get away, git," she yelled. The dog moved back a bit, then seemed to make a decision, turned, and ran.

"Hiya," Lidian called out, coming toward me. I got out of the car. She was wearing a man's flannel shirt, torn at the elbows, and blue jeans. She was barefoot. She had the prettiest feet I'd ever seen.

"That's one ugly dog," I said.

She held out her arms, and we embraced. She smelled good, like soap and cooking.

"I was in the kitchen and didn't hear you come in," she said. "I was frying up some donuts for breakfast tomorrow."

"You look good, Lidian," I said.

"Do I?" She brushed some of her hair back. "I don't know anymore. I hardly look."

She had aged some, of course, and the lines around her eyes and those that ran from her nose to lips had deepened. Her eyes seemed darker, more hollow. Had she lost weight? I couldn't decide. She seemed tireder, too, and her smile came a bit slower. Still she was Lidian, and beautiful—tall, long-boned, her hair still long and dark—and she could still move my heart. Ten years ago, we had been lovers.

"Seems sultrier out here than back in Chapel Hill," I said.

"Oh, it's gonna thunder good tonight," she said, taking my arm. "It's good to see you." She made it sound like a question.

"Whose dog is that?" I asked. "Not yours."

She nodded. "It used to be Daddy's. Then when he—died—the dog just went wild. I mean, nobody could handle him. He just seemed to take to the woods to be by himself. He wouldn't come back to the house at all. He just got wilder and wilder. Mama kept putting out food for him, but he wouldn't take it. Don't know where he gets food. Kills some of the feral cats probably. They live all around here, you know. . . .

Well. It seems I originally thought the story wasn't about a man visiting his dying mother, but rather was about a much younger man visiting the young woman who'd once been his lover. Many of the basic elements of the ultimate story were there—the wild dog, the feral cats—but the characters and conflict—what the story was *about*—were totally different. And the story somehow didn't work. For the longest time, through draft after draft, I tried to figure out who these people were and what their problems were. At first, they'd been lovers. Later, they hadn't been lovers, but the narrator wished they'd been. In still another draft, they were just old friends. In one version, Lidian was a woman who had retreated to this farmhouse after the death of her parents, and was now gradually slipping into emotional isolation there. In another, she was on the verge of mental breakdown. In another, the story was less about her and more about the narrator's having to come to terms with his romantic fantasies about her. My confusion about these characters vexed me, draft after draft. Nothing seemed right, and finally I admitted I was stuck and filed the story away. Some years later, however, I finally realized it was a story about a man visiting his dying mother. My own mother had died the year before, so that pain was fresh in my mind. I'd been wanting to write a story about a man trying to deal with a dying mother but couldn't find a suitable story line. So I'd just made a bunch of random notes. And then I remembered "Lidian"—suddenly everything fell into place. That was the story line I could use! I began rewriting, and it went smoothly.

Revision. *Re*-vision—seeing everything again. And for the first time.

CHAPTER ELEVEN

REVISING AFTER PUBLICATION

t's a cliché, but we never stop growing and changing. We are constantly reevaluating and re-seeing our lives and our experience. To
what was only raw experience, we try to ascribe meaning. Indeed, I
believe that's why we're here on earth: not to be happy, or to find
wealth or fame (although I suppose these *might* be nice), but to find
meaning. We look back on the past and try to make sense of it, and
what seemed true one year, one decade, is true no longer. We search
for the best possible story of our lives, the one that makes the most
sense, has the most unity, the fullest meaning. This search entails
constant criticism, an ongoing self-evaluation. Vision and re-vision.

Why should it be any different in our writing? Our writing *is* ourselves, after all—our experience transmuted into dramatic meaning
through written words. So why shouldn't it change? Not only as a
work in progress—what this book has been about—but also after it's
supposedly "finished." We read great literature and it means different
things to us at different times of our lives—*King Lear* at sixty is a
different experience from *King Lear* at twenty-five. Just so in rereading
our own writing. Why shouldn't we later see different possibilities,
different meanings in it than when we first wrote it? Unlike with *King
Lear* or anybody else's writing, however, we *can* revise our own work
to accommodate a new way of looking at things, even after it's
published.

Many writers have done this. Irish poet W.B. Yeats was known for
going back to earlier poems and changing them to reflect his new
understanding of their meaning. Indeed, the act of *re-seeing* was often

the subject of these poems. The short-story writer Frank O'Connor said in a *Paris Review* interview that "after [a story is] published in book form, I usually rewrite it again. I've rewritten versions of most of my early stories and one of these days ... I'll publish these as well." In another *Paris Review* interview, Joyce Carol Oates has said that she revised her story "The Widows" both before and after its serial publication, and then again before it appeared in a collection—"a fastidiousness" she said, "that could go on into infinity." As indeed it could, except for Death, which will finally seal our lips and bind our senses and our stories. But until then, why not think of revision as an *ongoing* creative process? After all, as a publishing writer, you often get a few more cracks at a story after its initial serial publication. You can revise it again for your short story collection. And again for a second edition. And yet again for your *Selected Stories*.

REVISING AFTER PUBLICATION CASE STUDY: RAYMOND CARVER

Revision can make a story entirely different, which is what Raymond Carver did with his short story "The Bath" in his collection *What We Talk About When We Talk About Love*, published in 1981. As you may recall, the story concerns a young boy who suffers a head injury just before his birthday. He's taken to the hospital, where he slips into a coma. What was at first thought to be a simple concussion turns ominous, and his parents are anxious:

> The mother went to the window and looked out at the parking lot. Cars with their lights on were driving in and out. She stood at the window with her hands on the sill. She was talking to herself like this. We're into something now, something hard.
> She was afraid.

While they await their son's fate, the parents receive anonymous, harassing phone calls from the angry baker from whom the mother had ordered a birthday cake, now simply forgotten and uncalled-for in the aftermath of the accident. The story ends with the son's life still in balance, and the mother answering yet one more call:

> The telephone rang.
> "Yes!" she said. "Hello!" she said.

"Mrs. Weiss," a man's voice said.

"Yes," she said. "This is Mrs. Weiss. Is it about Scotty?" she said.

"Scotty," the voice said. "It is about Scotty," the voice said. "It has to do with Scotty, yes."

In "The Bath," the mood is ominous, edgy, anxious. The fate of the boy is held in suspense, although things certainly don't look good. The only communication between the baker and the parents is anonymous and harassing. Indeed, the baker becomes almost a physical embodiment of their dread. Paradoxically, he's both a minor and a major character—minor in that he is present almost entirely as a spectral voice over the telephone, major in that he does become the embodiment of their foreboding. Nothing good will happen to these characters, we feel. They are disconnected from one another. They are doomed, and can do little about it beyond communicating anxiously and anonymously, while waiting for the worst.

As you can see from the sections quoted, stylistically "The Bath" is spare and stark. Diction is simple; sentences are short, clipped, terse. Modifying adjectives and adverbs are few, and modifying clauses nonexistent. Dialogue is spare. Description is terse. We feel that language has been pared to the bone. This style—as much as the plot—helps create the sense of bleakness that pervades the story.

Some years later, Carver completely revised "The Bath." In his collection *Cathedral*, published in 1983, the story is now called "A Small, Good Thing." The bare bones of "The Bath," plot-wise, are still here. The mother orders a birthday cake that remains uncalled-for after Scotty has an accident and slips into a coma; again the parents wait anxiously at the hospital; again the baker makes harassing phone calls. But the story takes a different tack, especially toward the end. In "A Small, Good Thing" the boy now dies in a heart-wrenching scene, just when the reader thinks he might recover:

The boy looked at them, but without any sign of recognition. Then his mouth opened, his eyes scrunched closed, and he howled until he had no more air in his lungs. His face seemed to relax and soften then. His lips parted as his last breath was puffed through his throat and exhaled gently through the clenched teeth.

213

The parents, bereft, go home. Again the baker calls—only this time the mother figures out who's calling from the machinery noise in the background. They drive to the bakery and angrily confront him, the mother screaming that her son is dead and that "It isn't fair." "Shame," the father tells the baker.

And then a truly marvelous thing happens. The baker has them sit down. And delivers a soul-searching apology not only for what he's done, but for his whole life:

> "Let me say how sorry I am . . . Listen to me. I'm just a baker . . . All I can say to you now is that I'm sorry . . . I'm not an evil man, I don't think . . . You got to understand what it comes down to is I don't know how to act anymore, it would seem. Please . . . let me ask you if you can find it in your hearts to forgive me?"

It is both a confession and a plea for understanding and forgiveness. He offers them some of his hot rolls to eat. He tells them they have to eat and keep going, that "Eating is a small, good thing in a time like this . . . ." They share the bread and talk, and "Although they were tired and in anguish, they listened to what the baker had to say," as he speaks of his loneliness, his doubts, his childlessness—and also of his satisfaction in making cakes and bread, things that will nourish people and serve them in their celebrations. The bereaved parents and the baker share bread, and talk through the night until the early morning, and "they did not think of leaving."

One thing that's obvious from the sections I've quoted is the difference in writing style. The style of "The Bath" is spare, terse and tense, as bleak and unadorned as its atmosphere, whereas the style of "A Small, Good Thing" is fuller, more open. Sentences are longer, often compound, often with dependent clauses. Adjectives and adverbs appear. Dialogue has changed—people talk more. Time is taken to fully develop a scene, as in the boy's death quoted above, rather than trying to render it in a few illuminative sentences.

But of course it's in the endings that the stories differ most. "The Bath" posits a world in which the possibility of human connection, of empathy and understanding, is absent, whereas "A Small, Good Thing" shows the possibilities of connection, of people being able to put aside their anger, shame and isolation to share bread and talk and "not think of leaving." It's a story of redemption and reconciliation. In "The Bath" the baker is almost a symbol of dread; in "A Small, Good Thing," he is very much a fully fleshed human being, his unkindness unwitting, his pain revealed, his redemption within grasp. "The Bath" is about hopelessness; "A Small, Good Thing" is about hope.

In a story for all intents and purposes "finished," Carver saw other meanings and possibilities. "A Small, Good Thing" is a re-vision, a re-seeing of not only a story, but also, we feel, Carver's way of looking at the human condition. If fiction represents a moral examination, as John Gardner maintains in *On Moral Fiction*, his illuminating book on the function of literature, then the results of that examination for the early Carver and the later Carver are radically different. This is not to say that one story is "better" than the other. They are both wonderful, and readers will prefer one to the other. Personally, I find "A Small, Good Thing" richer than its earlier version. Others may find it sentimental—I don't think it is at all—and prefer the "tougher" version of "The Bath." And the re-vision certainly doesn't replace "The Bath." Carver did not, after all, renounce the earlier story and want it stricken from all future printings of *What We Talk About When We Talk About Love*! Perhaps the true meaning of the two versions is the tension between them. The two are meant, in some sense, to be seen together. The overarching meaning of the stories is the view they offer, when seen together, of the possibility of creative as well as personal change.

REVISING AFTER PUBLICATION CASE STUDY: TIM O'BRIEN

Tim O'Brien shows us another perspective on revision after publication. His short story "Ghost Soldiers" was originally published in *Esquire*. It's a story about injury, brooding and revenge, which O'Brien later revised as a chapter in his novel, *The Things They Carried*. In both short story and novel chapter, the plot remains much the same, not changing as radically as Carver's did in "A Small, Good Thing." Yet the story is much different, primarily in the narrator's voice, which in turn changes the story's tone, and in some sense its meaning. At the beginning of both versions, the narrator, a soldier in Vietnam, is shot in the rump. Ineptly treated by an inexperienced medic, Jorgenson, he's sent to a military hospital for a long, painful and embarrassing recuperation. In the original story, the narrator is a brash young man, full of youthful bravado. He talks like this:

> Getting shot should be an experience from which you can draw a little pride. I'm not talking macho crap. . . . All I mean is that you should be able to *talk* about it . . . the sound of the shot when it comes about ten decades later. . . .
>
> Diaper rash, the nurses called it. They . . . patted my ass and said, "Git-cha-goo . . ." It made me hate Jorgenson the way some guys hated Charlie—ear-cutting hate, the kind atrocities are made of.
>
> . . . In early May . . . they transferred me over to headquarters . . . Fairly safe, too. . . .
>
> I wasn't complaining. . . .
>
> But Jesus, it *hurt*. Torn-up muscle, nerves like live electric wires: it was pain.
>
> Pain, you know?

However, when "The Ghost Soldiers" appeared years later as a chapter in *The Things They Carried*, the narrator's voice through these same passages was very different:

> Getting shot should be an experience from which you can draw some small pride. I don't mean the macho stuff. All I mean is that you should be able to *talk* about it . . . how the sound of the gunshot arrives about ten years later. . . .
>
> Diaper rash, the nurses called it. An in-joke, I suppose. But it made me hate Bobby Jorgenson the way some guys hated the VC, gut hate, the kind of hate that stays with you even in your dreams. . . .
>
> At the end of December . . . they transferred me over to Headquarters Company. . . . For the first time in months I felt reasonably safe. . . .
>
> I didn't complain. . . . I figured my war was over. If it hadn't been for the constant ache in my butt, I'm sure things would've worked out fine.
>
> But it hurt.

The voice has changed, we feel. How? For starters, slang words such as "crap" and "ass" have been replaced by more neutral ones such as "stuff" and "butt." Hip, breezy colloquialisms such as "I wasn't complaining" and "fairly safe" have been changed to more standard speech: "I didn't complain" and "For the first time in months I felt reasonably safe." "A little pride" becomes the more measured "some small pride." The hyperbolic imagery associated with a young man's voice—the bullet arriving "decades" later, or hate being "ear-cutting, the kind that atrocities are made of"—has been changed to the less hyperbolic "ten years" and "gut hate." The high-pitched, exaggerated description of pain in the original story ("But Jesus, it *hurt* . . ." etc.) has been refined to the more sedate, reportorial, "But it hurt." Period. Certain incidents have also disappeared; for example, the almost adolescent bathroom humor of the nurses patting his behind and saying "Git-cha-goo." So: slang has been replaced by more standard diction; speech rhythms have become less colloquial and more measured; hyperbole has been exchanged for more objective description.

The narrator has subsequently changed from a cocky young soldier, full of bravado, to a much older, more contemplative and presumably wiser man who is looking back on his experience—the story—from a perspective of years. Does the meaning of the stories change too, as happened in the two Carver stories? I think so. The original "The Ghost Soldiers" is about a young man's learning about the limits of revenge and his capacity for forgiveness. In the later version, due to the narrator's older voice, it's more a bittersweet *recollection* of that event. A series of small changes made throughout the story—words and phrases, really, not grand changes of plot—have created this difference. Simple stylistic revisions have created an overall re-vision of the story. Part of the reason for this is aesthetic unity, of course, since the overall voice of *The Things They Carried* is that of an older man looking back on his war years. But another reason—although we must beware the autobiographical fallacy here—may be the difference between the young Tim O'Brien and the older writer. It is not only the narrator of the story who has aged and changed and matured, but Tim O'Brien too.

Both Carver and O'Brien revised their stories—saw them again in new ways—after publication. And so it may be for all of us. At the beginning of this book, I said that revision ends when a story is perfect, no sooner. That was meant as a warning, an exhortation and an inspiration. Now it too must be revised. Because perfection is never attained, or attained only for a time. And so revision need never stop. Some of our stories, just as with some aspects of our lives, may never be reenvisioned. Nor need be. But others may. In an earlier chapter, I suggested periodically reviewing your journals to mix and match story ideas and images. Just so, you might periodically reread your "finished" stories—even if published. Any story, even those we thought done and filed away, may come calling on us again, teasing our imaginations with fresh possibilities, new insights. Re-visions. We see them more clearly now, or see them differently, and we're off again, trying once more to seek the elusive grail of Perfection, as we revise our lives and, with them, our art.

ABOUT THE AUTHOR

David Michael Kaplan's books include the novel *Skating in the Dark* (Pantheon, 1991) and the short story collection *Comfort* (Viking/ Penguin, 1987). His fiction has appeared in such publications as *The Atlantic, Redbook, Mirabella, Playboy, TriQuarterly,* STORY, *American Short Fiction* and *Mississippi Review,* and has been heard on National Public Radio's "Sound of Writing." His stories also appear in many anthologies, including *The Best American Short Stories 1985* and *Prize Stories 1990: The O. Henry Awards.* Kaplan is an associate professor of English at Loyola University Chicago, where he teaches fiction writing.

INDEX

More From Story Press!

The Joy of Writing Sex by Elizabeth Benedict. Finally, here's the book to help you craft intimate scenes that are original, sensitive and just right for your fiction. Elizabeth Benedict's instruction, supported with examples from the finest contemporary fiction, focuses on creating sensual encounters that hinge on freshness of character, dialogue, mood and plot. You'll also find spirited opinions from some of today's most prestigious writers—among them, John Updike, Dorothy Allison, Russell Banks and Joyce Carol Oates. *#48021/$16.99/160 pages*

The ABC's of Writing Fiction by Ann Copeland. With a teaching style that's dynamic and offbeat, Ann Copeland offers an authoritative wealth of instruction, advice and insight on the writing life. Penetrating alphabetical mini-lessons and unexpected words and phrases—culled from 15 years of teaching fiction—encourage browsing, free associating and random discoveries. *#48017/$18.99/256 pages*

Fiction Writer's Workshop by Josip Novakovich. In this interactive workshop, you'll explore each aspect of the art of fiction including point of view, description, revision, voice and more. At the end of each chapter you'll find more than a dozen writing exercises to help you put what you've learned into action. *#48003/$17.99/256 pages*

Turning Life Into Fiction by Robin Hemley. Writers' lives, those of their friends and family members, newspaper accounts, conversations overheard—these can be the bases for novels and short stories. Here, Robin Hemley shows how to make true stories even better. You'll learn how to turn journal entries into fiction; find good story material within yourself; identify memories that can be developed; and fictionalize other people's stories. Exercises guide writers in honing their skills. *#48000/$17.99/208 pages*

The Fiction Dictionary by Laurie Henry. The essential guide to the inside language of fiction. These are terms from yesterday, today—and even those just being coined for the language of tomorrow. Some you've heard of; others may open up exciting new possibilities in your own writing. You'll discover genres you've never explored, writing devices you'll want to attempt, fresh characters to populate your stories. *The Fiction Dictionary* dusts off the traditional concept of "dictionary" by giving full, vivid descriptions, and by using lively examples from classic and contemporary fiction . . . turning an authoritative reference into a can't-put-it-down browser. *#48008/$18.99/336 pages*

Creative Nonfiction by Philip Gerard. Nonfiction is in the facts. Creative nonfiction is in the telling. With this engaging book, you'll learn how to tell a story with power and grace to create compelling, unforgettable pieces. Philip Gerard's clear and passionate instruction covers every step of the writing process—from finding an original subject to conducting a stirring interview to working with an editor. Plus, you'll get the opportunity to follow in his footsteps as he shows you, step-by-step, how one of his own pieces came together. *#48016/$17.99/224 pages*

The Art & Craft of Novel Writing by Oakley Hall. Using examples from classic and contemporary writers ranging from John Steinbeck to Joyce Carol Oates, Hall guides you through the process of crafting a novel. In example-packed discussions, Hall shows what works and why. You will learn the key elements of fiction and gain inspiration along the way. *#48002/$14.99/240 pages/paperback*

These selections are available at your local bookstore or directly from Story Press. To order from Story Press, send payment, plus $3.50 postage and handling for one book, and $1.00 for each additional book. Ohio residents add 6% sales tax. Allow 30 days for delivery.

Story Press
1507 Dana Avenue
Cincinnati, Ohio 45207
VISA/MasterCard orders call TOLL-FREE
1-800-289-0963
Prices subject to change without notice.
Write to this address for information on STORY magazine.   6555